Bio   Dietrich, Marlene.
Die
        Marlene

DATE DUE

MY 22 '89			
JE 13 '89			

MARLENE

MARLENE

by

Marlene Dietrich

Translated from the German by
SALVATOR ATTANASIO

Grove Press
New York

Copyright © 1987 by Marlene Dietrich
Ullstein Verlag GmbH
Frankfurt/Main-Berlin

Translation copyright © 1989 Salvator Attanasio

Published by Grove Press
a division of Wheatland Corporation
841 Broadway
New York, N.Y. 10003

Library of Congress Cataloging-in-Publication Data

Dietrich, Marlene.
    Marlene/by Marlene Dietrich: translated from
the German by Salvator Attanasio.—1st ed.
        p.   cm.
    ISBN 0-8021-1117-3
    1. Dietrich, Marlene.   2. Entertainers—
Germany—Biography.
I. Title.
PN2658.D5A3   1989
791.43'028'0924—dc19
[B]   88-21642
                                       CIP

Designed by Irving Perkins Associates

Manufactured in the United States of America

This book is printed on acid-free paper.

First Edition 1989

10   9   8   7   6   5   4   3   2   1

A BRIEF NOTE

This book is dedicated to no one in particular.

There is no "Tom, Dick, or Harry" in my lexicon.

I have written this book for those who enjoyed seeing me on the screen and on the stage, for those who made it possible for me to work, to earn money, to pay my taxes and to enjoy life's fleeting pleasures.

Perhaps they will read this book.

Perhaps they will laugh a little with me.

FOREWORD

I decided to write this book in order to clear up numerous misunderstandings.

Too much nonsense has been said about me by persons who wanted to make money by exploiting my name. How could I have stopped them? By the time I learned about their books, it was always too late. Nor did I know that these gentlemen who had the gall to spread slanders, to usurp a person's private life, were protected by the laws of their own countries. There should be no need for me to emphasize that none of my so-called biographers ever had the courtesy to consult me—which speaks volumes about them.

These people have neither honor nor dignity; they belong to the breed Ernest Hemingway called "parasites." My only defense—a sad one admittedly!—against them has always been to ignore their "work." Whenever, after a stage performance in the United States or abroad, someone handed me one of these books to autograph, I always refused.

I have no interest in talking about my life. But since my career and the parts I played on screen and stage seem to meet with general interest, after some inner struggle I decided to write these memoirs so that in the future there will be no need to ask what is true and what is false. Facts are unimportant. I would like only not to distort the different segments of my life, primarily for the sake of those who like or remember me. I never kept a diary. I never took myself seriously enough to record the trivia of everyday life, for which I lacked the necessary self-centeredness. Where others might have succumbed to it, I was always indifferent to the glitter of fame. I found it troublesome, crippling and dangerous. I detested it. Unlike most actors and actresses, I hate to behave like a "star" and to be a target of the curious on the street or at an airport. Admiration from unknown persons leaves me cold. The fame that can completely alter the personality of a human being has no power over me. Why? That's how I am, and I can't be otherwise.

I possessed a certain "laisser-aller," surely rare for so young a girl as I was at the start of my career. In contrast to what my "biographers" assert, I was never concerned about being a celebrity, a topic of conversation, or about having photos of myself on the front pages of newspapers. Nor, despite the disapproval of the studios for which I worked, did I ever concern myself with the photos and articles that appeared about me in the press. When I gave an interview arranged by the studio, it was only to comply with my contract.

Everyone knows how difficult it is to recall the early years of your life. We all have impressions, memories that do not always match reality, or that have blurred with time. My mother, who could have told me many things, is no longer alive. She died shortly after the war. We crafted her coffin out of school desks and stood outside in the rain for the ceremony because the chapel had been bombed. That was in 1945, and I was still in the American army. My superiors allowed me to take care of all the formalities of my mother's death. I took a plane; during the flight we ran into a violent thunderstorm, and the landing in Berlin was a near mishap. But finally I could bury my mother. This event severed the last bond that tied me to my homeland. We all lose our mothers, friends, children; we are repeatedly torn from those we love. How can we escape our fate, our sorrow, our own extinction? Perhaps by thinking that—for our children and our families—our lives have not been entirely useless, that we have been able to ease their sorrows and their pains.

My name really is Marlene Dietrich. My schoolmates could easily attest to that. Tough luck for my "biographers" who claim that it is a stage name. As a child I was thin and pale; I had long red-blond hair and a translucent complexion, the white skin characteristic of the redhead, and a sickly look thanks to this long, red-blond hair. My parents were quite well-to-do, and I received the best education imaginable. I had governesses and private tutors who taught me High German, that pure language unspoiled by any dialect. I have remained loyal to High German, and I am shaken by the mutilation it constantly undergoes today, by the indolence with which most contemporary writers handle it. This loyalty is also a way of not forgetting my childhood.

PART
ONE

A GIRL FROM
A GOOD FAMILY

I

Everybody said that I was still too young to go to school. In the winter, early in the morning, I would squeeze my eyes tightly and tiny tears would change the pale street lamps into long, slim, glittering beams of light. I played this game every morning, and my tears would flow easily. Actually, I didn't have to cry at all. The wind and cold did the trick well enough if not better. I knew all the closed shutters of the stores, all the jutting stones that I could jump over on one leg—with closed or crossed legs—or slide on if it had snowed during the night. My feelings were just as familiar to me: the certainty of having lost my precious freedom, fear of the teachers and of their punishments, fear of loneliness.

The school gate was heavy. I had to push against it with all my might to open it. A leather band muffled the loud clang of iron on iron, and again I was trapped as every morning. I had been prematurely enrolled in school a year earlier than usual, and since I could already read, write, and count, I went directly into the second school year. I was younger than my classmates and even

3

younger than the little girls who were in the first grade. That's why I was so lonely.

Later also, even though not a few of my schoolmates cribbed from my French compositions, I remained lonely and was still excluded from their whispered secrets, their intimacies, and their fits of laughter. Yet I had no desire to know what they were keeping secret from me. Thus, the prison of school contained an additional bar expressly for me because I was too young. I didn't doubt for a second that age is of decisive importance. All grown-ups first ask a child what its name is, then, its age. Yet it's not the name but the age that always elicits approving nods. Since the obvious satisfaction of grown-ups seemed to correspond to the number of years, I liked to make myself older.

My fate in the school was peculiar and, I thought, undeserved. I knew that no matter how many years went by I would always be too young. I had to find someone who would stand by me, an intelligent person to whom my age would be of no importance. Then Mlle. Breguand, Marguerite Breguand, came into my life.

She had dark brown eyes, tied her black hair together in a loose knot, and always wore a white blouse, a black skirt, and a narrow soft leather belt around her waist. She was the only native French teacher in the school; the other teachers of French or English had learned these languages in Germany. Mlle. Breguand spoke fluent German with a French accent. She taught the advanced classes, pupils who had already mastered the ground rules of French grammar.

One day, during lunch break, she addressed me as I was trying to devour my sandwich. I was standing all alone at one of the high windows in the school corridor and was sadder than the rain falling outside. She stopped in front of the window, looked out, and asked me: "Do you have a real reason to be sad?" I pressed my lips over the almost indigestible piece of bread and shook my head. "Because it's a sin to be sad." (She spoke German but said the word "sin" in French.) At this moment the bell rang, the recess was over, and she walked off.

The next day, at the same hour, she came back to me; I

answered all her questions. Now she would come every day at the same hour to the same spot. My age seemed to be of no concern to her. What was important, obviously, was that I was there and that we spoke to one another. She was so happy to be able to speak French with me. When the bell rang, I would follow her and carry her books. She would turn her head around to speak to me, and sometimes she came to a halt with a mild exclamation of surprise over my extensive vocabulary. Finally she would enter her class-room, turn around to look at me, and close the door. Then, radiant with joy, I would run through the empty corridors to my class-room before the last ring of the bell.

She banished my loneliness, my childish worries, my sad-ness. She embodied both my wishes and their fulfillment. I spent all my free time thinking up gifts for her: blue-red-white ribbons that my mother had once worn at a French ball; French landscapes I had cut out of magazines, a bouquet of lilies of the valley on the First of May, a cornflower, a daisy and a poppy on the Fourteenth of July. I bought Christmas and New Year cards made in France and even thought of giving her a French perfume, but my mother suggested that so expensive a gift might embarrass Mlle. Breguand and that I should wait patiently until I grew a little older. Mlle. Breguand often waited with me in front of the school if my governess was late, and sometimes she would accompany us for a stretch, but only up to the point where she had come to the end of the story she had begun.

On the last day of school, before the vacation season, she would never fail to give me her address, which she wrote down on a page torn from her notebook. She had divined my secret hopes and knew how to soothe my sorrows.

Finally came the day on which I became one of her pupils. At last I was in her class! Yet she didn't give me more attention than the other children got. At times she would cast a glance in my direction as if she wanted to make sure of my attention. Our familiarity floated like a pale blue ribbon in the motionless air of the class and filled my heart with the ecstatic happiness praised by poets, but which leaves others untouched. After school I would run home quickly to work on my French compositions, to find splendid expressions that would astound her and to draw out the best from a language whose richness she always praised. Her comments in her beautiful handwriting, composed in telegram style, contained moderate praise that earned me tender looks from my mother. Thanks to Mlle. Breguand the school was no longer a prison, but a big city of sorts in which I knew how to find my secret love. Every morning, throughout that winter and spring, I went to school with a light heart at the thought that another happy day lay before me.

But when classes resumed in the autumn of 1914, all the pupils and teachers were ordered to gather in the auditorium.

Thunderous speeches were delivered, of which we didn't understand a word. I tried to find Mlle. Breguand's face. I didn't see it. The English and French teachers were seated next to the Latin and Greek teachers. She wasn't there. I then combed the rows of the science and mathematics teachers. Neither was she there. She surely must have heard the big school bell that summoned us. Where was she? Then slowly the terrible truth dawned on me with a chill. Marguerite Breguand! France! French! You are a Frenchwoman! You, Marguerite Breguand, you are a French-woman! Germany is at war with France! That's why you're not here. We are enemies. These thoughts actually made me faint.

I was made to drink some water, and they said the air in the auditorium was too stuffy. The speeches came to an end, and we returned to our classrooms chattering like magpies. Now we had to knit for the soldiers during school hours. The youngest of us made mittens, the older ones sweaters. Scarves, too, a simple task. Wool was stored in the gym. The dead languages were still being taught, but what was going to happen with English and French? New teachers would replace the old ones now fighting at the front. If we were lucky, they'd be old and drowsy. And we were lucky. The school rules were made less rigid. Every morning in all classrooms, from eight to nine o'clock, from the fourth grade through the fifth form and from the seventh through the eleventh, academic instruction was replaced by knitting lessons.

The soldiers marched through the streets with flowers clasped to their rifles; they laughed, they sang, kissed the women.

Flags hung from windows as people celebrated the war against France. *The festival of the war.* The barbarians were celebrating the declaration of war with a flower clasped to a rifle.

Nobody could have forced me to participate in the war against France. I loved Marguerite Breguand, and I loved France. I loved the soft and familiar French language. I was the first to wear mourning. I had lost Mlle. Breguand; I had lost the French language; I had lost a promise that was not kept, an honorable, pure promise that my teachers had made to me—they who had been telling us: "A promise is a promise."

We had been promised a peaceful childhood: school, holidays and picnics, summer vacations with hammocks, beach, pail, shovel, and a starfish that we could take home with us. We had been promised plans, plans to be forged, carried out, actualized; dreams to be dreamed and made to come true. A secure future—and it was up to us to take advantage of it. And now? No more plans, no secure future, and no knowledge that could be of any use to the war. Since we couldn't form a military unit, we knitted. We sat in the classroom barely lit by the daylight and knitted to warm the soldiers digging trenches far from home. They made us knit to make us feel useful, to fill the gaping void caused by the war. The wool was "field gray," rough and constantly tangled. Field gray. For me the fields were not gray, but wherever the fighting was going on, they probably were.

Life in school sank back into a gray monotony, becoming again what it had been before Mlle. Breguand's guest performance: a prison. But I didn't forget her. Each time I was punished for speaking French (the language of our enemy) and had to drop ten *pfennigs* into the class till, this donation was made in her name.

My passionate love for France overcame the first shock: It went underground and survived all the prohibitions. I didn't tell a soul about it. With head held high, I bore my secret in the depths of my heart.

The first members of my family who fell in combat were distant cousins and an uncle. Their deaths left no void in our small family circle. My mother showed no grief. Her great concern was, and had always been, her childrens' health. My father was on maneuvers when the war broke out. He went to the front without returning home to bid us good-bye. It seemed to me as if he spent all his time writing to us; his letters seemed to have kept him out of the fighting. He never related anything about the war, but instead described the various countrysides, the villages, and the woods through which he trudged, and the seasons that he saw come and go.

Summer vacation was drawing closer, and with it the mountains and the scent of the pines at sunset. Some teachers had stayed put and had organized summer courses to which I was sent. I loved the lessons outdoors, the feeling of freedom, the cheerful and sunburnt teachers. Nobody talked about the war. Yet not too far away was a POW camp, off limits to us.

One day I was sitting on the veranda busy with my homework. The last sunbeams cast a yellowish light on my paper. Suddenly I noticed that I had written the date of July 14 in my notebook. The Bastille! France's famous day! The holiday of holidays! *"Allons enfants de la patrie."* By the time it was twilight, I had gathered as many white roses in the garden as I could carry. I ran to the edge of the woods. The thorns pierced my summer dress. I cried in pain and fear. But I was firmly determined to go through with my adventure, come what may.

I stood still right in front of the barbed wire.

Some figures were discernible behind the fence. Too late to make a retreat. They had seen me. I was small, but I was wearing a white dress and carrying a bouquet of roses of the same color. The men had black beards, black eyes; they didn't stir. Bells were pealing in the village. Peace, suppertime—and again the fear of being discovered, of not being able to transmit my message to them. For a long time I just stood there, motionless. The bells ceased to peal.

"Let's go," I thought, "let's go! After all you're a soldier's daughter."

I drew a rose from my bouquet and held it up to them. I couldn't notice any movement on the other side. They just stood there, rigid and stiff like tin soldiers. Then I drew a little closer to them, and in my childish voice and in my best French, I said:

"Today is the Fourteenth of July. I thought the roses would make you happy." I pushed a rose through a hole in the barbed wire fence; a hand suddenly moved, grabbed, then other hands also dared to reach out. Breathlessly, I quickly handed over all my roses, as though accomplishing a glorious and forbidden feat. No other word was spoken.

I ran, and my heart pounded as though it were about to burst when I secretly slipped into the house through the cellar door. The anniversary of the storming of the Bastille came to a quiet close. Nobody had noticed my absence.

On the following day a teacher came by to see my mother. I had been seen. The teacher was ready to forgive me, to forget this "childish" prank, but the mothers of my schoolmates had demanded my expulsion from the summer school.

My mother remained quite calm. No anger, no nervousness. I was ashamed of myself for her sake and broke into tears. I didn't get to hear the familiar phrase: "A soldier's daughter doesn't cry." When I raised my eyes she was standing there, motionless, looking at me and weeping.

Now that I was left to my own devices for the rest of the summer, I gave a lot of thought to the notion of justice; confused thoughts, questions without answers, buzzed through my head. The war was unjust. Good and evil, these poorly defined concepts, have a clearly etched meaning in the world of children. They are like a primal law: unchangeable, always explainable, inexorable and mighty. Outside the world of children, on the other hand, good and evil seem to be changeable, deceptive, and invented arbitrarily.

I lay on the grass and thought about God and about Mlle. Breguand.

Both were somewhere, very far from me. God would come back after the war; I was as much convinced of this as I was of His absence. Yet I wasn't so sure in the case of Mlle. Breguand: First of all because she was a young woman, and then because I knew her less well than I knew God. I could rather easily foresee what God would do. Mlle. Breguand's image, however, was blurred and yet fascinating, full of surprises; it would suddenly turn up, flooded with light and vanish again as suddenly as it had appeared. Why should she have to come back after the war? The peace, perhaps, would not reconcile the French and the Germans, and besides, I might be too old to still be at school. God, on the other hand, had to come back, as He is responsible for us and, unlike us, does not reckon in years. He would come back to us again and reward those who suffered in the war permitted by Him. Yet none of these reasons spoke for the return of Mlle. Breguand.

Deep down I thought it was proper that God and Mlle. Breguand should keep their distance for a while, because men were slaughtering each other and making a mockery of human and divine laws. Summer came to a close, and sadly, I boarded the train that brought me back to the city.

I sang "Deutschland, Deutschland über Alles" in the spacious school courtyard amid my girlfriends. But I kept my mouth hermetically closed when the imprecation "May God punish England" reverberated from the walls. And again more victory celebrations, again holidays in exchange for gold pieces we were told to elicit from our mothers and grandmothers. Holidays in the event of death in the family. Once more, girls absent from school, more girls in black, food ration cards, lists of the wounded, lists of the missing, lists of the dead. Family gatherings with coded words, phrases overheard through closed doors: "The children mustn't notice anything. Careful, speak softly, there are children in the house."

Grief of the grown-ups. In the church, religious services for the missing. Tears hang like silver pearls from veils that flutter in the cold gusts and summer winds. The hope that you will never have to experience war when you are grown up.

Our mothers. How do they bear this ordeal of fate? How do they still muster the courage to cook, sew, help their children with their homework, attend to them, listen to the melodies they play over and over again on the piano, go for walks with them on Sundays? All these women bereft of their husbands! They press us to their hearts; we embrace them in our turn, and the men for whom they yearn will soon be corpses. How sad . . . If at least we could cry. But we can't. We have our children's sorrows, our daily disappointments, our world in which things are going wrong, going to pieces without any reason, resisting our efforts, desperate efforts, to cover up our stupidities, to hush up our memory gaps, to hide our ignorance, forgetfulness and inattentiveness, to atone for our sins—on paper and in our heads—to veil a lie with more and always new lies! And this terrible and insufferable anxiety against which only illness can be of some help, fever, doctors and bed, always the same routine—the bed, a haven, a bulwark, a fortress. It resists the assaults of teachers and principals who draw the parents to their side—and silken soft angel arms that cradle us like babies, protected in warmth, in security.

Children are condemned to silence and solitude in advance. They may not let on that their own fears bring them close to those who are suffering at the front every day and who live in fear of ambush and mutilation. If grown-ups were to listen to us, would they stop slaughtering each other? But we are only the passive witnesses of history's upheavals. We attend, as usual, to our affairs morning, noon and night, as though God were with us and blossoming apple trees bedecked the entire earth. Why send us to school if we are going to lose the war anyway? But no! We shall not lose the war, and we must go to school. God is with us, don't you know that? God, do You know that You are with us? Us the Germans? How do You choose what side You are on? Do You support the best ones? The best pupils? Are You only on one side? Then You cannot be God, or can You? You let the just and the unjust come to You. Are we the just? We are victors. Doesn't that mean that we are the just? Don't ask questions. Do your home-work. Attend to your daily chores. And, finally, don't forget music.

My mother taught me a waltz by Chopin that I was allowed to play as a reward, if I had diligently practiced Bach and Handel. Sometimes we changed places, and then she played, her finger-nails touching on the keys with a delicate click. I knew this sound from earliest childhood. It belonged to a house full of flowers, to my mother's perfume, to her evening gown, her beautiful hairdo, to the smell of my father's cigarette coming through the open door of the library where he strode back and forth on a thick rug and listened to my mother playing the piano. Everything was ready for the guests.

The fingernails had stopped striking the keys. I took my place again at the piano and noticed how precipitously my mother had left the room. The doorbell had rung. I heard my mother race to the door. It could not be the mailman, but she ran. She ran because she was waiting; all day long she waited for letters from the front, for something else. In the way she raised her head, you could feel that one-half of her being was steeped in anxiety and sorrow, and the other was restricted to performing the duties of day-to-day living. "My fate is that of millions of women," she would say. For her that was neither good nor bad. With deeply bowed head, she read a letter from the family, and then she told me about the death of a relative, as if she had been expecting it for a long time.

She was always dressed in black. A black band was put over my left sleeve as a sign of permanent mourning for all the family dead. Mostly, I wore dark blue dresses and coats. Gray was also a mourning color, but one could go over to gray only after several years. Little white cuffs and collars constituted the only modification of this outfit's severity. I wore braided black ribbons on the pigtails that hung below my shoulders. Before the war I was allowed to wear my hair loose, held only by a headband—something now allowed only on Sundays or holidays. During the war there were no holidays. I dreamed of an armistice and peace; I dreamed also of the warm, wild, and fragrant sweep of hair that once fell on my face and on my neck.

Toward the end of the war I was vaccinated against smallpox, and a red band adorned my arm: black and red, the German flag. I painted for myself my own black and red homeland. Harmony, harmonicas, accordions, violins. No teachers, no soldiers. Twilight instead of dark nights. Plains and rivers, houses with straw roofs, children in big feather beds, a cow for each one, golden wheatfields in the sun, sweet-smelling lupines, moist and dark earth, green clover and sour sorrel, lavender honey-scented pillows, hammocks for summer afternoons, carefree, fleeting time. The hammock sways, the back of the hand grazes the grass, now this way, now that. Back and forth without stopping. Nobody calls you. You eat whatever you like. No thunderous voices, no battle, no war. Silently, I swore allegiance to my flag when the moment came to remove the red band. But the black band remained on my sleeve.

In the late afternoon we examined the lists of the missing. My mother always walked more slowly as we neared City Hall. I didn't dare to ask her why and silently adjusted my step to hers. She would never let go of my hand; when she stopped there, only her head moved up and down as she looked through the names. I would watch her and try to guess when she would take the two steps sideward and with her head held high begin to read the next list. There were also many other women and young girls. But there was none of the pushiness that usually prevailed in front of the shops, in the endless lines at the doors of the bakeries. Those who were scrutinizing the list of the dead and wounded were polite, considerate of others. Why, I thought, couldn't we behave like this in times of peace as well? Behave as though we were still at war? I didn't share these thoughts with my mother, since I was sure that she thought likewise, viewed the problem as insoluble, and had decided to live as useful a life as possible. But it was not the war that taught my mother life's fundamental values. She knew them from way back when she taught me to read. She didn't use a blackboard; she would explain the pronunciation, the syllables and the punctuation with the help of the poems by Ferdinand Freiligrath written in splendidly colored letters that hung under glass in our living room!

> O love, as long as you can!
> O love, as long as you will!
> For the hour will come, the hour will come
> When you stand by the grave and lament!

Her deepest convictions did not rest on experience but on her intuition. She was always so sure of them, as if she had arrived at them by herself. When she quoted philosophers and poets for emphasis, you might think that, in a friendly way, she was allowing them to share her personal views. Otherwise she was much too young to have had personal experience in all the areas she seemed to know so well. She had had a very sheltered childhood, and she had shocked the city's respectable society by her early marriage. She had become a mother at seventeen.

And there she stood now before the list of the missing. She was looking for a name she didn't want to find and holding on to a little girl's hand as darkness descended and the street lamps lit up. Still two more lists, hope, don't forsake me, "his" name will not be on it. Please, let it not be there. . . . Now the last ones . . . Her finger followed the black letters behind the glass pane smeared by countless fingers. The pressure of her hand slackens; she bows her head; her eyes are moist, but they shine with a relief and a joy only I can see. "We're going home now, Paul. We want to open the canned food I set aside for a very special day like today, and we'll spend a restful evening. If you want me to, I'll also do your homework." *Paul* was the name she called me when she was happy, and she uttered the word "canned food" in French to avoid the harsh German sound. It was so easy to love her.

I needed no affirmation, no proof, to be certain of her love. I don't remember when I sensed for the first time that she loved me. Surely already before my birth. I was her daughter, that sufficed for me. Now she no longer kissed me, she no longer took me in her arms as she once did when I was still very small. The older I grew the more reservedly she expressed her tenderness, the less she kissed me. She gave me a kiss on the forehead or on the cheeks, always very lightly; at times she would scold me for some kind of venial sin and then just walk off. Her feelings for me were surely the same as mine for her. She didn't want to know whether I loved her or not; she was simply convinced of this. She considered it more important that I should feel secure with her.

It was her task to dispel the insecurity and the anxiety that the war had brought. Every day she would have me repeat a dozen times: "When I'm with my mother, nothing can happen to me." With her I would go fearlessly through the city enveloped in darkness; and with my hand firmly in hers, I would have unflinchingly faced the enemy lines, the plague, the poison gasses, or the lion's den. Nothing could upset her plans, her hope. She always remained herself. She was trustworthy. Everything was clear to her. Perhaps she didn't love, perhaps she was just trustworthy. It didn't matter. She was there—strong, courageous, full of compassion. She deliberately placed her own feelings and desires in the background. Never was she ill or inaccessible. When she retired to her room and no one was allowed to follow her, she always made known how long she wanted to be alone. And on no account would she ever exceed this time. Her outer appearance was in no way inferior to her inner qualities. She was extraordinarily beautiful.

One of her favorite occupations was memory training, as she called it. If I asked her, "May I call my girlfriend and ask what homework we're supposed to do for tomorrow?" I was forbidden to touch the phone. In winter I would be bundled up like an Eskimo, and in rainy weather I would be wrapped in rain gear from head to toe and then be sent on foot to procure that valuable piece of information for myself. Yet I also knew that, at bottom, she loathed to act that way. She forced herself to do this to improve my memory and deliver a finishing blow to forgetfulness forever. She was successful. God bless her!

I felt a deep respect for my mother throughout her life. She possessed a kind of natural nobility. Her behavior, her authority, her intellectual attitude were like those of an aristocrat. Just looking at her made it easy to respect her, to put up with all the strict rules of everyday life and the more drastic rules of my wartime youth. These rules were so indisputable they seemed to be familiar and friendly, lasting, unalterable, irrefutable. Protective rather than threatening, no mood, no whim underlay them. Since my mother had laid them down and had been able to create a corresponding discipline, she must have understood all the wonderful secrets of a child's emotional world. She herself was like a kindly general. She followed the rules that she laid down; she set a good example; she furnished the proof that it was possible. No pride in success, no pats on the shoulder. The only aim was humble submission to duty.

First and foremost duty, the daily obligations.

And love of the duty to which you submit. Love of the work which you do, love of absolute trustworthiness, love of habit that must prevail in the daily struggle against the charm of the new. My mother knew how to structure a familiar activity so excitingly, precisely on the basis of its familiarity, that it, too, could be as exciting as a wholly new adventure. "To recover" something lost or forgotten made her eyes light up, quickened her movements. Her voice would rise uncontrolled and wild: "There! Just as I told you. See! Oh, look, just look! I knew it!" And she would stand there, beaming with joy, with pleasure because she had known what is useful and what is not. I felt as though I were in church and thought to myself: "Who am I, then, with my trivial thoughts, my petty cares, when she's standing there, here before me, and setting such a good example to me in this house in which our two lives are rooted?"

"To recover," love of the known . . . what can all this have meant to my mother without that other imperative by which she was completely controlled but which she did not teach me, which she did not praise—loyalty. She didn't deliver any homilies to me on the subject, but to sense the depth of her feelings, it sufficed to observe her childlike dismay when she discovered that someone had deceived her. In the matter of loyalty my mother proved to be a fanatic—"fanatic," yes, for here kindness or sympathy were irrelevant—an inexorable crusader under the banner of loyalty.

As a passionate "prosecuting attorney" she voiced sharp, decisive and irrevocable judgments. She was lenient and took time to think over violations of a rule she considered overrated. But she changed her tune, with flying colors, so to speak, when you were carried away by your own excitement. At such times she would not tolerate mention of guilt or extenuating circumstances. "When you're excited," she would say, "you easily lose your head. Your feelings run away with you."

It had become second nature to me to hold my feelings firmly in check, even before my mother decided that my dresses had to be made longer to cover my knees.

I also knew that one of her supreme fundamental rules of

behavior, easy to grasp but difficult to practice, enjoined: "Bear the unavoidable with dignity."

Dignity ruled out wailings and complaints; consequently the twin rule stated: "The tears you shed over something unavoidable must remain secret tears." A "logical mode of thinking" was another early achievement that was supposed to make learning easier and serve as a memory prop to a still untrained mind. But it was also the light that illumined the way to a clarification of problems. O logic, when I learned to love you, mother smiled. She smiled at me, at me who had grown up in a war she could not have prevented.

Such was my mother's loyalty—loyalty to appreciation, loyalty to hope, loyalty to the conviction that her body had been strong enough to give a new being a strength that would last throughout the war. "Your teeth are perfect," she would remark when I brushed them. "They'll hold. That's hereditary—you can be grateful for that," she would add, as though to reassure herself. She stubbornly believed in heredity, in the "stable" as she put it. She would take some of my own meager rations of milk, cheese, and meat to give them to her own mother.

My wonderful and gentle grandmother got the lion's share of all family rations. She was not only the most beautiful of all women but also the most elegant, most charming, and most perfect person that ever lived. Her hair was dark red and her eyes of an iridescent violet-blue. She was tall and slim, ever radiant and cheerful. She had married at the age of seventeen and was always taken to be as old or young as she herself wished to appear. She wore expensive clothes and even her gloves were made to measure. She was naturally elegant and didn't concern herself with what was fashionable. She loved horses, went riding every morning very early, and sometimes she would pass by our house just before school and throw me a kiss through a veil in which the early morning air mixed with her perfume. My mother never objected to any of her decisions, even though they might lead to a reversal of my daily program. My grandmother showered me with love, tenderness, and kindness. She awakened in me the longing for beautiful things, for paintings, for Fabergé boxes, horses, carriages, for the warm, soft roseate pearls set off against the white skin of her neck, and for the rubies that sparkled on her hands.

She would let me balance her shoes on my little finger and say: "This is how light they must be." Before the war I had always impatiently awaited the French shoemaker who would come in person every season to take orders for new shoes and to deliver already ordered shoes, but I was never allowed to see him. "School is more important," she would say, "and besides, shoes are a serious matter." My grandmother was at one and the same time very real and very mysterious, a dream image, perfect, desirable, distant, and fascinating. But her love was *here*, present. Her worries concerning those she loved were as passionate as her love for them.

Before I rang my grandmother's doorbell, my mother would pinch my pale cheeks, and I would utter a faint cry of pain. My grandmother would come running down the wide staircase, her skirts aflutter. Tirelessly she would repeat my name, crouch down to my height, and, radiant, sway back and forth with me. We would always talk about beautiful things, never about the letters that arrived from the front, never about the war or mourning. My mother planned our visits carefully so that my grandmother wouldn't notice that my cheeks were becoming progressively paler. She wanted to spare her mother any concern, any unpleasantness. On the way home my mother was always silent and sunk in thought. Sometimes she would lay her hands on my cheeks, turn my head toward her and adjust herself to my step.

On the day the telegram arrived that led to my mother's journey to the front, two older cousins and an aunt moved into our house. I took care of the household as I had been instructed to, and I was an obliging hostess without neglecting my usual chores.

My mother received a *laissez-passer* from General Headquarters, so that she could get to the Russian front "and again give strength to her husband," as the telegram read. My father was seriously wounded and not transportable. He had succumbed to his wounds by the time my mother came back. Now a widow's cowl and veil, which hid her face, were added to her black dress.

When winter arrived she again left the house to transport her husband's corpse in state. She identified him and accompanied the mortal remains to the city where her mother-in-law lived. For my mother, a mother's love was always more important than conjugal love, and so it was normal that her husband's mother should bury him where he had first seen the light of day.

At this time most of the men of our big family had fallen in combat. Women in deep mourning often came together to our house. My mother, resolutely and affectionately, would attend to their physical and spiritual well-being. She believed in the effectiveness of abundant and healthy nourishment and went from room to room with bowls full of bouillon and cups of herbal tea. She combined the meat rations to prepare a broth that occasionally even contained an egg. The herbal tea was tasteless; it was supposed to calm the nerves and induce sleep. At spring-cleaning time my mother had work for everybody. My aunts, great aunts, and cousins in black, contrasting with the white walls, stood on ladders, scrubbed, cleaned and re-hung the curtains through which the April sun shone. On those days supper did not proceed as quietly as usual. Those gathered around the table gossiped and sometimes even laughed.

Although the course of the day had remained the same, the rhythm and atmosphere had changed. My mother now moved around in a somewhat more leisurely manner; even the ringing of the doorbell couldn't quicken her step. She moved slowly, languidly; she held her head the way weary people do. She no longer listened attentively to what was being said; she no longer waited expectantly. She comported herself as if someone was sleeping in the next room.

Sometimes I woke in the middle of the night and discovered my mother, fully dressed, lying on my bed and fast asleep. I was happy to see her near me. But I didn't exactly know why that made me so happy. I had heard her say: "If only I could sleep." And my aunt had answered: "The war has robbed us all of our sleep."

This war did not seem ever to come to an end. Peace was a long forgotten dream, and we had ceased to make plans for so distant a hope. Our victories were rarer. That was why the war dragged on so. Only our complete victory would bring it to a close. We prayed for victory, we prayed for peace, we prayed for the dead, the forgotten dead. They had already been gone for so long; we had not seen them again, even once, before they departed from us. If we had not been told, no one would weep over them. It's easier to tell the truth than it is to console women's hearts. Naturally, everything I thought up in order to soothe the pain did not work, and I began to doubt many things that before I had accepted respectfully and automatically.

Yet I hardly had time to reflect on those confusing realizations. Everything revolved around school, which demanded my full attention and involvement. I was exhausted and became even paler. After lunch I had to sleep. Once in bed I enjoyed this midday rest, but it brought disorder into my activities that had been skillfully divided to take up the whole afternoon, those brief periods that began at one o'clock and ended at seven when I would go to sleep. It was like this throughout the period of my school days. Sleep before midnight—in my mother's view a miracle drug. She clung as loyally to it as to loyalty itself. This principle and the halo with which she surrounded it had, I believe, nothing to do with the fact that I, like all the children of my age, was undernourished. Throughout her youth and up to her marriage she had known the same discipline: She was sent to bed at the stroke of seven. She recounted this full of pride—Was she actually proud of something that concerned herself?—and obviously attributed great importance to it.

I had to get up early in order to do my homework. Long sleep was lost time. For months I was up before daybreak, shivering with cold and fatigue in the light of a petroleum lamp. We had to save electricity, fuel, save our Fatherland. Although pale and thin, I felt strong and healthy. Morning, afternoon, and evening we ate turnips—turnip marmalade, turnip cakes, turnip soup; the roots and the leafy tops of turnips were cooked in a thousand ways . . .

Nobody complained over these meager meals, the children even less than the grown-ups. If I was hungry, there were potatoes in the afternoon and in the evening. Potatoes, true friends of childhood. There they lay, white, tender and mealy, easy to eat and digest. They didn't give us stomachaches. They were still warm when everything else on the table was already cold, arousing the anger of mothers, governesses, and aunts.

We had no milk, but I didn't miss it, and I knew no girl who did. In the summer we drank soda sweetened with saccharine when we were thirsty. In the morning we were given cocoa with water, and at home there was always water whenever we wanted it. Outside the house, however, it was considered impolite to ask for something to drink.

Physical self-control was difficult to learn, but it would never have occurred to anybody at that time to grumble. Each one helped his or her neighbor and drew a lesson from this ordeal of fate. Grown-ups submitted to it calmly and with composure, and they set an extraordinary example for us children. We emulated them without any expectation of reward: No praise, no honors crowned our successes. Negligence was synonymous with sin: Neglecting the body, neglecting feelings and sentiments, neglecting compassion for others. In everything that concerned the body, neglect was called stupidity; and in relation to feelings, it was deemed unseemly. And when we sinned neither out of stupidity nor of impropriety, judgment was pronounced in a firm tone: "That's not done."

Every time my mother wished to end a discussion, she would say: "Later you'll be thankful to me." Then I would argue further, but silently, since I had reached the age when you simply must contradict those who lay down the rules. I didn't call the basic principles into question, of course. Only the unpleasant orders and the daily chores that appeared unnecessary or obsolete to me.

The war had repealed many rules and habits. The country found itself in a state of emergency. The fact that our education continued as though we were still at peace prompted us to doubt the intelligence of grown-ups. We shook our heads, perplexed; we felt ourselves to be mature and wise, but at the same time powerless and ignorant.

For example, the importance that my mother attached to lacing my shoes was really something exaggerated. Even after she had tied them very firmly to the very top, with an energetic finger, she would then pull out each hook up to the knot and re-do it all over again to make the shoelace really sit tight: "When you are bigger, you should have slender ankles; they must be supported so they don't spread." I certainly did not share her interest in my ankles. Nor did I like to wear laced boots or even to look at them. I considered my ankles my mother's property, and all that I did for her a favor. Slender ankles and wrists had something to do with the "stable," and that seemed to be important. I loved this childish feature in my mother; it brought her a little closer to me when she had lost her laughter and seemed to be so quiet and distant. To my regret I resembled my father. To me that was a misfortune.

But my mother assured me that children who resemble their fathers are lucky children. My father: tall, imposing stature, leather smell, shining boots, a riding whip, horses. My remembrance was blurred, indistinct, enveloped in darkness by a power that did not permit a clear portrait of him. That power probably was death.

I passively accepted this blurred portrait of my father whenever I was reminded of him. Most of my schoolmates no longer had fathers. We didn't miss them; we hardly grasped that they had gone forever.

We lived in a women's world; the few men with whom we came in contact were old or ill, not real men. The genuine men were at the front; they were fighting until they fell. After the war many years went by before men existed again. Our life among women had become such a pleasant habit that the prospect that the men might return at times disturbed us—men who would again take the scepter in their hands and again become lords in their households.

The women did not seem to suffer in a world without men; they were calm, relaxed. The visit of one of my aunts' cousins, who had been transferred from the East to the West, proved that I was right: Feverishness spread throughout the house, feet ran hurriedly upstairs and downstairs. Voices trembled, sounded altered, impatience and reproaches lay in the words and gestures; dishes clattered long before suppertime; the house seemed to have been shaken by an earthquake.

The cousin arrived almost secretly. He took a look at me, lifted me high in the air, pressed a long kiss against my cheek and then set me down again on the floor. The iron cross on his chest became entangled in my dress and pulled a thread that stretched between us while the soldier steadily gazed at me. Suddenly, unnoticed by him, my mother stood beside him. The thread broke the moment he turned around and said: "Isn't there anyone around here to greet a weary warrior?" I noted an unusual expression on my mother's face: "She's getting big, cousin Hans," she said. "Yes, I can see it," he answered.

This dialogue seemed stupid to me. My mother out of the blue announces I was getting big! It was not anger that saddened her voice, but something that I had never heard before. She took cousin Hans by the arm and they left the room. She was speaking to him, but I couldn't understand any of their words, which were lost on the way to the other wing of the house.

While they were drinking tea in the garden, I was doing my homework and heard my cousin Hans's laughter. His voice boomed so loudly—at least so it seemed to me—I had to close my window. Before I went to bed I made a curtsy before all the people in the room, except before cousin Hans. Suddenly I had the feeling that I could not bow before him and, instead, just extended a hand to him. He grabbed it, stroked my cheek, and turned again to the conversation with my mother. Everybody must have felt relieved when he left.

The ashtrays spilled over with cigarette butts, and ashes were scattered all over the floor. Two "field gray" shirts were soaking in the laundry room in a milky water full of green soap flakes; the back parts had been inflated with air and towered above the water. I stuck a finger in the sleeve, but it immediately filled up with air again. I suddenly realized that cousin Hans's shirts were to be washed and then sent to him at the front. This thought struck me as grotesque, idiotic, ridiculous, so that I, always taking two steps at a time, ran up the attic and, desperate, huddled in my favorite hiding place. I curled up inside a wicker chest and broke into tears over cousin Hans, over the "field gray" shirts, over the trenches

23

and the packages prepared by women whose minds were be-
fogged by a desperate sorrow—suddenly after so many day-
dreams I had come face-to-face with the war.

The wars described in the history books, all the wars with
which I had to concern myself and whose dates, causes, and
outcomes I had to memorize have never especially interested me. I
never understood the Wars of Religion. To kill on religious
grounds went beyond my powers of understanding; I kept every
thought on this theme from me, as you would scare off an angry bee.

I had to experience that extraordinary evening in order really
to understand the meaning of the war we were going through.
The soldier in our house, the mood he brought with him and left
behind, his steps that resounded on the floors, his bulky body, the
dangers he had experienced and that awaited him after his departure, the kiss he had given me, his "field gray" shirts, the certainty
that he would never come back again, all this for the first time
clearly brought the war before my eyes. It seemed that up to this
moment I had lived in a kind of fog. I wept further in my wicker
chest, and the tears dripped on my knees.

"I'm crying over the war," I answered my mother as she
leaned over me in the darkness, lifted me up, and locked me in her
arms. "Now that the Americans are fighting against us the war will
end soon," she said.

"When they fight, must we pray for them?"

She deposited me gently on the floor. "Do that, if you wish."
She stretched out her hand. "And what if you dried your tears
now?" In the dark I couldn't see her face too well, but her voice
betrayed to me that she was smiling.

II

The mailman brought us small packages from the front.

"The war is taking a bad turn for us," wrote cousin Hans. "The
men in the trenches on the other side obviously pity us. At night
when the guns are silent, they throw cans of food over here."

Their corned beef had a heavenly taste, which is engraved on our memory forever. It was reassuring news, proof that people, whatever the risk, were still thinking for themselves even if in opposition to the politics and the masses of their countries. A further hero was added to my secret love for France—the American soldier. I prayed for all the American soldiers who had come from so far to put an end to the war.

I had already prayed for a long time. I didn't believe, admittedly, that God heard me or that He wanted to hear me, for even more strongly than before, I was convinced that He really wasn't at all interested in humans. But it made me unhappy not to be able to confide to anyone my anxieties and cares that concerned the entire world. Would God, since His wrath may have subsided again, perhaps grant me some attention? No wrath lasts eternally, I thought, so I would try my luck and since the things for which I prayed were important, God will have nothing to object to if he hears me. In the morning I prayed for the Americans, and in the afternoon I thanked the Americans instead of thanking God knowing, as God also would know, that I meant the corned beef, and that if He had not commanded them to send it to us, they must have arrived at this decision exclusively on their own. Therefore, one also had to thank them for it. But my sympathy didn't rest on the fact that the Americans had come to the help of the French. I should have been grateful to them for that, but this wasn't reason enough. I thought it over and came to the conclusion that Italy had done the same. It had, however, earned only contempt because betrayal was a sin. Even when the breach of faith helped my beloved France.

One of my favorite pieces on the violin was the "Serenade" of Giuseppe Torelli. I played it before and after my lessons; it was a lullaby. Each time I played it, my mother would stand at the open door; sometimes she would also come into the room, sit down at the piano, and accompany me. So before all else I was punishing myself when I decided no longer to play this piece for as long as the war lasted. Gounod's "Berceuse" served me as a substitute. The lovelier the melody the better it pleased me. Because my violin teacher loathed lovely melodies, I procured them myself, and since I never listened to her anyway, I would play them in my own way and give them a cloying melancholy. It was said that I had an extraordinary aptitude for the violin. That made my mother very happy, and she congratulated me for each success, no matter how slight, in this area. I loved the tender, plaintive tone of the strings, but I didn't like the boring études, the only pieces I was allowed to play. It was different at the piano. My piano teacher raved about Chopin, Brahms, and the melodies of the great—and less great—Romantic composers. Yet the greatest among them fully sufficed to fill out the piano lesson hours. At other times I played scales and exercises, which are infinitely easier than on the violin. On the keyboard the notes are present; you don't have to form them. All you have to do is to strike the keys without wondering whether the sounds are in tune. On the violin, instead, you constantly have doubts about the purity of the tone, even when the teacher nods approval.

Had I begun with the piano instead of the violin, I might have been a good concert pianist. Yet when I practiced the violin, I became conscious of the difficulties, and I entertained no illusions. Besides, the social prejudices of that day stood in the way of a career as a professional performer. My teacher, however, had a different opinion; perhaps she wanted to encourage me. At any rate, this pale, slender, willowy woman with beautiful musical hands but an overly long nose (when she played, her head inclined leftward over the instrument, the violin became an endless extension of her nose) constantly predicted great fame for me on the podium in the music world. A fame that you couldn't buy, that could be achieved only through work, work, work. She always repeated this word three times.

She looked at me on one occasion and said: "You know if one isn't beautiful, life's not a bed of roses. But if one loves music, if one dedicates oneself to it with talent and perseverance, life becomes beautiful and appearance no longer counts."

I was sure that by these words she was not only thinking of herself, but also of me. I was not beautiful, I know that, and I liked that woman who had the courage to talk to me that way.

Her name was Bertha and she looked like it. Or rather like a bird named Bertha. She could also have been a fox called Bertha. Her red-brown hair was her most beautiful feature. Although she gave me violin lessons for years (later I had male teachers), I never learned whether she, like everyone during the war, had lost brothers, friends, or cousins. She never spoke about herself. In winter she would first warm herself the moment she stepped inside, rub her hands, breathe on them, and then hold them around the cup of tea that I would bring to her in the music room.

In summer she would bring us flowers that she grew in boxes on her balcony, or a tomato of which she was especially proud. At Christmas she gave us a pink-colored, pale blue, or green glass wrapped in colored paper. She would hold it out to me and say: "Here, put it under the Christmas tree for your mother. Let's see if she guesses from whom this gift is." She allowed herself this pleasure every year. Her last name was Glass, and she always asked me if my mother saw the connection. I never dared to ask her whether she posed such riddles to all her pupils.

She was the first to suggest to my mother that I become a violinist.

My piano teacher was a plump lady whose appearance alone induced trust. She laughed and chuckled over every little thing. When we played four-handed waltzes, she would throw her head back in pleasure. She was pretty but never spoke about what beauty means for a woman. She had daughters, none of them married, and only female cousins, no males. Of all the women I knew, she was the only one who didn't have a husband in the war. I was convinced that this explained her *joie de vivre* and her cheerfulness. My mother said: "No, she was born that way and remained that way because she has no husband in the war." She would send my mother taffeta scarves she had sewn herself and painted with pussy willows and the first bars of Chopin's waltzes. The material was stiff; the colors flaked from one Christmas to the other, so that many notes of the melody disappeared.

My mother had great respect for my teachers; she criticized none of their decisions, their methods, their habits, none of their gifts. She wrapped the scarves in tissue paper, placed the colored glasses in the first row of the buffet, and was always ready to show off these presents and praise their great importance and usefulness.

My gym teacher never came to the house; she sent no gifts, but on every holiday she invited our families. She would stick my head in a leather collar with chin props, hoist me to the ceiling of the gym, and make me hang from there—I felt for an eternity. When I was down below again, I was made to lie down on a table and was massaged with a kind of bubble soap. All students received the same treatment; it was supposed to strengthen our neck and spinal column, which supposedly eliminated tendon and joint damage caused by bad posture.

My teacher wore her black hair tied in a thick braided bun on the nape of her neck, and she dressed in a black jersey costume with pleated skirt. With a shrill voice she would count one, two, three, one, two, three. She treated us all the same; to her we were only a row of bodies to be hung like sausages in a smokehouse.

Posture was a very important point of physical fitness. Of this we were all convinced. Nevertheless, we hated to be suspended from the ceiling in that way. Yet on the way home we felt in top form and quickly forgot the torments we had undergone.

Two concluding remarks on my teachers: There was also a small, shy woman who twice a week taught me knitting and crocheting. When she left our house, her pockets, crocheted out of red wool, always bulged with gifts. Where my mother conjured them from, as if by magic, was a mystery to me. She must have had a hiding place for such things. The small, shy woman's name was Martha. When she left without her presents, my mother would call her back with "Martha, Martha, you have vanished"—words of an aria from the opera *Martha* by Flotow. Those were the rare occasions when my teacher smiled. And when she climbed the steps to the front door, you could see her pointed teeth which looked all worn out.

Finally, my mother bought me a guitar, and a new teacher was added to the rest. But she was quite different from her colleagues, much younger, with straw blond hair and red cheeks. She adorned her head with braids, wore peasant blouses and skirts and short black cardigans that kept her warm. She spoke with a strong

Bavarian accent. She was taking care of a sick sister whose hus-band—a local doctor—was at the front.

This guitar player's name was Marianne, and she seemed to take no notice of the war. The dozens of colored silk ribbons that hung from her instrument were as joyful as the musician herself. She sang folk tunes and mountain songs. I deeply loved her clear, strong voice. And I, too, enthusiastically collected ribbons for my own guitar. Some were painted, others were embroidered with texts, songs, and poems. It made one think of a bouquet of field flowers swaying to the rhythm of a melody in a light breeze.

I sang short Bavarian and Austrian songs, my breathless, weak voice supported by powerful chords. I dedicated much time to my guitar and daydreamed about it. "Go ahead and dream," my mother would say, "but be careful you don't become dizzy."

My guitar was coated with a dark brown lacquer, and a slim black stripe had been left around the sound board. I was head over heels in love with this instrument and hugged it every night before going to bed. I felt a little guilty for not feeling the same tenderness for my violin; perhaps it touched me less because it was smaller.

Despite the war I never lost heart during my youth. My mother protected me, and despite all the storms that descended on her and her principles, she overcame all difficulties—entirely by herself.

The war came to an end. I didn't know much about the events and the politics of that time. We went to school, to the tutoring sessions, to concerts, to literature courses—all that was supposed to benefit our education.

I had a wonderful childhood. And much happiness as well. Despite my mistakes, my father's death, despite the war-scarred childhood years, my early youth was beautiful. I learned to renounce many "good things" and nevertheless live. Result: At the end of my youth, "I stood firmly with both feet on the ground." At that time young people knew nothing about the historic upheavals, and that was probably one of the reasons for my happy girlhood. Our defense mechanism, admittedly, did not prevent us from expressing foolish opinions about government policy with utter naïveté. After all, it's easy to criticize; it's much more difficult to govern. That was made clear to us at the time. And also: "Be quiet, if you've got nothing of interest to say, never just be content with destroying what you don't like. Life is not a bed of roses. Nor does it have the sweet taste of honey or sugar, but life is good if you struggle to make it so."

I saw my mother for the last time when I was with the occupation troops of the U.S. Army in Berlin. When I left Berlin, she brought me to my jeep, slammed the door shut, and said: "Now, for a change, think of yourself for once."

YOUTH

Thanks to my mother my life was very pleasant.

One day I was shocked to hear the words "boarding school." It was nighttime. My mother was discussing the matter with some aunts who were visiting us.

For a while my life went on unchanged. As usual, my violin case under my arm, I walked over to my new violin teacher, always accompanied, of course, by my governess.

She was an Englishwoman, and after some resistance on my part, I learned her language, perhaps to make up for my poor classroom instruction in English. My governess was a good woman, I suppose, but I didn't especially like her. Her guard dog expression bothered me, but I didn't really object to her doing her duty. The moment we arrived at my teacher's flat, she would sit down in the living room and happily sip the cup of tea that the teacher's wife offered her.

I began to practice the violin tirelessly. This cut into my other activities and took up all my free time. When I didn't go to the violin teacher, there were piano lessons, gymnastic lessons, or the prescribed walks. By seven o'clock I was in bed. The days were short and usually crowded. Fortunately, some nights an exception was made: The visits to concerts and the theater were like sunbeams after a rainy day.

31

I saw performances of all the classics: Shakespeare, Greek tragedies, everything that might enrich a young mind. At other times I might be taken to the opera.

Life apparently had again returned to normal. But I found that a meaningless expression, since I didn't know what "normal" meant. Everything now seemed to be going smoothly at home. My mother still wore black, but like my aunts she had discarded her veil of mourning. The widows were slowly getting used to their lot. Their lamentations had ceased, but you could still sense a quiet, restrained pain. I already knew sorrow to be a personal thing.

I had taken part in many Protestant burials, and I learned not to cry in public. I later had occasion to observe rites at Jewish burials. I came to the conclusion that Jewish customs might be better than our own. Jews can express their grief, weep and lament over the corpse being interred. In the Christian world we are taught to hide our feelings. As an inheritor of this traditional practice, I continue to be a woman who never reveals her deepest feelings, a reserved and lonely woman, imprisoned by her most sacred beliefs.

The boarding school, which until then had been only a whispered threat, became a reality. I was to go to Weimar, the city of my idol Goethe.

During my last year at school, I had begun to deify Goethe absolutely. It's no wonder that throughout my whole life I have devoutly honored his spirit and thought. His philosophy guided all of us, my schoolmates as well as myself, in our formative years. But I suppose it left an even deeper imprint on me. Since I had no father I needed a masculine model to relate to. So I raved about everything that revolved around Goethe.

I was happy when I was told I would be going to boarding school in Weimar, although the idea of leaving home made me very sad.

As always, I obeyed.

The boarding school was cold and unfriendly; the streets seemed foreign, and the smell in the air was different from that in my big native city. No mother, nobody I knew, no refuge to which I could flee, no place where I could secretly cry, no warmth.

We slept six in a room. That was harder for me than for the other pupils. I was used to a private existence. (In the meantime, I've learned it's no different in the army.) There must be a hidden intention in this kind of education. While you may "enjoy" its benefits, you also, of course, suffer under it. You mope, and you lie awake all night and cry because you want to be at home with mother. But the school finally wins out. You no longer cry for "Mamma" but learn to manage on your own. You learn to do what you must and keep your personal feelings at arm's length.

You fall in line going down the street in twos; you lead the other pupils (I wonder why I was always at the head) and meet people who are busy shopping or gossiping on a street corner. You feel desperate, rejected, excluded. We read Goethe's *The Sorrows of Young Werther* and shed copious tears. We would have liked best of all, as young people do today, loudly to proclaim our joy at discovering that so famous a writer knew our young souls. All young people feel misunderstood. It is an old affliction of youth. When you're suffering the torments of loneliness, poetry and sentimentality help—violins that sing deep in our hearts, dreams that inspire us even though they cannot solve our problems. That was what I felt at the time. During my stay in Weimar, I came to know a wonderful love that suffused my whole being with excitement, indeed an ecstasy that guided my life with a divine light and shielded me from evil and mean experiences.

Strange as it may seem, Goethe had become a veritable god to me. I read his books and followed all his teachings. Nothing could undo or harm me. His city became a refuge for me. His houses became my houses. The women he loved became rivals who made me mad with jealousy.

Many of my "biographers" make Weimar the city of my birth. This is simply not true. But what is true is that this city became the home of my choice.

It was a simple thing to do since almost all its inhabitants live under Goethe's spell.

His house on the Frauenplan, his Garden House, the house of his great friend Frau Charlotte von Stein were shrines—we would go there every day to cleanse our souls.

This admiration for a great poet and thinker bore fruit. It was a protective shield against all the temptations that threaten a young girl's heart, her body and soul. My passion for Goethe, along with the rest of my education, enclosed me in a complete circle full of solid moral values that I have preserved throughout my life.

And there was also Immanuel Kant! His laws were my laws; I knew them by heart!

"So act that the maxim of your will, at the same time, could always hold as the principle of a universal legislation."

"The principle directly opposed to morality consists in making the principle of individual well-being the dominant principle of the will."

"The moral law, as such, requires no justification, not only because it proves the possibility of freedom but because it proves that freedom really belongs to those who recognize this law and choose to submit to it."

Logic is not a feminine trait. Thank God I was bound to Immanuel Kant's categorical imperative and teachings and, during my youth, insisted on thinking like a man and not like a woman. Logic was demanded at every moment. If my conclusions were illogical, I was excluded from the conversation. To this day I've been unable to ignore this strict rule and continue to expect those to whom I am close to share my respect for it.

This education helped me through my whole, often more than eventful life and continues to serve me today. It was the best "capital" resource for my profession. But in my private life, too, decisions were determined by my capacity for logical thinking. This capacity is exclusively to Kant's credit, because in my youth there was no man who could have taught me this.

Logic is the key to an all-inclusive spiritual well-being.

The girls studying music, as I was, were allowed to attend the opera three evenings a week. We were overcome by the magic, the lights, the *trompe l'oeil* in the auditorium, fascinated by the violins, by all the music.

This period of my youth was wonderful. To be young seemed to be the most natural state of the world for all of us. Little did we know that such happiness would be of brief duration. Even so, I felt it was my duty to enjoy every single moment of it.

My mother came to visit me every three weeks to "straighten up" my room, which needless to say, was always in perfect order, and to wash my hair. Since there was no shower, she would use jugs to rinse the soap out of my hair, until there was no trace of soap left in the water.

It may seem unusual that a mother should travel so far just to wash her daughter's hair. But my mother was very proud of my hair, and she wanted it to stay beautiful. She didn't trust me on this point. That my hair has always remained attractive I surely owe to my mother's help. She would dry it with a hand towel, then have me sit on a chair in the visiting room. My face would be flushed from all the rubbing that was part of this treatment. My hair was in complete disarray and wet, and when we took leave of each other, tears would stream down my face. I wasn't the only one who underwent this treatment. We would all wash ourselves thoroughly in expectation of this day. But that was nothing compared to mother's "scrubbing."

Thanks to the music I was very happy even when I had spells of homesickness. The other lessons bored or oppressed me. I was poor at mathematics and still am. I was good at history and languages. My memories of those years are, on the whole, happy ones.

Then came the fateful day when my time at the boarding school was over. A decision had to be made as to whether I should or shouldn't continue my studies in Weimar. When my mother arrived, my violin and piano teachers praised my "triumphs," and she entered me in another girls' school in Weimar. I was to live there so that I could take further music lessons. I led an even more pleasant life than before. I could play as long as I wished or had to. I was freer, and could divide my time as I saw fit.

35

Naturally, I still went to concerts, to the opera, and to the theater. I frequently visited my favorite haunts, the libraries, and regularly wrote my mother, who always answered punctually.

But soon disaster descended upon me. Out of the blue my mother showed up in Weimar, took me out of the boarding school and back to our home in Berlin. Was she concerned about my new freedom? In any case, she seemed troubled. And she answered my anxious questions evasively.

However, she did leave me time to say good-bye to my friends and teachers. Sadly, I visited Goethe's Garden House for the last time. Since I was used to obedience, I raised no objections. On the way back I was very quiet. In Berlin I had a new violin teacher, Professor Flesch of the Music Academy, who accepted me only after I had played hours on end for him.

Everything was different now. Bach, Bach, Bach, always Bach. I had to practice eight hours a day. My mother and I almost lost our minds.

I was the first to give up. The doctors examined me and explained that the pain I was feeling on my left ring finger was due to a tendon inflammation; my whole hand was placed in a cast. Bach's solo sonatas were responsible for my debility. It was a crushing blow. Now I would never become a violin "soloist" celebrated in the musical world. My mother's disappointment was even greater than mine. The old violin she had bought for me now lay wrapped in a silken cloth in its black case. For my mother it was one more broken dream. As for me, for the first time in a long while I had nothing to do.

I started receiving formal instruction all over again, now at home. I started reading Goethe again to maintain my connection with him. Then, one day I discovered Rainer Maria Rilke—I say "discovered" because in school no teacher had ever spoken about him. From then on I had a new god.

I thought his poetry so beautiful that I learned long verses by heart and loved reciting them aloud.

My mother gradually got over her disappointment, though she still hoped that my hand would heal. She approved of my doing lots of reading because, in her opinion, one should always be "doing something." Tirelessly, she would repeat "do something" when she found me daydreaming. Even now I still hear her voice, and I find myself always "doing something."

Finally, the cast was removed. The swollen hand lay motionless on my lap. I observed it, perplexed. Telephone calls to doctors were made again, but their prognosis was not very encouraging: The hand would always remain susceptible to a recurrence. At this time I greatly missed my father, and I'm sure my mother would have liked a man at her side, a man who would have helped us come to some decision.

Surprising as it may seem, I took my father's place—against my mother's will.

I decided to become an actress because the theater was the only place where one could recite beautiful texts and beautiful verses like those by Rilke, which at one and the same time broke my heart and restored my courage.

So I set the violin aside once and for all and tried to obtain entry into the theater world. Just a try, I explained to my mother.

At that time Max Reinhardt ran a drama school in Berlin. I showed up there for an audition. Naïve as usual, I planned to play the part of the girl in Hugo von Hofmannsthal's play *Death and the Fool* after I had been told by someone that Rilke was not a "theater author."

We had to audition before a formidable number of men sitting in chairs for what seemed to me hours on end. Then we were asked to recite an excerpt from Faust, "Gretchen's Prayer." When my turn came, I was told to kneel. The idea of falling to my knees in such a place was embarrassing to me, and I hesitated— long enough, in fact, for one of the teachers to throw a pillow at my feet. I didn't understand. I looked at him and asked: "Why did you throw the pillow at me?" "So that you can kneel on it," he answered. This confused me even more, for in my view it was ridiculous to use a pillow for this scene. Nevertheless, I recited my verses and was then told to return the next day.

There were so many girls that I felt I was back in grade school. One of them was named Grete Mosheim, and we shyly exchanged a few words. Grete Mosheim later became a famous

37

actress. But on that day, in that school, she tried, like all of us, to attract the teachers' attention.

At any rate, the fact that we were allowed to attend the Max Reinhardt Drama School was an encouraging sign for the future.

The school's schedule filled most of our day and in addition, there were exercises that had to be practiced at home. We were warned that we had picked "a dangerous profession," but we were determined to accept the challenge. Dangerous or not, I was enthusiastic about it. We never regretted our work, we never regretted the long hours spent trying to understand what the teachers were talking about. We learned. Simply setting a goal for yourself is in itself already very important, distant and vague as it might be.

When I came home every day, I would tell my mother what we thought we had achieved, or what we had tried to achieve, and my mother listened to me patiently.

Like other young girls at that time, I knew little about what was going on outside the narrow frame of my little world. Although it might seem strange now, back then we had no interest whatsoever in politics or political events. Our attitude was diametrically opposed to that of most of today's young people.

My generation and, in particular, the young girls I knew, were affected only by the daily happenings in their immediate circle: the household, personal achievement, weddings, and children. Even as we grew older and inflation hit the country, our attitude didn't change. I was aware that prices could fluctuate wildly. But like all the young girls and women of my generation, I simply took note of the fact and didn't worry about it further. With the lightheartedness of youth, we thought all these sweeping changes were transitory and would soon disappear. Our own problems seemed to be far more important, and we weren't in the least inclined to ask ourselves about the reasons for the insecurity that gripped Germany in the twenties. Much later, when I had finally grown up and studied this period, I realized that these events had left no mark whatsoever on me. Today I wonder whether that wasn't a good thing after all.

Max Reinhardt ran four theaters in Berlin. His school was

located in the rooms on the top floor of one of these theaters. We never met our principal, and yet his reputation terrified all of us. He himself no longer taught, but he still picked the teachers who were to work with us.

I can understand why Max Reinhardt, once I became famous, liked to say that he had "discovered" me. But—unfortunately— that's not the case. I had no special talent and I knew it. Everybody knew it. Grete Mosheim and I, as well as all the other students, were content merely to attend classes and to play any of the minor roles offered here and there. Grete Mosheim was the first to stand out among us, leaving us all behind, far behind.

Rudolf Sieber, the assistant to Joe May, who was filming *The Tragedy of Love* in Berlin, had an unusual idea for that time—namely, to have the roles of spectators, pedestrians, etc., played by unknowns rather than by professional actors. He contacted the Max Reinhardt Drama School and asked whether the students would be available to be the face of the crowd. The offer was enthusiastically accepted. So one lovely day, Grete Mosheim and I showed up at the studio.

Rudolf Sieber told us he was looking for "demimonde ladies" of distinction. He decided that my friend Grete Mosheim looked "too serious" for the part. I, however, was told to appear for work the very next day. That's how he thought of me.

I was proud he had chosen me as "a face in the crowd," proud that I had made it, proud not to have looked too young, too innocent, too . . . well, too much of everything that I really was.

Grete Mosheim later got the leading role in the play *Old Heidelberg*, a terribly sentimental melodrama in which we had all hoped to get a role. But, unlike me, she was the "fine lady" type. Along with several classmates, I accompanied her to her first rehearsal, shed hot tears, and wished her lots of luck.

We missed her but continued to follow our own paths, which led us here and there. For instance, I played the role of a maid in the first act of one play, then by subway or bus I would go to another theater, where in the second act of another play I was a matron, after which I wound up the day as a prostitute in the third act of a third play. Each night was different from the night before.

All of us always went from one place to another and did what was demanded of us. Naturally, we didn't receive any money for all this. Working as extras was part of our training.

Most theaters, compared to those of today, were small, but when I was sent to the Schumann Theater where Max Reinhardt was staging *The Taming of the Shrew*, I was amazed at the enormous size of the interior. It had formerly housed a circus. I was to play the role of the widow in the fifth act. I had only three lines to speak, but this was more than had ever been given to me before. The leading man complained that people in the first row could not hear me. I had to await the final verdict. Elisabeth Bergner was playing the shrew. Austrian by birth, she had later lived in Switzerland and finally settled in Berlin. She had patience with beginners and was able to convince the theater director to take us on in the cast. Naturally, there was no amplifier in this giant hall, so we tried everything "to project ourselves beyond the stage" in the way we had been taught at school: "Hold your nose, bring your voice into your head and say *Ning, Nang, Neun, Neun.*"

Dr. Joseph worked tirelessly with us, without a break. With a rope laid over his shoulders, he literally pulled us through the rehearsal room while we struggled against it, weakly repeating: *"Ning, Nang, Neun, Neun."* His method worked. We became actresses. My three lines in *The Taming of the Shrew* were:

"Then never trust me, if I be afeard."

"He that is giddy thinks the world turns round."

"Lord, let me never have a cause to sigh, till I be brought to such a silly pass."

In Shakespeare's original text, the widow's role contained more lines. But they were deleted for reasons unknown to me. During the rehearsals, I familiarized myself with the rules of the theater. When my turn came, I spoke my three lines. I never got to see Max Reinhardt. We all hoped to catch just one glimpse of him. But, as always, he made himself scarce.

I declaimed my lines with as much "resonance" as possible. Later, when I said good night to Elisabeth Bergner, I never imagined that one day she would become my friend.

I had also come to know an actress named Anni Mewes, who

would call me several times a week. Once she asked me: "Can you fill in for me in a play? All I have is one line. My dress will fit you beautifully. But don't tell anybody about it. Just go there and make your entrance after the following dialogue. Get a pencil and write it down."

I really enjoyed doing favors for others. Also, it allowed me to visit many different theaters, recite many odd lines, but not many dialogues. The roles were utterly unimportant, but then again somebody had to play them.

While I played Anni Mewes's small role, she was probably dancing or otherwise having fun in some "night spot." The parts were so small that no one ever caught on to our trick. Sometimes things were not so simple, and Anni had to explain certain details more exactly. This was the case with the play *The Great Baritone* starring Albert Basserman.

I had to get myself ready in her dressing room, which she shared with some other actresses, and then go on stage and deliver a single line: "You are wonderful." Anni Mewes had explained to me that it was extremely important to wear her gloves and leave the last button open. After my partner embraced me, I had to extend my hand so he could kiss the inside of my arm. I followed her instructions conscientiously.

The only role I played worth mentioning was in George Bernard Shaw's *Misalliance*. I had several lines to say in this one, and for the first time in my so-called theatrical career, I drew a ripple of laughter from the audience with the words: "But papa."

I also remember a comic incident from this time. The play in question was being staged by Max Reinhardt in one of his small, intimate theaters with Elisabeth Bergner in the leading role.

She entered the stage by descending an imposing, arched staircase. Below stood a table around which sat four people playing bridge. I was one of them, and all I had to say was: "I pass."

As was the fashion in those days I was wearing a pale gray custom-tailored dress. When I tried it on, I was surprised to discover that it was brightly spangled with pearls and diamonds, but only on the back. When I asked about this, I was told that during the entire scene I was not to turn around, not even once, so that there was no need to adorn the front part of the dress.

I understood and said nothing.

I relate this anecdote to show how unimportant my roles were. Yet, because I sat with my back to the audience, I could all the better see and enjoy Elisabeth Bergner's splendid entrance on stage via the staircase. The first word she spoke was "Damn!" I was so fascinated to hear this word spoken that I often forgot my "I pass," but nobody noticed this. The other actors continued as though nothing had happened; nobody made mention of my omission. I was an insignificant extra (or supernumerary as they say today). So when I read the chapters that my "biographers" devote to this time where they claim that I had become a "famous actress," I can only laugh. I was completely unknown, a mere beginner, one among hundreds of amateur actresses, just another pupil attending the Max Reinhardt Drama School.

But I was not discontented with my lot; I was quite happy just to be in contact with great actors and actresses. I did what was asked of me, as I also always did later both in my life and in my work.

I made still other appearances in many plays, mostly in silent roles, usually magnificently made up. As a rule, I spent more time getting myself ready than actually performing. The leading performers never spoke to us, and we were afraid of them. But we didn't engage in any "star cult." We observed them so attentively only because we admired their performances. Learn, learn, learn—that was our motto and our job.

I was one of the "silent observers" in Frank Wedekind's *Pandora's Box*. Believe it or not, I knew nothing at all about the play because I appeared only in the third act. To this day, I don't know what it is about.

I took pains to appear older, to look like a grown woman. At home I rehearsed in one of my mother's dresses, walking and swaying my hips like a kept woman. And every day I worked with Rudolf Sieber, with whom I was—and was to be for a long time— head over heels in love.

I took more singing lessons, visited the Max Reinhardt

Drama School, and learned a lot of classic roles I knew I would never play. I avidly learned the entire modern repertoire of ingenue roles, without, however, convincing my superiors who would make a face after the audition. Emotion-laden monologues did not suit my tone. So I had to acquire another style. I had to slip with great difficulty into the skin of another woman. I didn't like this woman. But, being well mannered, I learned all her outrageous lines.

There were more rehearsals, and I was ready to captivate the public with my presentation of the "femme fatale."

And again it was a flop. My teachers explained I was too young for this type. Another disappointment, but my zeal for work did not suffer.

My mother was relieved when I stayed home to work or read. She didn't particularly care about what I was doing as long as my nose was stuck in a book.

She cared as little for "the theater" as she did for "the film." But she put up with it all against her will, probably in the hope that I would meet someone who would break my attachment to the stage once and for all. But I was stubborn.

Rudolf Sieber had suggested I wear a monocle so as to appear more provocative. At that time the monocle symbolized the height of the macabre.

My mother gave me my father's monocle that she had kept for years.

Wearing one of her dresses, with my father's monocle tucked in my eye, my hair done up in hundreds of curls and locks, cosmeticized by some listless makeup artist who didn't have the slightest interest in lowly beginners, I walked on stage and took a few steps toward my future husband. I was as blind as a bat, but the monocle stayed in place. Rudolf Sieber must have laughed to himself when he spotted me in this getup. But he didn't show it.

He even managed to get me a small role in a film—again I had only one line. I loved Rudolf Sieber, not because he helped me but because he was blond, tall and clever—everything that a young girl longs for. The only problem was that he wasn't at all interested in young girls.

At that time—according to rumor at least—he was having a stormy love affair with the daughter of a theater director, a very beautiful movie actress.

And so I suffered. Luckily for me, the scenes in the gambling casino had to be shot over and over again, and since I was a "crowd extra" I was often called to the studio. I would see Rudolf, but he never spoke to me.

It was unthinkable to take this matter up at home. My mother had withdrawn into herself. She expressed no opinion of any kind. Nor did she ever speak of my adventures in the "world of film," a phrase offensive to her ear. For her film and circus were one and the same thing. And the circus was the complete opposite of the life she had imagined for me. In her eyes that world would prove disastrous for a young girl of my age.

She was so worried that she had terrible nightmares. She was afraid that I would allow myself to be misled into a sinful life and ruin myself forever.

She did not realize that I was immune to such dangers. Although she had brought me up to be this way, she wasn't at all sure she had succeeded.

To return to my outlandish outfit: I was led to the gambling table, then Rudolf Sieber and his assistants told me what I was to do and where I was supposed to go. At times he would run up to me to give me advice. Hopelessly in love, anxiety-ridden, I would wait for these brief encounters.

When I returned home after three days under his direction, I told my mother: "I've met the man I want to marry." My mother didn't faint on the spot or lose her composure. Instead she said to me, "If you really want that, we'll see what we can do." But she never allowed me to meet Rudolf Sieber outside the studio, despite his telephone calls and his invitations to dinner in a restaurant or to go for a stroll.

Yet he didn't give up. He came to the house to speak with my mother (after making an appointment, of course), but after this meeting she was no happier than she had been when all I did was talk about him.

He could not know that at home I was not the same girl as at the studio, the girl with the monocle in her eye playing the most depraved prostitute. Though, of course, he knew that that was only a role. Otherwise he wouldn't have courted me the way he did. He could see I was only bluffing. He was nice; he was gentle. He gave me the feeling that I could trust him, and this feeling was sustained during all the years of our marriage. Our trust was reciprocal and total.

We were young. Such mutual faith back then was extremely rare in the decadent, cynical world of Germany in the twenties. Rudolf meant everything to me.

We got married after a year's engagement during which we were never alone. There was always a chaperone with us, always a "spy" who kept a watchful eye on us. Rudolf Sieber must have had an angel's patience to endure all these restrictions. He never complained. On the day of our marriage, my mother placed the myrtle wreath on my head; the family members, in uniform or in civilian clothes, crowded into the church. And I, sentimental and romantic as always, wept when I looked at Rudolf who seemed so calm.

He loved me with all his heart without, however, sharing my penchant for sentimentality. He detested mawkishness. He gave feeling a higher priority and racked his brains trying to teach me the difference between the two. And he succeeded, as he did in everything close to his heart.

Even after we were married, he didn't have a simple life. We observed all the amenities and traditions, but he still felt he was not fully accepted by my family. I was not intelligent or clever enough to help him over this abyss that separated him from my relatives, but I continued to hope for the best, continued to look on the bright side of things, deciding that if I loved him, all the others would finally love him, too.

Fortunately, I was soon pregnant, as I wanted to be, and this worked to bring Rudolf closer to my family.

He was frequently called away on trips by the film work he was engaged in. Then I would be alone. Each time he left, he was considerate enough to bring me to my mother so she could take care of me; his young wife with the bulging belly would be better able to rest in her mother's living room than in her own.

That didn't bother me. I was carrying so many wonders inside me. A new life was developing within me. Another heart was beating next to mine, everything that was happening to me seemed wonderful, as if coming out of an ethereal novel written specially for me. I actually felt that I was the only person who had ever carried a child beneath her heart.

Whenever my husband returned from a trip, he would embrace me and kiss my belly where the child, our daughter, was growing. We searched for a first name, a first name for "her" and we found one that was to represent all my hopes and dreams: Maria. Maria!

She was born. I screamed and suffered as women throughout time have suffered. I screamed and suffered and brought a little girl into the world.

Nothing really extraordinary. I breast-fed her for nine months. Mothers who do not breast-feed their babies don't know what they are missing: inner happiness, of course, but also health for the newborn. Babies who are breast-fed do not cry and scream as much as bottle-fed babies. The house was peaceful between the two breast-feedings. The milk makes the mother's breast swell, which in turn, comforts the child and assures it peace and tranquility. All is quiet and peaceful, all attention is focused on the mother and the child . . .

So it was with our child, Maria. She was our supreme joy in addition to our marital happiness.

A home without a child is not a home. I was convinced of this even before I had a child. It belongs to the mysterious intuition that a young and ignorant soul possesses. Suddenly the whole world goes off in another direction, and everything revolves only around a child in a cradle.

This cradle becomes the center of the world.

I was sad for the first time on the day I had to stop breast-feeding. Although I drank many quarts of tea and beer and conscientiously followed the best advice, I could nourish her only for nine months.

Gradually I resumed my work—Maria was an uncomplicated

child who slept through the night and never woke up to demand her bottle—but the films I was making were nothing special.

When I began this book I decided to relate only the essential events of my life and career. My so-called biographers eagerly published a long list of films in which I had appeared at that time and supposedly played leading roles. This is not so. When Josef von Sternberg chose me for *The Blue Angel*, he was hiring an unknown. It was not until 1930, in Hollywood and after *Morocco*, that I really became a star. However, I consider such matters trivial and superficial, despite the typically American notion that an actress's career is determined by whether her name appears prominently over or under the title on the movie poster.

I didn't find being placed above the title worth all the effort. It involved too much responsibility. For one's peace of mind, it's better to stay below. But there were no such problems with *The Blue Angel*: The name Marlene Dietrich appeared as one of the supporting cast.

I had learned modesty from my early experience in the theater. My name on the programs was miniscule. You'd need a magnifying glass to decipher it. As I've said, Max Reinhardt never deemed me worthy of a glance. This was only right, I suppose, because he certainly had more important things to do than "discover" the hidden talents of young actresses like me. So my appearance on the Berlin stage held no great importance for me, except on one occasion . . .

I was told that I should introduce myself to a certain Forster-Larrinaga at the "Komödie," an enchanting little theater, also under Max Reinhardt's direction, on Berlin's Kurfürstendamm.

There I found auditions in progress for the next staging of a kind of new-style musical (also called "literary revue"). I was asked if I could sing, and in a shy voice I answered, "Yes, a little."

When I came to the theater everything was brilliantly lit up, which was unusual for auditions; normally a single electric bulb illumined the panicky faces of the candidates.

Yet I would be lying were I to say that I was scared. I was anxious only about the singing. Once backstage, notes were pressed into my hand. My musical training saved me. The words were simple, easy to retain and witty. The action of the revue *It's in the Air* took place in a department store. It was written by Marcellus Schiffer and Mischa Spoliansky, both of whom were very well known in Berlin at that time. My song (a young woman lost in a department store driven to buy everything offered "at reduced prices" whether or not she needs the items—terrific bargains) was to open the performance. That meant—and it really didn't surprise me—that my role was unimportant.

It was the first time that a revue of this kind was to be staged at the "Komödie." Five musicians, as well as a slender youth at the piano, were ensconced in a niche of the auditorium just above the front parquet rows.

The pianist gave me the key. A thin child's voice came out from between my lips. The pitch was much too high for me. I gave forth with a trembling falsetto that had nothing to do with singing.

"Stop! Next!" the director shouted. At this point, Mischa Spoliansky stood up and said: "Try it once more, only this time an octave lower."

The one who was to be "next" retreated to the background while I stayed where I was, as if rooted to the spot, scared stiff. What if I should disappoint the composer? We began again at a lower pitch. Mischa Spoliansky kept changing the key until suddenly—to my infinite surprise—harmonious sounds seemed to fill the theater.

Spoliansky made note of the key. The musicians and the composer began to whisper to each other. The other candidates moved toward the exit. The role was mine!

I went to the seats in the orchestra to thank the composer. Then I moved to do the same to the director. But I stopped short when I noticed all heads turned toward the theater's main entrance. Margo Lion, the star of the show, was coming down the center aisle toward the director. Her husband Marcellus Schiffer, the author of the revue, was at her side.

Someone must have said something about me, I thought, as she glanced in my direction. As far as I could tell, she didn't speak a word. She was a strange woman whose beauty did not match the preferred stereotype of that time. She was as thin as a bean pole and showed none of the voluptuousness that Germans at that time were supposed to prize so highly.

She was French, but spoke flawless German. She had "a satirical and ultra-modern way of singing," to quote a famous critic. A style that she was to retain. During the rehearsal, Marcellus Schiffer watched her closely from the corner of his eye. She was a professional down to the last detail. She was a consummate artist.

After rehearsing for a week, she summoned me to her dressing room. There she began to size me up with her pale blue eyes. The author, composer and director crowded around her. What did she want from me? Quite simply, I found out we were going to sing a new song together—a duet—called "My Best Girlfriend." I couldn't believe it.

When I finally got hold of myself again, I was told that the song would be a parody of The Dolly Sisters. We would be dressed in the same way. She was to sing high and I was to sing low. Then, one behind the other, we would cavort about the stage in great comic strides, finally bringing the number to a close at center stage.

We got down to the business of our song right away. The tailor shops made the costumes. I was elated that my modest request to appear in black was granted. Even our hats were to be black. Everything fell together perfectly. When our clothes were ready, I fastened big bunches of violets to both our shoulders to give our outfits, which I found a bit too mournful, a friendly touch of color.

Little did I know that after a play by Edouard Bourdet called *The Prisoners*, violets in the Berlin theatrical world of the twenties had taken on a rather special meaning. I had simply found the violets pleasant.

But on the day after the opening, when I read the review describing "an androgynous song" as the high point of the performance whose somewhat peculiar character was heightened by the violets on the shoulders of "the star Margo Lion and her cohort, a moderately talented beginner," to quote the critic, I was flabbergasted.

However, I didn't dare ask Margo Lion to explain it all to me. She probably would have laughed at my gaucherie and naïveté. "Androgynous!" I had no idea what the critic meant. Hadn't he noticed that Oskar Karlweiss had joined us in the last refrain? And what about the number in which all three of us danced together in a close embrace?

The production was far ahead of its time—and far ahead of anything I knew about at this point. As, for example, when the director insisted on the use of curtains rather than side scenes and focused the lighting on the performers, leaving it all to the audience's imagination.

During the performances (and I didn't miss a single one), I didn't make friends with anyone in the company. Margo Lion both fascinated and frightened me. For nothing in the world would I have missed that great moment when, in her wedding gown, she sang "The Blue Hour," telling the story of her deep longing in the time before the wedding.

Since I was a member of the cast, I was allowed to stay backstage. That's all I really wanted. I never sought direct contact with the leading performers or lesser cast members. My upbringing discouraged any kind of intrusiveness on my part. How could an unknown like me dare to speak to a great star whose name was emblazoned on the posters? Unthinkable! But life sometimes holds many surprises in store for us. Who could have imagined that several years later, during the Nazi regime, I would become a close friend of Mischa Spoliansky and his family, whom I was to meet in England? That I would play a role in the secret operation that rescued Oskar Karlweiss from the clutches of the Nazis and succeeded in bringing him via Spain to the United States, where he resumed his career and then, all too young, died?

After her husband's death, Margo Lion returned to her native France and later became famous in the movies and on TV. By that time I had formed a deep and real friendship with her. Nothing brings people closer together than shared tragic events.

It's in the Air enjoyed a great success, but suddenly its long run came to an abrupt, unceremonious end. There were no good-bye parties as is customary today. One otherwise fine evening the curtain came down, and we simply walked out of the theater for the last time. I had to go back to the "small" roles.

My performance in the revue had not brought me much recognition from the strict teachers of the Max Reinhardt Drama School. Again I began racing against the clock, riding the buses and streetcars, performing in countless productions with only a few lines to say, just as before.

Yet one day my luck changed. I was engaged for Georg Kaiser's *Zwei Krawatten* (*Bow Ties*). Hans Albers was to play the leading role, and Mischa Spoliansky was responsible for the music—two names that promised success. I played an American woman and had only one line: "May I invite you all to dine with me this evening?" This was the play in which Josef von Sternberg saw me when I repeated my line for the umpteenth time. The "Leonardo da Vinci of the camera" scrutinized the program with his eagle eye, found my name, stood up, and left the theater.

It's not true that he ran backstage as soon as the performance was over to meet me and sign me up for *The Blue Angel* right then and there. It is true, however, that from that moment on, von Sternberg had only one idea in his head: to take me away from the stage and to make a movie actress out of me, to "Pygmalionize" me.

One step followed the other, despite my husband's apprehensions. He allowed me to go for the screen test only after he had assured himself that von Sternberg's proposal was serious. My meeting with von Sternberg has prompted many false assumptions on the part of my "biographers." On the day after the performance of *Bow Ties*, von Sternberg arranged a meeting for me with the Ufa executives. This reception was ice cold. They did not like me, had no confidence in me. Von Sternberg flew into a rage, shouting: "If that's how things are, I'll go back to the United States!"

But, as we know, he finally got his way.

I had not been impressed by my first meeting with von Sternberg. When you're young and stupid (which is often the case), you have no aptitude for appreciating extraordinary human beings. I pointed out to him that I was not photogenic (my few movie roles had convinced me of that) and suggested he look for somebody else.

Despite all this, he arranged to give me a screen test on the same day he tested the most likely prospect for the job, Lucie Mannheim. She was well known and had set her heart on getting the part, even though it didn't suit her at all. She had a rather broad behind. In addition to her acting talents, she had a gift for winning over Emil Jannings, who apparently had a weakness for broad behinds. Despite my baby fat, I've never had a prepossessing posterior. I was well-cushioned all over except for this particular part of my anatomy. Nevertheless, my rear seemed pretty round to me. But probably not enough so for Emil Jannings.

To show his good will, von Sternberg's screen test of Jannings's protégée included shots of her most prominent feature. Finally, it was my turn.

I wasn't so upset at first because I didn't care whether I got the part or not. But by the time I squeezed into a tight, sequin-studded gown and had my hair curled by a hairdresser with a curling iron, with steam billowing up to the ceiling, I felt utterly defenseless and full of despair.

And there he was, the stranger, the man whom I would be seeing mostly behind the camera, the inimitable, unforgettable Josef von Sternberg himself. Someone was sitting at the piano. I was asked to climb on top of the piano, roll down one of my stockings to the ankle and sing a song, the notes of which I was supposed to have with me but had failed to bring. Since I thought I didn't have a real chance for the role, why should I carry the music around with me? Then why did I come? There was only one answer: Because it was expected of me.

Von Sternberg was patient: "If you don't have any music," he said to me, "then sing whatever you like."

"I like American songs," I answered, with some embarrassment.

"Sing an American song, then."

Feeling a bit more relaxed, I started to tell the pianist about the song I was going to sing. Of course, the pianist didn't know it.

Von Sternberg suddenly interrupted me in a tone that allowed no objections: "That's it!" he exclaimed. "That's exactly the scene I want. It's terrific! I'm going to shoot it right now. Repeat what you just said to the pianist. Explain again what he is supposed to play and then sing your song to him."

I am sorry to say I've never seen these screen tests.

For a few weeks I heard nothing from those in charge of the production. But I didn't worry about it. My daughter was taking her first steps, my husband was finally back from a very long business trip. Everything was going along as smoothly as possible at home.

Finally, the phone rang. It was von Sternberg. He wanted to talk with my husband. This call marked the beginning of a friendship that was to end only with the death of the great director. My husband paid careful attention. He wanted to represent his wife's interests properly, just like an agent. And just like an agent he was determined to haggle over the contract conditions offered by Ufa, clause by clause. The upshot of all these endless negotiations was a lump sum of five thousand dollars. Emil Jannings received two hundred thousand dollars, a difference requiring no comment. But, of course, Emil Jannings was a big star and I was a nonentity. Not only unknown but also inexperienced. In short, there was no reason to rejoice.

The "big wheels" at Ufa in no way shared von Sternberg's confidence in me, which troubled me further. When he showed them the screen tests, they were unanimous in their opinion that Lucie Mannheim was much better for the part. It was then that von Sternberg uttered the words that were to become legendary: "You have just confirmed that I was right. Marlene Dietrich is perfect for this role." Again, he threatened to drop the film altogether, pull up stakes and leave for the United States if I was not given the part. The producers were flabbergasted.

After von Sternberg's phone call, my husband met with the Ufa executives and signed the contract that bound me to appear in both English and German versions of *The Blue Angel* for the ridiculous sum (as my husband knew) of five thousand dollars. My husband suggested that I do something crazy with the money. So I bought myself my first mink coat.

The other members of *The Blue Angel* cast were not exactly sociable. Yet that was nothing compared to Emil Jannings, who hated the whole world, himself included. Sometimes we had to wait two full hours in our dressing rooms until Jannings was at last "ready to work." During this tense, difficult period von Sternberg would put to use all of his seemingly inexhaustible imagination to entice this psychopathic stellar performer onto the set; von Sternberg even whipped him when Jannings asked him to. When the atmosphere became sufficiently relaxed, we would finally be called onto the set. Jannings hated me from the depths of his heart and even had the gall to declare that I would never get anywhere if I insisted on following the directions of "a nut like von Sternberg," that I'd never become an important actress. Whereupon, like the well-bred young lady I was, in my best German, I answered, "Get lost!" meaning, "I'll continue to work with Mr. von Sternberg and obediently follow his directions up to the very last day of the shooting schedule. You have no right to speak to me that way. I'd find it distasteful to squeal on you, but you—especially you—will never get me to change my opinion. I may be a beginner and you may be a big star, but I know I'm better than you are, not professionally, perhaps, but as a human being." End of quote.

As soon as it was clear that I would be a member of the cast, I set to work under Josef von Sternberg's direction, and the legend of our creative association was born. You can never know whether the film you're making will someday be called "a classic." That's something that posterity must decide. You can never know beforehand what importance this or that film might ultimately achieve. That, at any rate, was the way it was back in those days. Today, stars invest their own money in a film and speculate on the anticipated profits that are expected to make their pockets bulge all the more.

The Blue Angel was the first great sound film following the First World War, and as such, it has all the imperfections of its time. Its success was due exclusively to von Sternberg's direction.

There were countless technical difficulties. For example, it was not possible to cut film carrying sound, which considerably prolonged the shooting period. And four cameras had to film each scene simultaneously to provide options for the final cut.

I found all this terribly exciting. To watch the great master at work was a boundless pleasure.

I was always ready when he called on me. However, I held myself a little to one side so as not to disturb anything, or to get in the way of the other actors. But I paid the strictest attention to the slightest sign from Mr. von Sternberg ordering me back onto the set.

In addition to Jannings, the cast included many other famous actors. They were, incidentally, all very nice to me. Poor Marlene, they must have thought. If she only knew what was in store for her after this . . .

But I had no idea of these ominous thoughts. I was still the nice, well-bred little girl who dutifully obeyed the instructions of her lord and master. He would not forsake me, I was sure. I was there for him, and he was there for me. Or so I told myself at any rate.

And I wasn't mistaken, as it turned out. Von Sternberg made two versions of the film—the German and the English—simultaneously.

Dubbing had not yet come on the scene. Von Sternberg introduced me to his American wife who, he said, would speak my lines if I had any trouble with English. All I would have to do is move my lips.

His proposal, with its underlying assumption that I might fail at something, shocked me. And I hated failure of any kind. So it was up to me to prove my worth, that I could do it.

We began the shooting. Each scene was filmed first in German and immediately thereafter in English. I was as good as in my best times at the Max Reinhardt Drama School—perhaps even better—thanks to the English I had learned at home.

But Josef von Sternberg wanted only American English. Panic on board. I didn't know American English. Von Sternberg undertook to make up for this difference. He didn't call on his wife's help. Nobody, I believe, could fault my pronunciation. Only my role counted.

In contrast to what the Max Reinhardt Drama School had demanded of me, von Sternberg did not want me to speak with a lower voice. He wanted it high and nasal. This was supposed to emphasize the Berlinese, which is quite similar to London cockney.

Von Sternberg, the magician, worked this miracle and sent his wife home. I don't think this entailed any great difficulties because, in fact, they had just been divorced. Von Sternberg never disclosed anything about his private life. Only much later when I came to Hollywood did I learn that his ex-wife never forgave him for the separation and that he understood her bitterness.

Von Sternberg had a most definite idea of what Lola in *The Blue Angel* should be like. He knew everything about her voice, her movements, her behavior. He influenced the choice of my clothes and encouraged me to make even further costume sketches, which I relished doing. I decked out my costumes with top hats and worker's caps, replaced my trinkets with ribbons, tassles, and braids—everything that in my opinion was within the means of a B-Girl in a sleazy, waterfront saloon.

One day von Sternberg said to me: "Seen from the front you should bring to mind Félicien Rops; from the rear, Toulouse-Lautrec." That was a concept that I could easily work with. I always liked clear instructions. Nothing is more pleasant than to know what's expected of you in life, in work, and in love.

"I didn't discover Dietrich," von Sternberg would often remark. "I am a teacher," he elaborated, "and this beautiful woman came to that teacher's attention. He shaped her appearance, highlighted her charm, minimized her defects, and molded her into an aphrodisiacal phenomenon."

There is nothing worse than the blurred, confused direction of performers when a director relies too heavily on his actors. At the time of the filming of *The Blue Angel*, it was not customary for young actresses to design their own costumes: Directors didn't have enough confidence in them. But under von Sternberg's sharp scrutiny I could do my own thing, and very well. The costumes that I wore in *The Blue Angel* have become a symbol for both my personality and the decade that placed its stamp on the film. At the time it appeared, the setting had already become somewhat dated. Though the film was shot in 1929 and 1930, its action referred to the beginnings of the twenties and even earlier. The fact that we could make our own costumes helped us to re-create the atmosphere, like conjurors. This is all the easier, the farther you revert into the past.

The word fashion had only a negative meaning for von Sternberg. He himself had designed the set for the tavern called "The Blue Angel." Together with several German writers, he had based the script on Heinrich Mann's novel, and he had the final say in everything—cast, lighting, props. His all-embracing culture fascinated me. He had an answer for every problem and no contradicting argument could upset him.

The experience of making this film awakened in me an ever greater interest in everything that went on both before and behind the camera. "The world behind the camera" became a virtual source of inspiration for me. Von Sternberg allowed me a great deal of latitude and generously passed on to me and everyone else he worked with not only his knowledge but also the secrets of his art.

He was the greatest cameraman the world has ever seen. Am I exaggerating? Not at all! Compared to films today, the cost of his amounted to no more than "a bag of peanuts" (if I may use the expression). Even for a film like *The Blue Angel*, the budget at his disposal was low and the shooting time strictly limited. One of his greatest talents lay in making everything appear opulent and radiant when in fact he worked on a very thin shoestring. He bubbled over with ideas, and the objections of producers that might have panicked less gifted directors left him completely cold. He always found ways to achieve the effect desired with less cost and never wasted time arguing with his employers of the moment.

He was also a superb editor and could work behind the cutting machine for several nights in a row without a break. He taught me how to cut and splice scenes together. Since my mind was being shaped by him, I had no idea that some directors couldn't do this work and had to rely on film cutters. Von Sternberg allowed me, his zealous pupil, to share his experience, granting me fleeting glances into the dark imaginative figments floating about in his mind, to which I, too, seemed to belong.

But this kind of close collaboration began only much later, in Hollywood. In Berlin, while shooting *The Blue Angel*, I was never allowed to see the rushes, a privilege reserved for the stars! But I didn't care one bit. I was happy enough to sit in and listen next morning when von Sternberg would comment on the work that had been done on the day before.

I simply wasn't ambitious, nor have I ever been. Perhaps that's what allowed me to survive all those years in Hollywood. It was the least of my worries. I just obeyed and did what I was supposed to do and felt quite good about it all. My German upbringing helped me to cope with sudden fame. I went on doing my duty without asking for any privileges. This continues to be one of my self-imposed limits. I have never—and I hope I never will—asked anyone for the slightest favor. As the well-behaved little girl I've always tried to be, I've lived exclusively on my own talents. I've had my share of bad luck, and sometimes I've been through hell, but I've always emerged from the pits, radiant I might add.

"Radiant, irradiant"—that brings me back to von Sternberg. Von Sternberg was creator, Lord of Light, an incomparable technician, the commander in chief of the film world. In the studio or on the set, he was a bulwark against bothersome intruders from reporters to office boys, the Almighty God to whom you looked up and whose voice you obeyed.

He knew it and accepted it.

When you're a consummate master in your field of work, you can draw a justifiable pride or even vanity from it. In Hollywood he would later say: "People should just leave us alone!" He was a director in the true sense of the word. He, in fact, directed everything and everybody, the electricians, the technicians, the makeup artists, whom he hated, the extras, whom he loved, and all the rest of us at his service.

My "healthy common sense," as he called it, surprised him. He considered me beautiful (which was far from being the case) and, consequently, stupid. He accorded me no special attention outside working hours. He was charming, understanding. And since he knew exactly how easily I could fall into any kind of a trap, he would also counsel me as best he could—which, given my young years, was no small thing.

I thought *The Blue Angel* would be a flop. I found it very ordinary and vulgar—two utterly different concepts in my view, but which here complemented each other perfectly.

On the set, at least that's how I imagined it, four cameras, turning simultaneously, stared at each of my steps (I say this only with the greatest disgust). And yet that's just how it was! Whenever it was my turn, I had to lift a leg, the left or the right, and the cameras were constantly riveted on me.

In the evening we all went home, took care of our children, led our own routine lives, and on the next day we went back to work. We were in the studio and shooting *The Blue Angel* but were all utterly indifferent to it. In the final analysis our attitude proved to be eminently correct. If you take your work too seriously, you become critical, something which most directors (von Sternberg among them) didn't appreciate very much. Von Sternberg was content to use me as a "springboard," as a living dictionary, and as an expert (so he believed) on Berlinese, which he, an Austrian by birth, didn't know very well.

How could a girl "of good family" be familiar with so indecent an idiom as Berlinese? I was very interested in this colorful, graphic jargon spoken by the denizens of Berlin's working-class quarters. I also liked their special humor. Humor, after all, is not a typical German trait. By nature we are more prone to solemnity. But Berliners are an exception, their humor is unique. Although it's not exactly black humor, it bears a slight resemblance to it. It's a kind of "gallows humor," plain and simple, as Ernest Hemingway described it, making it his own.

My social background, by definition, forbade my using this

notorious gallows humor, but somehow I acquired it anyway, learning to regard myself with a certain ironic detachment, and accepting with an air of resignation the tribulations that each day visits upon us.

Von Sternberg, who had spent almost his entire life in America, was totally obsessed with "this typically Berliner sense of humor." Between takes, he would spend long periods of time studying the way I used various expressions and turns of phrase that he wanted to incorporate into the film.

Thanks to his logical bent, von Sternberg filmed *The Blue Angel* according to the laws of logic, transforming me into an American vamp. He made the other actors speak English to me. None of them knew English, so he taught them their lines. But at the same time, he insisted that they retain their German accent, just as he insisted that I retain my "American" accent.

Although the English version, which continues to be shown around the world, is not as good as the German one, it proves convincing because it is authentic and not falsified. Actors today, even stars, use languages in films they don't really know. The public gets used to this, but in my view, by doing so, performers give themselves away.

The public takes everything at face value. Oscars are given to actors who have always been dubbed, who did not utter a single word in films for which they are awarded "Best Performer of the Year" honors. It's quite funny. But only those in the business realize it.

The public simply doesn't know "the film kitchen" from the inside, remaining instead in the dark and allowing itself to be taken in by the biggest cock-and-bull stories. All the better for the "fat cats" who dump this kind of film on the marketplace. They get richer. And me, I'm always the solitary moviegoer who knows that all, yes, *all* Italian films are dubbed, *even in Italian,* and that actors go on making other films elsewhere while their voices are being dubbed in remote sound studios. You call that acting? Not in my opinion, which, of course, counts for very little or nothing.

Unlike many film stars, as I've said earlier, I was very interested in the technical side of film production. Since my *Blue Angel* experience under von Sternberg, I've always been fascinated by the magical effect of cameras and light. The marvel of camera placements, of visual angles that can alter human faces and figures to make them appear big, strong, small, thick, thin, short or tall, has excited me ever since.

I was kept so busy during the shooting of my first two films in Hollywood learning the language correctly that I had no time for other things—but after these long months, I was always in the cutting room where the takes were being spliced together at the end of the day.

Von Sternberg has said about me:

"Again and again she claims that I taught her everything."

"It was impossible to exhaust her, she wore out others with an enthusiasm only a few could match."

"To a degree she was open and straightforward, which some might call tactlessness. Her personality was marked by an extreme refinement and an almost childlike simplicity. Never before had I met so beautiful a woman who was so misunderstood and under-estimated, the woman who was to enchant the world."

Since we all had to get up at six in the morning, the other ladies went right home to bed as soon as work had ended. In those days there were no limits on working hours. Very often we worked until three or four in the morning. Naturally, the technicians were paid overtime. I stayed as long as they let me in the hallowed halls of the cutting rooms, knowing well that the "Master" loved to teach amateurs and pros alike.

Today filmmakers know all about camera placements and visual angles. But TV cameras often distort contours much to the astonishment of bewildered viewers who wonder why an actress's face appears broad on one day and narrow on another.

For that matter all the secrets of camera placement also apply to amateur photographers. You should hold the camera high, slightly above the eye level of those you want to photograph. If you hold the camera lower, at about the subject's belly-button level, say, the face appears round and thick and bears no resemblance to what you actually wanted to photograph.

But back to studio lighting. The back light is the big bugaboo. If a performer near it is speaking to her partner, she is told not to turn completely away from it. If she does, the back light will give her a bulbous nose.

A side light can also play little tricks—but it's not quite so risky.

The key light, directly behind the camera, is the most important of all. The higher this key light is placed, the longer and narrower the face will appear on the screen. If an actress happens to be blessed with high cheek bones, such lighting sketches attractive, soft shadows on both cheeks.

Since at the present time there are no great film beauties as in the past, this knowledge is not all too important. The actors and actresses may be good, but beautiful they are not.

The only exception to this is Robert Redford. In addition to being a brilliant and versatile producer, he knows his camera. I take my hat off to him.

You must really exert yourself to become a real pro. But it's worth the effort. You learn your trade. You learn to cut, an essential process in completing any film. Directors today like to play it safe and shoot each scene from every conceivable angle. So when the cutter's turn comes, he has all the necessary parts to form a sequence. In the old days the great filmmakers never operated this way. They knew in advance what they wanted and at the right moment would shout "Cut!" thus saving both time and money. They didn't prolong the shooting period unnecessarily for hours on end, shooting from the left, the right, the front. They didn't give the cutter, or editor, lengthy "rushes" from which to make a film.

Josef von Sternberg got me used to the quick "Cut!" Later I worked in the same way with Ernst Lubitsch and Frank Borzage. All my other directors played it safe. Complying with studio directives, they would make endless takes, most of which, they well knew, would end up in the waste basket. Great creative talents don't have to do this.

For example, let's take a single room in its entirety. A door opens in the background. A person enters. Her facial features are not clearly visible since she is still far away. She closes the door, comes up to the camera and says: "Excuse the disturbance, but . . ."

An experienced director will stop here, because he knows he needs a close-up. On the other hand, a director who is not sure of himself will film the whole scene following the actress's line just as it stands in the shooting plan and to the very end. The result is a lot of wasted footage, unsuited for the final montage. I've always had a pronounced horror of waste. I can't stand this way of shooting, but, of course, I never said anything.

Von Sternberg attracted students from all over the world who wanted to study his craftsmanship. One of them even went so far as to measure the distance between my nose and the main spotlight hoping to track down the secret of his magic.

Here I'd like to explain the underlying purpose of the "main spotlight." It's the major light source for the close-ups and can make or ruin a face.

In my case the face was *created*.

The most outlandish stories have made the rounds: that I had to have my molars extracted so as to highlight my hollow cheeks; that young girls and actresses could use their facial muscles to suck in their cheeks to achieve the secret effect to be seen on the screen. None of these tales is true. Nor are those that claim that in the shooting of *Morocco* I ran through the desert on high-heeled shoes. But I'm getting ahead of my story. We're still with *The Blue Angel*. In this film von Sternberg used the main spotlight to give greater prominence to the roundness of my face. No hollow cheeks in *The Blue Angel*.

For that purpose the main spotlight was placed very low and far away from me. The secret face with the hollow cheeks was achieved as a result of placing the main spotlight close to my face and high above it. That sounds quite simple, right? And when pupils (or professional colleagues) stormed the set to measure the distance and the height of the main spotlight, von Sternberg would shift the mounting and say: "Put your measuring tapes away, boys. I can light Mrs. Dietrich just as well with any other tried and true technique." He couldn't for the life of him restrain himself from making biting remarks. Nobody could "measure" his artistic gift either in inches or centimeters.

In my favorite film, *The Spanish Dancer* (the awful English title *The Devil Is a Woman* was forced on him by the producers), von Sternberg sent the team out for a lunch break earlier than usual. By the time we came back he had dusted white the entire woods through which I was to drive with a cart. Nothing is worse than green when you're shooting in black and white. But since the action was taking place in the woods, the trees that had been placed in studio 13 were, of course, green, at least at first. On the screen they looked as though they had come out of a fairy tale, and I, sitting in the cart dressed in white, looked just like a fay. And how do you think von Sternberg attired the man I met in the white-dusted woods? He had him wear a black suit and placed a black sombrero on his black hair. *Black and white.* There were no color films at that time, but even today black and white remain unmatched as a form. It is strikingly suitable to certain films. *Color* beautifies everything. Photograph a garbage dump in color and it will look clean, orderly, glossy.

If von Sternberg had filmed in color, the result would certainly have been the *ne plus ultra* of good taste, clever effects and radiant beauty. Many may remember *The Devil Is a Woman*, the last film he made with me, as shot in color. This, of course, was not the case, but the images it created are so rich in light, shadows and halftones that one easily thinks it's in color.

While the filming of *The Blue Angel* was in full swing, von Sternberg brought an American to the studio—B. P. Schulberg, the general manager of Paramount Studios. He offered me a seven-year contract in Hollywood. "I wouldn't like to go away," I answered very politely. "I would like to stay here with my family." He was just as polite and then disappeared again. Von Sternberg had made him come over from America to show him some scenes from the film.

But since I had no intention of changing my mind and the shooting period for *The Blue Angel* was over, we all said good-bye to one another. Von Sternberg returned to America long before I myself traveled there and long before the film's premiere. Each member of the cast went his or her own way, continued, as best as possible, his or her career, and mourned the absence of von Sternberg's direction, of his authority, of his dynamics, of his friendliness, and of his magic whose divine and demonic powers he had let us glimpse without ever causing us any offense.

As I was writing these pages, I had the opportunity to see *The Blue Angel* in the original German version on TV. I had not expected to meet a first-rate actress in a difficult, brazen, at times tender role, a natural, relaxed actress who awakens a complex person to life, a personality that was not mine. I don't know how von Sternberg worked this miracle. Genius, I assume! In its ordinariness, the character of Lola reflected superbly the mentality of ordinary people.

I must confess I was very impressed by the *actress* Marlene Dietrich who successfully plays a sailor girl of the twenties. Even the accent (Low German) is just right.

I, the well brought-up, the reserved, still entirely unspoiled girl from a good family, unwittingly had accomplished a unique feat that I was never again to repeat successfully. All the women's roles I played later were "more delicate" than Lola's in *The Blue Angel* and, accordingly, easier to perform.

The contract I had signed with Ufa contained a clause which my husband had questioned. It stated that for a certain number of days after the making of this film, Ufa would have an option on my future career. I no longer remember how much time Ufa had to exercise this option, but that, too, was irrelevant. It was one-sided. The studios had all the rights, the actor none at all.

I wasn't even notified when the film had finally been edited and the last of the work completed. Nor did the studio exercise its option on the date fixed in the contract.

Everyone was convinced that *The Blue Angel* would in no way enjoy the success von Sternberg had predicted for it, but would end up a fiasco, a disaster. My husband and I thought that the option Ufa had received (for a pittance) would remain only on paper. None of the company's executives, moreover, had taken my future film career seriously.

During this time von Sternberg would often phone me from

Hollywood and ask me to join him. I didn't trust his proposals. I had enough of all the fantastic promises of a "great future career" in America. But one fine day he repeated that I should drop the "big wigs" of the German studios and tell them all to go to hell.

Actually, I didn't care whether I went abroad or stayed at home. After long discussions, my husband and I finally decided that I would go to the United States alone. Our daughter would remain with him in Berlin until we could see what impression that strange country called America would make on me before we dared to "transplant" our little Maria and her governess. I was sent out on a reconnaissance mission, as it were.

I didn't agree with one of the clauses in the contract that Paramount Pictures had sent to me, which stipulated that I was to sign up with them for seven years. I categorically refused, an indication of the great value I placed on my independence.

Later, I received a new contract stating that if I was not comfortable in America, I could return home after my first film but could not sign a contract with another studio. The Americans obviously were ignorant of the sense of honor deeply ingrained in the German character. I would never have done anything of the sort, anything so shameful.

So I set out for America confident that I could return to Germany whenever I pleased. I fought for this right not knowing that a powerful, ominous force would be leading my homeland to its ruin and that all my plans would come to nothing.

All went well at first. My husband insisted I bring along Resi, my dressing room attendant from *The Blue Angel* days, and the journey began.

The giant ship scared me so much that I remained in my cabin most of the time. I was bored to death and already troubled by homesickness on this opulent ocean liner with its glittering shops and restaurants.

On the other hand, I wasn't seasick. The high, swirling waves (it was April) caused a lot of discomfort to the other passengers, including Resi. To top it all, Resi lost her dentures on the second day of the crossing. They had fallen into the sea, and throughout the trip I prepared her purees and soups and comforted her in her wounded pride. No argument could convince her that a stroll on deck would be good for her and that she didn't have to be ashamed of being toothless in the middle of a raging storm all bundled up in a shawl.

The crossing took six days because of the head winds. I would have despaired if von Sternberg were not waiting for me on the other side of the Atlantic. But since he was the main reason for my coming to America and I had a blind trust in him, I stuck out the bad weather. This German ship was the last connection with my past, and for a long time I was not going to hear my mother tongue again.

At that time I didn't know that constantly speaking a foreign language would matter so much to me, although I fully mastered English in the following years.

It was a strain for me to converse in English, and since von Sternberg improved not only my grammar but my accent as well, I was sometimes insufferable. Anyway, so he claimed. Mostly he would refuse to speak German with me. But after all I had Resi and, on the telephone, my husband. I had sent him three or four telegrams a day in German from the ship. Money means nothing to me when feelings are involved. Besides I thought I would be earning lots of it in America. Innocence, innocence, will you ever leave me?

It never left me.

In the course of my life I have squandered entire fortunes. They struck me as ridiculous, and they perished under the pile of checks that I would sign every day. I responded to the appeals of foundations and charity organizations without actually knowing what they were all about. It didn't matter to me. It's so easy to write your signature on a check.

I also made long telephone calls from the United States and sent out telegrams all day long. I learned how to spell my German messages in English, and to this day I wonder who taught me that. But it was necessary since the postal employees spoke no German.

Later, I also sent telegrams in English which made things easier. But I could never manage to be brief on the phone. I spoke with my daughter in the morning and in the evening. Otherwise I busied myself as best I could. I cooked, worked in the garden of my little house, waited to be called to the studio, tried to get used to the strange environment and to the homesickness that constantly plagued me—especially in the morning when the sun was shining and the palm trees stood motionless and I stood in front of the house on the lookout for the mailman. Waiting for the mailman was to become a habit during all the years spent far from my country, at any rate, for so long as Germany remained my country.

When I decided to renounce my German citizenship, America opened its arms to me.

To give up your homeland and mother tongue, even when forced to by circumstance, is an almost unendurable ordeal. Only German, this lovely language, has remained to me as a legacy. I came very close to forgetting it the more securely I settled in America and felt sufficiently at home in English. To be sure, I still don't have a perfect mastery of English (to the degree that I would like), but I'm familiar with it now, and that's the main thing.

Of all the languages I know English is the most precise, which makes my work easier. With von Sternberg's help I learned new words, new expressions every day—enough to grant the usual interviews and to survive them satisfactorily, that is, as far as the studio was concerned.

Although I was still young, these long "conversation exercises" in a foreign language were physically difficult for me. I didn't understand why I would almost faint from fatigue at sundown. Yet I seldom rebelled. I had a great respect for the efforts of others. Compared to the way things were to go later, the studio at that time radiated peace and tranquility. Perhaps everybody was taking a deep breath for the upcoming work on my first American film in the hope that it would be a success. At that time the postal workers were in no danger of being buried under avalanches of my fan mail. The unknown actress by the name of Marlene Dietrich wasn't a burden for anybody, and the reverse was likewise true. My only ventures in the outside world were limited to walks to a drugstore in the neighborhood or to visits to the movies with Resi.

The Blue Angel had not yet been distributed in America, so I could go where I pleased without being recognized.

Although the Paramount executives had purchased the film, they deliberately kept it under lock and key, since they wanted to show it in the movie theaters only after my first American film. They were afraid "The Blue Angel image," the image of the "dissolute young girl," would stick to me; in any case they wanted to avoid my being permanently pinned to a type.

In my opinion I have always played "dissolute young girls," and they were, as von Sternberg once said, certainly more interesting than the "nice roles."

YOU ARE SVENGALI— I AM TRILBY

"I then put her into the crucible of my conception, blended her image to correspond with mine, pouring lights on her until the alchemy was complete."

—Josef von Sternberg

I believe I've always been very lucky.

Von Sternberg drew everyone he met under his spell. I was too young and too stupid to understand that. But I admired him, and as a well-mannered student of the Max Reinhardt Drama School, I took pains to follow my director as well as possible.

I never gave up this devotion, this recognition of supreme competence and authority during my entire acting career.

On the day of my arrival in New York I was wearing a gray dress, my favorite travel outfit in Europe. A charming envoy of Paramount Studios, a Mr. Blumenthal, explained that I couldn't leave the ship in "those" clothes. I was at a total loss. Resi, my dressing room assistant, was still sick. Blumenthal persuaded me to go ashore in a black dress and a mink coat, *if* I had one.

The sun was shining and it was nearly ten o'clock in the morning. I couldn't decide whether to make myself so sartorially elegant at this time of day. But it was made clear to me that I had to follow instructions.

My big overseas trunks were in the hold, so I had to go down there, keys in hand, hoping to find some clothes that would please my American hosts. Finally, at ten o'clock, I set foot on the New York waterfront attired in a black dress and a mink coat. Naturally, I was ashamed to be wearing such an outfit. But it seemed to correspond to the customs of the country. After this incident, I resolutely refused to follow the studio's orders in such matters and dressed as I pleased.

I wore trousers most of the time. Since we lived in a hilly area not far from the beach, they were more practical than dresses and stockings.

Everything seemed simple to me, but this was an enormous self-deception. I realized it only very much later, of course. Von Sternberg battled the Paramount publicity agents on my behalf. He took everything upon himself without my ever having to interfere. From this I drew the conclusion that it was up to him to guide me, to advise me, and to explain America's strange customs to me. And in the process he must have gone through some bad moments. I was stubborn and still young. In retrospect I realize that he showed infinite patience.

When I started to work for von Sternberg, I didn't under-stand very much. The moment I got a call from the makeup artist, I would rush over to the studio as early as five or six-thirty in the morning.

There new difficulties would come up. In general, takes of my red-blond hair (probably because of its reddish gleam) were made in subdued lighting. So I was advised to have it bleached to make it look more natural, more ordinary.

My hair looked too dark on film. Since I refused to have my hair bleached, and since von Sternberg backed me up, the studio had to give in. In normal life I was a blond, but on the screen I turned into a brunette. This completely confused the "Big Bosses" at Paramount. A floodlight was beamed on my hair from above, from the side and, above all, from the rear so that the tips of my hair lit up, creating a halo effect.

My hair constantly drove me to despair. Nobody liked my "baby hair." It simply couldn't be curled, combed through, or given a form suitable to the face from which some fabulous aura was supposed to emanate. From six o'clock in the morning on we dabbled with curlers; hair dryers irritated my scalp—in vain. Finally, we resorted to curling irons so that I could let myself be seen before the camera again.

By noon the curls were gone. The script girls would almost go crazy, as my hair style turned out different from the day before. So we retreated to my dressing room and tried to save the situation. Everybody joked about it, except me and my hairdresser, Nelly Manley. The photographs taken at that time prove that we did a very good job nevertheless.

When there was no time to curl my hair, we used spit, also a very effective expedient. During the filming of *The Garden of Allah*, in 1936 in the Arizona desert, the trouble with my hair became a little drama in itself. It was impossible to restore the coiffure of the day before. I came to hate working on that movie: My curls, the bombastic script—everything annoyed me. Yet once you've committed yourself to make a film, even if you find it bad, you must drink the cup to the dregs.

Backlighting became very fashionable. To realize this it is enough to look at photos of that time. But backlighting also has its disadvantages. The cameraman always insisted that you never turn your head to one side, otherwise the light behind the actress would fall on her nose, which would immediately resemble W. C. Fields's proboscis.

Consequently, most of the scenes with a partner were very stiff, to put it mildly. While speaking to one another, we would stare straight ahead instead of looking into each other's eyes, even during love scenes. We all looked splendid in the circle of light emitted by the reflector in back of us, but we remained rooted to the spot. Who was at fault? The actors, of course! Of me it was said: "She never moves." One day when I timidly tried to move so as to look at my partner, the cameraman rushed over to me and insistently asked me never to do it again. I obeyed.

At the beginning of our collaboration, Josef von Sternberg didn't belong to the cameramen's union. So, like a skilled diplomat, he had to content himself with making "suggestions" regarding lighting and camera angles.

Here I would like for a moment to revert to my arrival in America, that "unknown country." As it was to all Germans, America was a riddle to me. In Germany we had heard about Indians slaughtering groups of white settlers, but little else.

Today, and I say this without the slightest ulterior motive, I love America and Americans, including those who committed mistakes and those who have been "badly treated." I've known some gangsters who were friendly to me and whose "moral code" was absolutely compatible with mine.

I came to America at the height of Prohibition.

As the ship moored and I stood in the morning sun in a black dress and a mink coat, I was both fearful and enthusiastic. Officials of Paramount Studios came to my rescue, and I was taken to the Hotel Ambassador. Two hours later, I was told, I had to be ready and properly dressed for the "cocktail hour" (I didn't know what that expression meant) at four o'clock in the afternoon. But my own priority was to find new dentures for Resi, my dressing room attendant.

I spoke with the members of the reception committee about it. Once they realized it didn't involve me, they refused to help me. Yet, with Teutonic stubbornness, I managed to find a dentist in this unfamiliar city, left Resi in his office, and then went on to the press conference organized by Paramount. I was much more concerned about Resi's new dentures than the press conference. Who would have thought that the young actress, hailed as "the discovery of the century" by von Sternberg, was wandering about New York looking for a dentist for her dressing room attendant? It was unthinkable. Loyal as ever to my principles, I didn't care what people might say. So I managed to locate a dentist, and after he treated her, I returned to bring Resi back to the hotel.

On that night the vice president of Paramount, Walter Wanger, said that he would come with his wife to pick me up and show me around New York. I phoned Sternberg in Hollywood and told him how things were going. He advised me to do what was asked of me, but to phone him immediately should any difficulties arise.

So Walter Wanger appeared at the Hotel Ambassador. He waited for me at the reception desk. "My wife's not feeling well," he explained, "so we'll have a tête-à-tête dinner." Credulous, I asked no further questions and went with him to a restaurant. Later I learned that this type of establishment was called a "speakeasy," in which all the guests surreptitiously reached under the table for a bottle of Scotch or Bourbon.

I sat stiff as a board in this dark hall in which everybody was drinking. Walter Wanger had met a friend named Chrisie (I no longer remember how one properly writes his name). In the course of the conversation, Wanger said: "In one of your interviews you said that you'd like to hear Richman. Well, here he is." And in fact Harry Richman entered the tiny stage and sang a song that had been a favorite of mine for a long time, "On the Sunny Side of the Street." To see this singer, whom I admired, in the flesh moved me to tears, and before I knew it Walter Wanger had dragged me off to the dance floor.

Annoyed over this abrupt, authoritarian gesture, I, in turn, made a move to go back to the table to get my handbag. The moment Walter Wanger released me, I grabbed my handbag and made my quick exit from the speakeasy. I ran through the streets of this unfamiliar city without knowing where I was heading. Finally, I hailed a taxi driver and gave him my address, "Hotel Ambassador."

Once in the hotel (the doorman paid for the taxi), I phoned von Sternberg in Hollywood and told him about my adventure. He was quiet for a moment and then he said, "Come here tomorrow by train. Ask the doorman to reserve seats for you. Don't talk with anybody, *anybody*, understand? Leave New York immediately."

I woke Resi up; we packed our possessions in the trunk and didn't sleep a wink until we were seated on the "Twentieth Century" en route to Chicago. There we were to board a Santa Fe line train. I slept for two entire days, woke up, ate the tasteless meals that were served in our luxury compartment by polite waiters, after which we again went to sleep, all the while wondering why we ever came to this darn land.

Von Sternberg had promised to meet us in New Mexico. Naturally, I thought he meant Mexico. I had never heard of New Mexico before. The heat was unendurable. We spread bedsheets over the seats of the compartment and joked, but our hearts were heavy.

Every time the train came to a stop—and that was very often—we wanted to get off to stretch our legs, but the heat drove us right back to the compartment. It was as though a red-hot pillow was being pressed on our faces. Von Sternberg, at last, showed up on one of the stations along the way. He was unruffled. We went with him to his compartment, and he suggested that we try to relax. Now everything was going well—as always with him, he had "taken us over." The train rode on and on, but at last we arrived in Pasadena. We weren't far from Los Angeles.

Automobiles, drivers, trucks were waiting there to load our luggage. And not a single journalist. Thank God. I felt good, full of confidence, ready to shift all my problems onto von Sternberg.

Resi, who had gotten used to her new dentures, was insatiable. So was I. Hunger tormented me around the clock, which worried me very much. Up to then I had never given any thought to going on a diet. Yet on the way to Hollywood and to the splendid sylphs who ruled there, I suddenly felt too fat. I really was fat, but up to then I had paid it no attention. Yet now that I was on my way to Hollywood . . .

Von Sternberg refused to share my worries on this score. He found me perfect; I matched the image he had of me to perfection. I was the only one who thought that I had to satisfy a definite "ideal of beauty." The woman, whom von Sternberg wanted to bring to life on the screen, was by no means to be thin and sexless, but well fed, full of life, with ankles, breasts and sex appeal—in short, the dream of the little man.

I didn't see things exactly from this point of view. He must have found me hard to bear. I insisted on wearing black in my first

American film so as to appear slimmer. Black is not easy to photograph but, as always, von Sternberg was infinitely patient and said: "Fine, I'll take the risk of photographing you in black, if that's what you want." At that time I didn't yet know enough about photography to appreciate the significance of this promise and the difficulties that he would have to overcome. So I wore black, glossy black (the most difficult to photograph). When I had to speak tender words, I would position myself behind a broad armchair. And he endured my stupidity, day in, day out.

Up to now I've mentioned only the visual aspect of shooting a film. Now I'd like to speak of a second, equally important element: sound.

The work of the sound engineer is decisive. Whereas the cameraman must wait until the next day to see the results of his labors, the sound engineer, who listens in on everything directly, can demand a new recording as soon as a scene is filmed. All he has to say is "Bad for me," and the performance, even of the greatest actor, is ruined. At this moment the sound engineer's assistants come out of the dark to place the microphones elsewhere. Often they turn directly to the actor, something that von Sternberg had always forbidden. "Explain the problem to me," he would repeatedly say, "and I'll speak about it to the actor if I decide it should be done that way."

Despite my inexperience, I understood his reasons: If you ask an actor to speak more loudly it can alter his performance. When the sound engineer was dissatisfied, von Sternberg simply suggested that we emphasize our words more. The firmer the voice, the better it registers on the microphone. A very simple technical trick. What made the whole thing so difficult was that those responsible for the sound received tapes without pictures. Since they couldn't see the actor's lips, they could depend only on what they heard. Many directors who ignored this filmed the same scene a dozen times until the actor was exhausted and his acting unnatural. The sound engineers, of course, were satisfied.

The sound engineer's "Okay" let us breathe easier, especially when I no longer worked with von Sternberg.

Once, in *Golden Earrings*, I had to run screaming through a forest behind the man who deserted me, screaming louder the more I distanced myself from the camera. I was breathless when I came back to the director, and the sound engineer standing next to him said, "Why did you strain yourself like that? There's a microphone behind *every tree*." "But if that's the case," I tried to explain to myself and to him, "then they must have picked up my voice as if I were very near. And since the camera doesn't move, as the image becomes smaller and smaller, my voice still sounds as though I were close to the camera."

The sound engineer assured me that these technicalities would be solved in the "echo-chamber" and that my voice would sound properly distant.

I couldn't make any sense of it at all. Why all that work for the technicians afterward when it would be easier to handle these minor details on the spot? But I hate arguing and raising my voice while shooting a film. So I just shut up, but . . .

The von Sternberg–Marlene Dietrich collaboration in the United States began with *Morocco* in 1931. I had terrible difficulties since I had to speak correct English and appear mysterious at the same time. An aura of mysteriousness has never been my forte. I knew what was expected of me, but I wasn't in a position to create this atmosphere. *The Blue Angel* had been something altogether different, the role of an ordinary, brazen, sexy and impetuous floozie, the very opposite of the "mysterious woman" that von Sternberg wanted me to play in *Morocco*.

The first scene was shot in the Paramount Studios in Hollywood. The action took place aboard a ship putting ashore in Casablanca or some other exotic port. Leaning on the rail, I stared into the distance (camera left, please); when I turned around and reached for my only suitcase, it suddenly snapped open and all my belongings fell out. Thereupon a gentleman (Adolphe Menjou) came up to me, wanting to help me gather up my belongings, and said, "Can I help you, Mademoiselle?" At that time the word "mademoiselle" immediately enveloped any woman bent over the mess of an opened suitcase in an aura of mystery.

I had to answer, "Thanks, I don't need any help."

Paradoxically, I could have really used some help on that particular day. Unlike most Germans, I didn't say "SSSanks," yet my pronunciation of the English "th" in thanks was far from perfect. And hundreds of people had shown up on the set to get a look at the newcomer Marlene Dietrich (two unusual words).

I knew exactly what I was doing wrong. As best I could, I spoke with what I really thought was an American accent: "Thanks, I don't need any *belllp*," pressing my tongue against my palate, hoping to produce a guttural sound. Von Sternberg, aware of the moment's importance but, as always, infinitely patient, made me repeat my answer God knows how many times until I pronounced the word "help" properly. Today I understand that this first line and this first scene were of the greatest importance for the success of the film and of the unknown German woman called Marlene Dietrich. (When I asked von Sternberg if I could change my name, he answered: "Soon it will become quite well known.")

At the end of the day I broke into tears. Not in front of the technicians, but in my dressing room in front of my makeup artist Dot, the dressing room attendant, the hairdresser . . . it was too much for me. I wanted to go back to Germany. If that's what my life was going to be like from now on, the whole business no longer interested me. I had left my husband and daughter behind in Berlin; I would return to them immediately.

Von Sternberg was standing outside my dressing room; after knocking lightly he came in.

He restored my morale within twenty minutes.

"Never break off your contract, rule *numero uno*. Never give up, rule *numero due*. In other words, stay." That's what he said to me.

How tiresome it must have been for him to bother himself so over a young, impressionable woman who understood nothing of his aims, his wishes, not to mention his plans for his Trilby, his Eliza Doolittle, his Galatea—the dream of creating a woman according to his own ideal, like a painter who captures an image on his canvas. How could he ever have stood me? It's impossible to answer this question. I understood nothing of his concerns or obsessions; I knew nothing of his aims. He had decided to make me a star overnight, but that left me indifferent. In reality, he was molding an unknown Berlin woman. I was young, vulnerable, of course, and I was there to enchant the great American public, but in my own eyes I was still what I had never ceased to be, a German woman merely concerned with fulfilling her obligations, nothing more.

I didn't want to go to evening parties. He agreed. For me only my home counted. He agreed. I wanted to get my daughter out of Germany. He agreed. He even went to great pains to phone my husband (I didn't trust myself) to ask if I could take Maria with me back to the United States. In short, he set me on my feet once and for all. Anyway, we both believed this, at that time.

He was father confessor, critic, instructor, the one who adjusted himself to all my needs. Adviser, business man, agent, spokesman, he helped me to live in peace with myself. He was my absolute lord, whether it was a matter of buying a Rolls Royce, of hiring a chauffeur, or of teaching me that signing checks is a serious business. He taught me a myriad things, in addition to English and my chosen profession—acting. God knows how much I've learned from him! I don't think I ever properly thanked him for all that. But, so far as I recall, he didn't like to be thanked.

He also taught me to understand the American legal system, which, particularly in California, is so different from the European. In fact, he had come to know it quite well since his divorce, which had occurred long before we met in the States. He had put up a big fight against paying alimony to his ex-wife, whom in the end he hated. He even spent three days in jail once because of his refusal to meet the alimony payment deadline. This experience had pleased him extraordinarily. But this is all he ever told me about his private life.

Nor did he want me to talk about him. Now that he is dead, I'm free to do so. He created me. Only at one other time have I seen such a miracle, when Luchino Visconti was making a film with Helmut Berger. The eye behind the camera, the eye that loves the creature whose image will be captured on the film, is the creator of the wondrous effect that emanates from this being and calls forth the praise and enthusiasm of moviegoers all over the world.

All that is exactly calculated in advance and is in no way fortuitous. It is a mixture of technical and psychological knowledge and of pure love. Von Sternberg had already created stars before me: Phyllis Haver, Evelyn Brent, George Bancroft, Georgia Hale, but the "Leonardo da Vinci" of the camera wasn't content with his "material," as he called actors and actresses.

I had satisfied him. I was disciplined, punctual. Always and everywhere I followed his instructions, and I made my suggestions (which he often took) always at the right moment. In short, I tried not to disturb him. I grew up with discipline. I knew nothing else in my life. That may sound odd to all those who read a lot about personalities in show business, so it calls for some explanation.

When I arrived in Hollywood, I was what is called a "spoiled brat"—as far as my manners were concerned. Josef von Sternberg was the only person I allowed to patronize, instruct, and control me. Otherwise I remained my true, independent self.

The character trait that aroused his interest in me was the fact that I was a "disciplined" person. It wasn't my beauty or my physical attractiveness that fascinated him. Rather, it was my unique capacity for discipline, an almost unknown quality among actresses he had known, that drew him to me.

I was conscious of problems that concern directors and actors interested in camera technique and in everything that goes on behind the camera. He dreaded the day on which, perhaps, I would become an ordinary star or a woman fascinated by her own image and simply be like one of the actresses that had crossed his path by the hundreds.

Never will I forget the wonderful moment when I climbed up to the set, a dark and hollowish set where he stood in the faint glare of a single light bulb. Lonely? Not really. A strange man whom I was still to get to know.

He dismissed my entourage (makeup artist, hairdresser,

dressing room attendant), but he allowed me to stay while he lit up the scene. Today I regret that I didn't write down the instructions he gave the electrician—the voice of the lord who created the visions of light and shadows and changed the bleak, barren set into a painting suffused in a magic light.

The team adored him because the technicians wanted the same effects he did, and they admired his way of "lending a hand." For example, when the cameraman thought a scene that von Sternberg wanted was "impossible," von Sternberg himself then would take the camera and show him what to do. When you want to have a say in a matter, you yourself must be able to carry out the instruction you give to others.

He designed all my costumes; Travis Benton, the costume designer at Paramount, was very fond of him because of his ability and sudden inspirations. Both created my film image; I, spoiled brat that I was, merely had to slip into it and let myself be fawned upon.

They worked together on several films. The crowning achievement of this collaboration was the costumes in *The Devil Is a Woman*, in my view the most beautiful film that was ever made. Von Sternberg always reserved the right to accept or reject what Travis and I—always following his instructions rather freely—had thought up. We worked during lunch, between takes and until late at night. By then Travis and I were experts in fighting off fatigue. Perhaps because we adored von Sternberg. Many people claim to have made my costumes from the days of *The Blue Angel* on. That's not true. Travis Benton alone actualized von Sternberg's ideas. He remained at my side up to the last film. Today Travis is no longer alive, but how I wish that he were still among us, with me, to help write this book.

On the other hand, I never trusted the cameramen. They constantly resisted giving von Sternberg what actually was his due. The reason for this is obvious. But after von Sternberg was accepted into the cameramen's union and could put his stamp on the work of the camera people, he gave his genius free rein. Naturally, the "clan" of cameramen in the studios was not overly pleased, but that didn't prevent them from imitating him. At the time when von Sternberg did not yet belong to the union, he behaved more than properly toward some young apprentices and so taught them one of cinema's most beautiful styles. All of them became renowned cameramen and were thankful to him. Nobody ever disappointed him. Indeed, that was our greatest concern: *never to disappoint him.*

I, the leading performer in the film, was the fifth wheel. He kept pushy photographers and reporters at bay, and I led a relatively peaceful life. I had a lovely house with a garden, the blue skies above the roof, and a man who told me what I should do.

What more did I want?

In 1932 I went to Germany to get my daughter Maria. Paramount Studios had strictly forbidden any mention of my maternity. I wasn't ready to submit to this proscription, and once again von Sternberg battled the studio executives who were of the opinion that motherhood didn't suit the role of "femme fatale" I was supposed to portray.

He also won this battle. I brought my child to America, and Maria became 150 percent American. And she has remained so, even though I often thought of leaving this country with her and hiding ourselves somewhere. But we have survived.

Maria loved America from the very start, above all California. She practically lived outdoors, and she was happy. During the day I worked on my film, then I came home, cooked, and read her bedtime stories like every mother. It was a pleasant life for all of us, even for the nursemaid, Becky, and my housemaid, Resi. I took care of the cooking and everything was as it should be.

We would walk to the Pacific to swim and to watch the sunset, go on the pier for a ride on the annual fair's roller coaster, eat crabs, eat some more, play catch on the beach before returning home, tired but overjoyed at the thought of the ritual phone call to Berlin after which we would all go to sleep.

Maria was happy as only children can be; she didn't miss her mother tongue as much as I did, since she was too young to appreciate its value. She spoke fluent English, and the eternal California summer invigorated her. She swam in the pool, played tennis beautifully, brimming with health and bronzed by the sun.

She learned to read and write without a teacher; in short, she was at the right place at the right time. If Hollywood had not been to her liking, I would have returned to Germany. No film, no fame can be more important than a child's feelings and sensibilities. I was there in the morning, I was there in the evening.

Maria was an industrious, brilliant pupil—and also able to judge grown-ups. She was eager to learn, a joy to all of us.

She was also very beautiful. I took hundreds of photos of her in all kinds of outfits, in bathing trunks, in a swimsuit, in a dress in front of the Christmas tree, in summer light, in pants, in a shirt, wearing a baseball cap, dressed for Halloween . . .

Hollywood in no way disturbed us. As soon as the news got around that I loved being with my child, we were left in peace. The sight of airplanes writing my name in the sky one evening left me cold, a reaction that must have offended all those who had worked hard over this publicity stunt. I did find it pretty, however. My daughter and I looked up at the night sky for a moment and then returned to our reading while the airplanes continued to paint their letters on the clouds.

My daughter said: "Look, the stars are shining through your name." The sky was star-spangled. But I simply could find little to relish in this much vaunted example of "fame" so important in the motion-picture business.

The memory of this evening calls to mind a question that interviewers have asked me probably a thousand times: "Do you believe in astrology?"

I have often read that I will not board a plane or venture on the street without first consulting my astrologer. That, of course, is pure nonsense, although astrology has always interested me, even as a young girl. But I've never deeply concerned myself with it.

Lexicographers define astrology as a pseudoscience. I don't agree with the definition that Webster gives: "Divination that treats of the supposed influences of the stars upon human affairs and of foretelling terrestrial events by their positions and aspects." The expression "human affairs" disturbs me. I would prefer "human beings."

Fine, one can discuss the nature of this influence, but I simply can't get into my head how one can fundamentally deny or so arrogantly dismiss it.

In school we learned that the moon attracts the earth's water masses—ebb and tide are directly related to it. Also nobody argues with a peasant or a gardener who knows when the moon is "favorable" for sowing or planting. Nobody denies the effect of the full moon on the sleepwalker, nor does anyone deny the little known fact that the police increase their alertness on the night of a full moon. The moon is known as an instigator of riots to the New York police. On full moon nights the number of police on duty is doubled not just out of concern for the security of sleep-walkers but also because of the awareness that human feelings are more impressionable than usual and more calls than usual come over the emergency hot line.

Astrological investigations have found out more and more about the powerful energies released by the stars. But let me be plain about this: Astrology as it exists and is practiced today, is not a profound science. The only area in which it has its justification and can be very helpful in our lives are the character studies that some great astrologers have developed. When you have to deal with many people at work and in personal relationships, it's helpful to know under what constellation a particular individual was born. The ascendant is more difficult to determine, though in professional relations it is of lesser importance (not so for lovers, of course!). Knowing zodiacal signs helps to save energy when you face a Leo (don't dare contradict him or her) or have to deal with a dominant Taurus, and you can consider yourself lucky to have an Aquarius as a friend or a boss—just to mention a few examples.

In short, what conceit to think that we humans, composed of the same elements as the rest of the world, are preserved from forces whose effects are perceptible everywhere. Perhaps one day we shall know everything about the influence of the stars. For the time being we can only make conjectures, but there is no doubt about their mysterious and at times overwhelming effect. Although we cannot clearly explain the origin of these forces, we should not be so brazen as to completely deny their existence.

In 1932, when I was making the film *Blonde Venus* (what a

title!), I received a strange letter in the mail. The message was written neither by hand nor on a typewriter. The words had been cut out of newspapers and pasted on a sheet of paper. The message filled me with fear and horror: It was a threat to kidnap my daughter.

From that moment on, every morning I would take her to the studio with me. And as always von Sternberg protectively took over. His film took up most of his time, but now he actively engaged himself with all his energies in a dark, secret scheme to frustrate the plans of the gangsters.

I wasn't even allowed to notify the police, which completely confused me. I was deeply worried, unable to perform normally. My daughter no longer left my side. She would stay in the hall, seated on a little ladder, and watch me at work.

The look on the face of this child, who rose above all the dangers and splendidly asserted her strong personality, was a lesson to all of us. Maria knew about the kidnap threat hovering over her. I had told her everything. She remained calm, and the peaceful expression on her face also helped to reassure me. I believe Maria inherited this courage from her father. She is braver than I. She slept on the floor of her room near her governess. I would roam through the house, converse with the men hiding behind the bushes in the garden, make coffee for all of them and wait impatiently for the day when my husband would come from Europe to help me. And, as always, he came when I needed him.

On the day the gangsters expected payment of the extortion money, my friends Maurice Chevalier and von Sternberg, as well as my husband, were stationed at the windows of the house with rifles. The police had made it clear to me that under no circumstances was I to give an order to shoot. I was a foreigner, I had to remain calm and keep my mouth shut. They would "take care of the matter." But they got off on the wrong foot and stupidly botched everything.

Still, we managed to pull through this horrible situation and survived. Maria had kept a cool head throughout the ordeal, an extraordinary achievement in my opinion. If the "professors" and other bookworms are to be believed, in all probability she was doomed to suffer a "trauma" for the rest of her life after this adventure. Fortunately, they are always mistaken.

The windows of the house on the corner of Roxbury Drive and Sunset Boulevard are still barred. When the bars were installed, our dreams of sun, freedom, and joy, of a carefree life were shattered. The holidays had come to a close. We were prisoners. Gone the visits to the movies, the strolls along the quiet streets of Beverly Hills while we looked up at the moon, gone the picnics to the beach on the Pacific Ocean, gone the roller-coaster rides amid laughter and shouts of pleasure during which I would hold scarves, hats, popcorn, and candy in one hand and place the other over my daughter's shoulder.

From now on my job was to carry on as though everything was normal to avoid frightening those associated with my child. In my head, however, fear took on the shape of a black raven, or rather, it lay like a serpent coiled in our hearts ready to strike at any moment. But I was young and strong. Later as my daughter grew older, I was again in danger, and I nearly had a breakdown. I was hardly able to carry on and could only muster enough strength to perform the simplest chores. But at the time of this threat, I did everything to give Maria the impression that life was a bed of roses. Every day I would invent a thousand pastimes to dispel the curse of the criminals threatening my daughter.

Fear dominated me and my home; it never left me. Von Sternberg gave us advice. He held the reins firmly in hand; he took care of everything personally, even though he was shooting a new film.

This project took up his whole day (I don't know how it was with his nights). Yet he was always there, trying to calm the "hypersensitive wreck"—as we say nowadays—this woman who trembled with fear and anxiety and depended on him completely. Any other director would have retired to his villa, informed the producers that he would wait until his leading performer had recovered, and meanwhile lolled around in the sun.

Not so von Sternberg. He let me work regularly. He shot his film. He and I made this film regardless of our personal problems. It was not a great work, but a good film. Von Sternberg worked tirelessly day and night and tried to improve it while his actors and actresses slept with the aid of sleeping pills.

I have never taken any. I needed them as little as did Maria who enjoyed a child's deep, solid slumber. She never heard me when I entered her room quietly and left; she never once woke up when I took her in my arms and laid her next to me in my large bed. She clung to me the way I clung to her.

I was up at five o'clock in the morning, ready to go to the studio with her, to have my hair done and my tired face made up. On the way we played all kinds of games. The ride in the car was hard on us. Fear churned in my stomach, and Maria was simply allergic to this means of transportation. I always had lots of lemons with me to counter the nausea. Nevertheless, I often had the Cadillac—sixteen cylinders, no less—come to a stop so I could be sick on the side of the road.

This condition never lasted very long. The moment I stepped into the studio, my face was smooth and beautiful as it was supposed to be: I watched for von Sternberg's glance and his recognition.

When the film was finished, I kept the guards who had been Maria's companions during the horrible kidnap scare. At the beginning of the holidays they accompanied us to New York up to the ship, up to the last echo of the traditional call: "All ashore that's going ashore!" Locked up in our cabin, we were finally safe and secure. And this, too, was thanks to von Sternberg who had made all the arrangements for our departure.

Upon our return to the United States, this horrible scare still pursued us, and Maria continued her life as a loner deprived of the company of children of her own age. She had many friends, but they were all grown-ups. She learned to ride horses, with a saddle and bareback, dive, surf—and all the sundry sports native to California—always in the company of governesses and guards. And von Sternberg, of course, also kept an eye on her. Tutors came to the house and gave her instruction.

She spoke English before she could write German—her

mother tongue—but without becoming confused in the process. Her education was of no special interest to me. I was concerned only about her well-being. Von Sternberg tried several times to bring up the problem of her education, but I was as stubborn as a donkey. Later I took Maria to Switzerland where she was to learn French, since the study of foreign languages was the only education I thought meaningful.

In 1933 when von Sternberg wrote the script of *The Scarlet Empress*, he gave Maria the role of Catherine the Great as a child. She spoke her only line—"I want to become a ballet dancer"—in perfect English, and she would listen to all the dialogue like a professional actress. She called that "re-acting." Von Sternberg would smile and, most unusual for him, would embrace her.

My husband was detained in France by his professional commitments, and since he came only seldom to the United States, von Sternberg (his first son was born much later) was a father and a friend to Maria. But the happiness my small family gave him was fragile and surely not real in his eyes. At first I didn't understand his feelings. Certainly my own "emotional" shortcomings were sad and distressing. This was an area where I was still quite immature. I simply didn't know how to read certain subtle signals. In fact, I tried to pretend they didn't exist . . . but who knows?

I cannot repeat often enough how young and stupid I was. What I most regret is my inability at that time instantly to recognize intellectual superiority. Why "instantly"? Well, because your eyes will open when you find yourself in the presence of an extraordinary person. I was raised with this principle and have never deviated from it. But, unfortunately, I have not always unconditionally followed it in my private life, and von Sternberg had to pay for it. My entourage, furthermore, contributed to deepening the misunderstanding. Becky, my daughter's governess, and Resi, my housemaid, had a hard time adjusting themselves to American customs that they found silly. And who was the recipient of their wailings and lamentations? Von Sternberg, of course! He always found himself again in the role of family head, representing the real mentor who was still abroad. He was the one who assumed all responsibilities and had to listen to the often unjust and ridiculous complaints: The bread didn't taste like it did in Germany; American priests celebrated Mass differently . . .

On my arrival in the United States von Sternberg had given me a Rolls Royce convertible (by the way, it can be seen in *Morocco*) and hired a chauffeur. I was not allowed to drive the car. Some say—and it's not a bad idea!—that men resort to this trick to prevent a woman from going off secretly by herself.

I never took off secretly. Moreover, I have never felt any such desire. I felt comfortable in this peaceful, agreeable life, a serenity unknown to the power-seeking women (conceivably their number is ever increasing today) who buzzed around Hollywood at that time.

On April 1, 1933, in Germany it was publicly announced that all Jews occupying positions—often for many years—in large or small institutions and enterprises were to be dismissed. Ufa, a major film producer, was headed primarily by Jews, among them Erich Pommer and R. Liebman.

Shortly after this announcement someone approached my husband, who had been assistant to many directors and who worked for Ufa, and offered to put him in charge of the firm and its studios in Babelsberg, a suburb of Berlin. My husband replied that he would think it over and discuss the offer with his lawyer and then meet with his visitor again on a mutually convenient date.

He knew that as an "Aryan," tall and blond, he corresponded to the ethnic type the Nazis wanted to see lead and represent their world famous film company.

On the same afternoon my husband went to his bank and withdrew all the money from his account. Then he went home, threw some clothes into a suitcase, took his passport out of his desk, drove to a gas station, and before darkness fell he was already on the way.

He drove for a while, stopped on a secondary road, smeared his license plate with dirt and stopped again only to refuel. He didn't roar over the superhighways, instead he tried to attract as little attention as possible. He drove to the French-German border and into France toward Paris, the city he knew and loved.

My husband spoke fluent French. So it was not difficult for him to find a place to stay and a job.

Only then did he phone me in California.

Since at that particular time I was working on a film, I hadn't phoned him in Berlin for quite a while—partly because of the time difference, partly because it was not so easy to make outside calls from the studio, and also because, like myself, he was seldom at home. When I heard his voice from Paris I was very happy to hear of his decision and that everything had gone so smoothly. We hardly gave any thought to the loss of our home and our valuable furniture. We thought only of the moment, of the present—just as young people still do today.

He guided me further even in his self-imposed exile and gave me good advice as he had always done. And I, his companion in exile, was a good student who submitted to his orders.

Josef von Sternberg was very close to him and often sided with him in our discussions. He engaged him as an assistant director for one of his films, and he would scold me when I didn't act according to my husband's wishes.

I suffered under this separation from my homeland, but it is easier to get over homesickness when you are young.

The Hitler regime asked me to return to Berlin and become the "queen" of the German film, and my reply to this offer is well known. What is not as widely known is the way I played—and quite sadistically—my game with the Nazis. I reminded them that I was under contract with von Sternberg but that I would be more than happy to be able to make a film under his direction in Germany.

This conversation took place in Paris at the German embassy. I had been pleading with the American authorities to let my German passport expire, but they had insisted that all my papers had to be in order if I wanted to become an American citizen. So I had to apply for an extension of my passport. I went to the German embassy, of course, to attend to this formality. Von Sternberg knew nothing about it. And I had turned down my husband's offer to come with me to the embassy. I was afraid that his short temper would get the better of him. I had to act diplomatically and couldn't allow myself to be carried away by my feelings.

So I ventured into the lion's den, the occupant of which was Count von Welczeck, Hitler Germany's ambassador to France. Alongside him stood four tall men who were introduced to me as the Princes Reuss. All these dignitaries remained standing, as though nailed behind the high armchairs. The ambassador explained that the extension of my passport would be granted immediately and added that he had still another special message to pass on to me. I should return to Germany and not try to become an American citizen. As an inducement, he promised me a "triumphal entry into Berlin through the Brandenburg Gate." End of quote. I thought of Lady Godiva and suppressed a smile. I was extremely polite, gave my contract with von Sternberg as an excuse for my hesitancy, and explained that if they would ask him to make a film in Germany, I would be more than glad to accept their offer.

There was an icy silence, which I finally broke: "Do I rightly understand that you refuse to have Mr. von Sternberg make a film in your country (I said: 'your country') because he's Jewish?" Suddenly they all began to stir and to talk at the same time: "You are infected by American propaganda. There is no anti-Semitism in Germany. . . ."

Then and there I realized it was time to go. I stood up and said: "Well, then we're all agreed. I'll wait for the result of your negotiations with my director, and I hope the German press will change its tone toward Mr. von Sternberg and me."

As the ambassador (his Czech name confused me) let me know: "A single word from the Führer and all your wishes will be fulfilled, *if* you are ready to return."

Escorted by the four princes, I walked through the long corridor to the exit, and I was trembling when I set foot on French soil again, on the street on which my husband was nervously pacing up and down. He took me by the arm and helped me to get in the car.

On the next day the duly extended passport was sent to my hotel. These "gentlemen" knew everything. They knew when my contract with Paramount would expire and when the next one would come into force. They were up to date on everything. I seemed to have pleased the horrible dwarf. What an honor!

My friends and my family, jokingly, would often ask me whether I wouldn't like to return to Germany and kill him— another form of gallows humor. I never felt up to a mission of this kind, intellectually or physically. Today I'm sure I was right. But at that time I always acted on my gut feeling in which I had confidence, the good gut feeling of a Berliner. According to Noel Coward I am "a realist and a clown." I know the realist; I also know the clown, but he makes only an occasional appearance. I can sometimes play the clown and be very funny, but this is a characteristic that often remains hidden. The clown comes to the surface when I feel embarrassed by something or when I learn something essential about life. But the clown departs the moment my feelings begin to run deep. Then I am helplessly vulnerable to all possible offenses—even to a voice on the phone with an odd ring—and I can let myself drift, leave myself exposed to a world alien to me in the hope that somewhere someone will emerge from out of nowhere and save me. That's how I am, a creature whose character has been shaped by loving people, from my mother all the way to my husband and to my daughter, people who protected me.

I grew up surrounded by love throughout my whole childhood, and even as a young girl life was a game—guided by a star of sympathy and understanding, which was far more important than all we learned in school, went beyond the traditional commandments, and was surpassed only by my experience as an adult.

Before von Sternberg took me in hand, I was utterly helpless, I was not even aware of the task awaiting me. I was a "nobody," and the mysterious energies of the creator breathed life into this nothingness. I'm not entitled to the least recognition for the roles I played in his films. I was nothing but pliable material on the infinitely rich palette of his ideas and imaginative faculties.

The films that von Sternberg made with me speak for themselves. There is nothing, and there will be nothing in the future, that could surpass them. Filmmakers are forever condemned to imitate them.

Many books have been written on his work. But none offers a truthful picture of his extraordinary talent. None of them originated "live," so to speak. As for me, I was there and saw everything. I saw the *magic,* even though I was still young.

Von Sternberg looked for a very definite figure to play the male hero in *The Scarlet Empress*—filmed in 1934—and the type was not to be found in Hollywood. So he decided to pick the lawyer John Lodge. John Lodge was the proverbial gentleman: refined and well educated. He had never acted before, yet he corresponded to the concept von Sternberg had in his head, and he proved to be very convincing in this role. Von Sternberg didn't want to subject him to any sound tests and contented himself with shooting a short scene. He designed a magnificent, though perhaps not all too authentic costume, and Lodge conquered the hearts of all American women. He was *the* Russian hero, the romantic figure par excellence. On the first day of shooting John Lodge, who had never seen a camera aimed at him, began to stutter. Since von Sternberg wanted to spare him a humiliating failure, he asked me to perform all alone and no longer to depend on a partner, and he himself taught John Lodge how to behave in front of a camera.

John Lodge became our friend, and he won von Sternberg's unlimited respect. He made few films after *The Scarlet Empress,* but I'm sure he was never sorry to have had the experience of being an actor. He's too intelligent a man to regret the past.

Now to get back to me: so von Sternberg had me perform "all alone." This was asking a lot. At first, I refused, but I soon understood what von Sternberg wanted and I obeyed. Today *The Scarlet Empress* is a classic. In 1934, however, it didn't enjoy the hoped-for success. But now we know that this film was ahead of its time; certainly this is the reason why it is shown in film museums, in programs and film workshops, and also why millions of moviegoers see it on the silver screen throughout the world. The younger generations rave about *The Scarlet Empress.* Young people write me, and talk about the costumes—particularly about my boots, which moreover were white!—and other impressive details of the work they seem to understand thoroughly . . . much more than the public of that time. They are also fascinated by the artistic direction, which, of course, was in von Sternberg's hands. But he didn't believe wholeheartedly in *The Scarlet Empress*. Once he told the members of the cast: "If this film is a flop, it will be a grandiose flop, and the critics will rage. But I prefer to see you in a grandiose flop than in a mediocre film." Von Sternberg was to be proved eminently right. The critics' rage was immense.

I didn't attach any great importance to their reactions. First of all, because a film gradually fades as a phenomenon once it's in the distribution process, and then also because I never read even one article on *The Scarlet Empress*, nor did I follow the film's box office receipts. Work on a new film had begun; I spent hours on fittings and was concerned with keeping as close as possible to the new image that von Sternberg wanted to create. With him my roles were always different.

I constantly ran the risk of letting my roles or my profession slip into my private life. That was unavoidable. Despite this I've always taken great pains to keep these two spheres of my life apart. As I've said earlier, I was utterly indifferent to the opinions of others, save von Sternberg's.

The studio publicity people kept on trying to bring about an association between my roles and my person. Indeed, their work primarily consisted in hatching stories for the press and the countless large-circulation movie magazines that were not read by intellectuals. The life I led in Hollywood was not a good hunting ground for these characters hell-bent on piquant anecdotes. That's why I can't really reproach them for having fabricated an "exciting" life for me. I wasn't familiar with their articles, but when I think about it, I figure that these publicity agents must have really loathed me. Yet even had I known about it at that time, I wouldn't have cared. I complied with the terms of my contract. When I was scheduled to give an interview, which did not happen often, I learned to politely sidestep inappropriate questions.

The alleged "myth" or "legend" is still very much alive, and day and night it mobilizes hundreds of prospective reporters and writers. I could well do without them. When the new adventure of my life began, "the stage," I thought I could destroy the "myth." In a certain way I succeeded, since I was in direct contact with the public. Yet my so-called "biographers" were not to be dissuaded.

In their confused heads *The Blue Angel* was a von Sternberg creation, while he had merely brought to life on the screen a character of Heinrich Mann's novel *Professor Unrat*. Neither von Sternberg nor I invented the woman who ruined the poor professor. Naturally, von Sternberg and the two other scriptwriters Carl Zuckmayer and Liebmann made some changes (that always happens when a novel is filmed), but nevertheless, they preserved the characteristic features of the main characters.

I should like once more to repeat: The roles I have played in films have absolutely nothing to do with what I really am. It's stupid to associate these roles with myself. For a time I was busy compiling excerpts from the films von Sternberg had made with me for the Museum of Modern Art in New York. Most of my admirers were flabbergasted by the result. In contrast to the widespread opinion that I am always the same immovable creature who is looking over her left shoulder, who hides her face under hats and behind veils betraying no emotion whatsoever, and who doesn't see anything outside the range of the camera, this compilation showed an actress who contradicted all these clichés.

Although I edited the film myself, I must say that it's outstanding; unfortunately, I didn't keep a copy or even a list of the scenes. I edited according to a sense of proportion and feeling. From all my films I chose settings that, instead of meshing like the parts of a puzzle, contrasted with each other in relation to the person, the atmosphere or the camera angle, the lighting conditions or the costumes. I vaguely remember that the film was again cut apart since we had used some material belonging to the sacrosanct MCA. I don't know why I didn't receive a copy before the originals were given back. It must have been a question of money, as always.

That reminds me of another episode, certainly a "classic" for an enthusiastic younger generation of directors or cameramen. My second film in Hollywood, *X.27* (*Dishonoured*), was made in

1931. The choice of a film title was always an occasion for terrible controversies between von Sternberg and his producers. He very seldom agreed with the decisions of the studio officials and battled to change them step by step with more or less success. In the case of *Dishonoured* the producers were firm: They refused to back down. The struggle must have been bitter and endlessly long because I remember that the Paramount top brass threatened to "turn off the money faucet."

I had already changed my clothes and was waiting to be called to the studio when von Sternberg stormed into my dressing room to discuss this problem with me. In addition, he had to find a solution for the sequence of the great ball scene which was to be shot that day. He wasn't getting enough extras? Under no circumstances would he cut this decisive sequence! Loges were to be set up around the huge ballroom like balconies in an opera house. I sat in my dressing room and listened to my director without saying a word, without any idea occurring to me that might have been of some help to him. And yet at that time my head and hands were free of other concerns. Maria was still in Germany with my husband; nobody in Hollywood was giving me any trouble, and von Sternberg was watching over me.

My makeup artist Dot, my hairdresser, and I decided to go for lunch. When we came back from the studio canteen, I resumed my wait in the dressing room. Suddenly von Sternberg's assistant summoned us to the studio. Dot put the last touches to my face, the hairdresser fussed for a second or two over my still unruly hair, and then we went out. There were almost no structures on the set except for two theater loges placed one on top of the other, slightly raised, which could be reached by a ladder.

I was to take my place in the lower loge. Above me were men and women with confetti and pockets bulging with New Year's Eve trimmings. They had already received their instructions. As I sat down, I saw a huge mirror behind me, also slightly raised. Six couples were dancing in a tiny circle that was marked in crayon on the floor.

Their image was also reflected in the mirror in which innumerable male and female dancers appeared pressing very closely against each other. The confetti rained down in front of me, the music came in, set the rhythm and, suddenly, I noticed that the scene to a hair resembled a giant ballroom in which thousands of people whirled around the dance floor. Von Sternberg had achieved the desired effect despite the cutbacks the studio had imposed on him. I was young and inexperienced, but I admired his flair for *magic*, that faculty I was to see at work for so many years. In the course of the shooting period, with an ever-growing admiration, I learned everything from Josef von Sternberg, that conjuror of the thousand-headed serpent called "film."

Beyond that, von Sternberg also had to concern himself with me: photograph me, make me laugh, dress me up, comfort me, advise me, guide me, coddle me, explain things to me, and much more. The responsibility he assumed for the actress that he wanted and for the woman that had come with him was something enormous. And, as always, he managed to do this despite the pressure of the Paramount top brass. He battled them tenaciously.

Paramount tried several times to separate us, but since my contract stipulated that "I could choose my own director," they gave up. "Why should we be content with one box-office success, when we can have two?" figured the Paramount executives. Von Sternberg's name was famous and so was mine. I battled, he battled and we won! In 1933, he permitted me to make *Song of Songs* with another director. The film, of course, was a flop.

In 1935, after his return from a long trip, von Sternberg began preparations for *The Devil Is a Woman* based on the novel *The Woman and the Puppet* by Pierre Louÿs. I knew that this would be our last film together, and I was as restless as a sack of fleas. Von Sternberg noticed this and once more tried to reassure me. I played the part of a girl who worked in a cigarette factory. At his request I had taken lessons and learned to roll cigarette paper around a little stick. I also learned to make the empty paper rolls swirl around in front of the camera, catch them again and stuff them with tobacco. That was not easy, but I was a good pupil. It wasn't these little tricks that worried me most, however, but the fact that I absolutely didn't look Spanish. The Spanish lace blouse and the pleated skirt didn't convince me. There was nothing

"Iberian" about my blue eyes and blond hair! But my biggest worry were my eyes. I thought that all Spaniards had dark if not black eyes. My hair was rubbed with Vaseline so that it looked dark enough to me. Von Sternberg said that I was really stupid (as always) because there were plenty of blond women in northern Spain. How was I supposed to know that? So I continued with preparations for the film; I tried on the costumes sketched by von Sternberg and worried further about the color of my eyes. Finally, I visited an eye doctor whom my makeup artist had recommended. He prescribed drops that widened the pupils so that they would appear black on the screen. Then he gave me a second bottle containing a liquid that would restore the pupils to their normal size.

On the way home I pressed the bottles against myself as though they were made of gold. I took them with me to the studio, explained their use to my makeup artist and my hairdresser. The Vaseline had been rubbed into my hair; the carnations (which had increased in number in the course of the shooting) were pinned on, and I felt I had been transformed into a genuine Spanish woman. Apart from my eyes. But stupidly I believed I could remedy this annoying minor detail.

With swaying dress, combs in the sticky hair between the artificial carnations, my face made up darkly (which made me more attractive than ever), I arrived punctually at Studio 8 at nine o'clock in the morning. I remember exactly. I used my little bottle only after the rehearsal. I went to my dressing room, sprinkled the drops in my eyes, and returned to my place, ready to shoot the scene. I looked for my essentials, the paper and the stick. But they were no longer there!

Von Sternberg shouted to the cameraman: "Let it roll!" and I just stood there and could no longer find my tiny stick and paper, everything was functioning perfectly except my eyes. I acted as though everything was in order, but von Sternberg immediately noticed that something was wrong. "Cut," he roared.

The hairdresser and the makeup artist ran over to my dressing room and brought me the other little bottle with the drops that were supposed to restore my pupils to their normal size. I dripped the liquid in my eyes and resumed my place on the set. The whole thing hadn't lasted for more than five minutes. I again sat down at the table from which I had suddenly stood up in a daze. I saw everything as from a great distance, a very great distance—the technicians, von Sternberg. . . . But no matter what I did, it was impossible to recognize anything directly in front of me. No stick. No paper. No tobacco.

Von Sternberg sent us all out to lunch, but before that he took me by the hand and pulled me away from the extras and technicians, out of earshot and he said: "Now tell me what's the matter." I told him everything. I wasn't seeing things normally, I simply couldn't help crying. "Why didn't you tell me you wanted black eyes?" he asked me.

I didn't know what to answer.

"Do you want black eyes?" he persisted.

I nodded.

"Fine, then you'll have black eyes, but don't ever use anything like these drops without first asking me." He made my eyes look darker, simply by the way he played with the light.

Some of my "biographers" stubbornly claim that *The Devil Is a Woman* is an autobiographical film. In Europe where the Louÿs novel is well known, no one has dared to make so improbable an assertion, all the more so because the story has often been filmed. Yet, although the film sticks strictly to Pierre Louÿs' story, several periodicals in the United States gave the impression that von Sternberg had drawn his inspiration from his life and mine.

Von Sternberg, annoyed over all the fruitless discussions, had had enough: He decided to separate himself from me. Naturally, I protested strongly against his intentions, became angry, and decided I would leave Hollywood and never come back. But he told me, loud and clear, that such a prospect was out of the question, that if I wanted still to be his friend, I had to stay in Hollywood and make films without him. These words broke my heart, but I obeyed, as always. At what price? I was like a rudderless ship. I realized that no fame could replace the security that he had given me, that nothing could compensate for his extraordinary intelligence, his professional ethics, the fascination that he exercised . . .

But von Sternberg didn't abandon me completely. He secretly supervised the mediocre films I made subsequently; sometimes he would even sneak into the studio and cut out particular settings or make changes. I myself organized the nightly exploratory forays. Von Sternberg's "resignation" stood to reason: He had enough of scandals, attacks, of the behavior of the Paramount executives.

If only I had had a presentiment of all the problems with which he wrestled, I would have been more understanding. But he seldom took me into his confidence, he didn't want to involve me in his disputes with the Paramount executives. He let me go my own way and attend to my own work, normally and calmly.

This is the story of my collaboration with von Sternberg. Is that all? No. Before I finish this chapter, I would like still to mention what I feared most in him: his contempt. A shocking experience. Several times during the day, he would send me back to my dressing room so that I could cry in peace. After talking to me in German, he would turn to the technicians and say: "Smoking break. Miss Dietrich is having one of her crying fits." Bathed in tears, I would flee to the dressing room with my makeup artist and my hairdresser.

I have never reproached von Sternberg for his sharp tone. He had all the right in the world to it. Because he was my protector. Because he was also my friend. What he said was always right. He was always right. I will never be able to thank him enough for it.

I'm sure he would fume if he were able to read these lines. I can almost hear him shout: "Cut!" But how can I be silent about such things when I'm talking about him, when I'm trying to explain what he meant to me and what no actress, even if she were led by the greatest of all directors, ever will experience? It's impossible to forget the days and nights in which we worked together side by side without his showing the least sign of impatience or fatigue. He was always there for me; he forgot himself, his own wishes and needs.

A master.

End of the panegyric. Excuse me, Joe! But I had to write that. I'm sure I can give no better portrait of you than anyone else working with you could have done. I simply remember you, all the years that I lived in your shadow. Yesterday . . .

I've grown older, and I've learned to realize the burden of the loneliness of your efforts and of your thoughts, your responsibilities with regard to the studio and, above all, with regard to me. And I can't do anything else, I simply must cry: "Nevermore," quoth the raven, "nevermore." Josef von Sternberg was an unparalleled genius, a singular genius in his generation and in the world of films.

He, who stayed so close to me and my family, was also the friend of all film fans. He was a workaholic, and the mediocre persons in his entourage detested him. His authority and knowledge are irreplaceable. His death has left a great void.

HOLLYWOOD

Hollywood—the most disreputable and most mythical place in the world.

I never went to the wild parties in Hollywood, never experienced those aspects which make it famous.

For me Hollywood (I use its name although this is geographically incorrect) is a place where you work as hard as anywhere else. You get up early and speed off in a train or car to get to the studio and clock in on time.

As early as six-thirty in the morning the actors and actresses had to show up at the hairdresser's to have their hair washed, dried and set. At nine we were in the studio. This means we had been on our feet since five o'clock. Certain professional groups are used to such hours. It's somewhat different for an actress, a woman who must always appear impeccable. I've known actresses who can be enchanting from five o'clock in the morning on, but you can count them on the fingers of your hands. Most of the time you're utterly exhausted on your way to the makeup artist; you slip inconspicuously into the booth and wait for a sympathetic word or two. A big thank you for all the men and women who helped me get to the studio at the right time.

At that time the unions were incredibly strict in the matter of regulations. As a result makeup artists, hairdressers and dressing room assistants were always there on time. Nobody was allowed to interfere in the next person's activity. I remember a hairdresser who was almost fired because she had drawn my attention to the fact that the seam of my stocking was crooked. I thought that was unjust, and that's why I hired her to work for me. Nelly Manley was present at all my films in Hollywood and Europe. She wept with me, hated my enemies, and untangled my hair during lunch breaks, foregoing her own snack. She remained with me up to the end. She was rather short and wore worn-out tennis shoes long before they became fashionable . . . which didn't prevent her from transforming herself later into an elegant lady who was accoutered by Schiaparelli.

Nelly Manley performed a dual function for me as friend and personal "guard." She didn't have an easy life in the studio where everybody was jealous of everybody else. But she survived. On the way out of the studio, we would often go by Bing Crosby's dressing room, and if I came to a halt to listen to him, she would push me forward. Perhaps she already saw the next day's headlines: "Dietrich in Bing Crosby's Dressing Room!" I wasn't a great fan of the famous singer, but I liked to listen to Richard Tauber records as much as Crosby did. The crooner confided to me that Tauber had taught him how to breathe properly and how to modulate his phrasing. This common passion brought us together.

Mae West's dressing room lay between the studio and my dressing room. What a remarkable woman! She was very friendly to me and often gave me good advice. She gave me the strength I lacked with a sensitivity that astonished me. But I wasn't the only one. The Paramount executives were just as captivated and carried away by her. She was never a "mother" to me, since she wasn't the motherly sort. For me she was a teacher, no, a rock to which I clung, an intelligent woman who understood me and who divined all my problems. At that time I don't think she was aware of what a great influence she had on me. I was so bad in expressing my feelings.

When I read Ernst Lubitsch's screenplay for *Desire*, I was horrified: The film was to begin with a close-up of my legs. My legs, always my legs! Yet for me they have only one purpose; they make it possible for me to walk. I didn't want so much fuss made over my legs. But Mae West advised me to take another view of the matter and to let the producers have their way. She always had a thousand good reasons for her opinion, and I listened to her. So the film *Desire* begins with a close-up of my legs. It's an extraordinary film and could have dispensed with such a beginning.

Mae West was wonderful, intelligent, shrewd, and understood her metier. She never was seen at Hollywood parties. Probably only starlets went to them. We never attended them. It was already difficult enough to screen off our private sphere, to attend to the day-to-day demands of our job, to spend a few relaxing hours with the few friends we had.

"GLAMOUR STARS"

No lexicographer has yet succeeded in exactly defining the word *glamour*. It just cropped up one day, but nobody can explain it or trace its etymology. I've often been asked about the meaning of this word and have always had to throw up my hands.

The greatest "glamour girl" was Mae West. Then came Carole Lombard. And then Dietrich. At any rate according to Paramount's view. MGM, of course, also had its glamour girls in Jean Harlow, Greta Garbo, Joan Crawford . . . At that time there were no "sex symbols." In my opinion this notion first came into being with Marilyn Monroe. Sex then was taboo. "We must do all that only and exclusively with the eyes," Mae West explained to me one day. And we all stuck to this. There was no scene in which we undressed or appeared semi-nude, nothing improper. I must confess I prefer that method to what you see on the screen nowadays. I don't like it, and I'm sure the public shares my dislike.

Today sex is tremendously important. It's the only thing that has something to offer people. Everybody is so frustrated that the pursuit of pleasure has become a veritable sickness. That's why "shrinks" are so popular; many people pay horrendously exorbitant sums to their "shrinks" for their life-supporting therapy (all the better for the "shrinks" when they can become rich that way!).

Despite that, I feel sorry for people who need such a deceptive form of assistance.

The word *glamour* means something indefinite, something inaccessible to normal women—an unreal paradise, desirable but basically out of reach.

I find all that pretty stupid. Of course, we're beautiful in the photos and also in life; but we were never so extraordinary as the image that was sketched of us. We clung to this image because the studio demanded that we do so. But none of us enjoyed it. To us it was a routine job, and we just did it well. If one had asked the Harlows, the Crawfords, the Lombards for their opinion, I'm sure they would have said the same.

Marilyn Monroe was an authentic "sex symbol," because not only was she "sexy" by nature but she also liked being one—and she showed it. And she came at a time when the censorship to which we all had to submit (cheerfully, I would say) no longer existed. The skirts rose to the hips, panties became visible and the eye of the public was riveted on them. The performance no longer counted.

The directors of the thirties respected us and didn't demand that we show our "derrière." They attached no importance to it. We had to do without "tricks" of this kind. And what we did we did very well. We stimulated the imagination of the public all over the world; we awakened dreams and filled the movie houses.

But we also played serious roles in which the notion of being "fatale" simply never came up. The films with Garbo and with me have made history. When today's young people come to see us decked out in boots and fancy robes and behold our so-called "hot" love scenes they become enthusiastic and love us. Perhaps because of something else . . .

I came to Hollywood too late. I would have liked to live there at another time. The anecdotes about the days of the silents made my mouth water. At that time a kind of rickshaw would bring the stars to the studio. If two stars couldn't stand one another, the rickshaw drivers had to take care that their paths never crossed. I heard that such was the case between Pola Negri and Gloria Swanson. There was also music in the studio. A small orchestra played a melody suitable to the scene being filmed. Since sound recording did not yet exist, the orchestra played while the camera was running so that the actors wept and laughed to the rhythm of the music. That must have looked very strange. The moment the actors and actresses opened their mouths, one heard a "Cut!" coming to the rescue and the words would appear in beautiful script on the screen before they resumed their performance in the next scene.

At the time of the silent films all Hollywood reverberated with talk of famous, notorious wild parties. The great stars would remain there till late at night. On the next day they could nonchalantly appear four or five hours late at the studio. Just to make an appearance was all that mattered. Nobody would have dared to reprimand them, to bawl them out. These men and women ruled over the studios; they could indulge all their whims, they could exhibit their mistakes, their defeats, their dubious behavior, their bad performances, in short, all that was later to be labeled "bluff" in Hollywood.

I learned these stories from the truck drivers who helped me climb on the tailgates of their vehicles and brought me to the studio when my costumes were too bulky for me to sit with them in a passenger car. "Hold on, sweetie," they would call out to me before starting off slowly for fear I might fall off. These drivers, the technicians, the makeup artists and dressing room assistants who showed the same patience I did during the hours-long fitting sessions were my best friends.

I never saw the big studio bosses. I was looked on as the recognized queen of Paramount Studios, a distinction of which I wasn't aware, of course, and I was not supposed to be bothered. So my not too extensive fan mail was received by personnel especially appointed for that purpose who always lamented that I didn't get more letters. That made me suspicious, but later I learned that the people who liked my films were not the type who wrote fan letters "to his or her favorite actress."

I even had to get used to the previews. They were often held in the little town called Pomona. There the films were shown to a public that had no idea what it would be seeing. The poster simply read: "Major Studio Preview." A strange custom. In addition, cards were distributed in front of the movie house on which the public was invited to express its opinion of the film. These cards were then passed on to the studio and evaluated.

You don't have to have a Ph.D. in psychology to realize that a chance moviegoer who is asked to transform himself or herself into a critic will do his or her best to highlight mistakes, gaps, errors, etc. Nevertheless, the studio people conscientiously evaluated the cards and even forwarded them to the director and proposed certain changes to him. The directors I knew immediately threw them into the wastebasket. But I also remember a good example of the stupid influence of these previews.

After Josef von Sternberg finished shooting his first film for Paramount, *Morocco*, the film, as usual, was shown in Pomona. Gary Cooper played the leading male role. After the first half of the film, the auditorium was emptied. Finally, we watched the remainder of it all by ourselves. I asked for permission to leave, convinced that this showing signified the end of my Hollywood career. I began to pack my trunks the moment I got home. During my absence my big shepherd dog had almost devoured the black doll that had been my little mascot since *The Blue Angel*. I read it as a bad omen and packed my things even more feverishly. I wasn't sorry for myself but for Josef von Sternberg and all the others who had believed in me. On the other hand, I was somewhat relieved that now I wouldn't become a movie star and could go back to my family in Germany.

I didn't sleep a wink the whole night, as one can easily imagine, and I was ready to take off in the morning. At half-past nine von Sternberg phoned and asked me to see him in his office. There, I imagined, I would be told of my dismissal.

He had me sit down on the other side of the desk and threw or handed me a newspaper. "Read it," he said. There before my eyes was a short article by a Jimmy Star—a name I didn't know. After giving a summary of the film the reporter wrote: "If this woman doesn't revolutionize the film industry, then I don't know what I'm talking about."

I sat there, flabbergasted, and said: "But I've already packed all my trunks; I'm ready to go home now. I thought that I might have disappointed you."

"You can go back to Germany whenever you please," replied von Sternberg, "but surely not because you think you've failed here in America."

He was calm, as usual; his look, which I knew so well, rested on me. A faint cigarette smell hovered in the air; von Sternberg looked indifferent. I was as though paralyzed. Again, my overly proper upbringing and its imperatives. What should I do now? To me "to revolutionize the film industry" simply meant that I wasn't the flop I thought I was. How does one get up from a chair? How does one leave a room? I no longer knew. I remained seated, motionless.

"You can go now," he said, "but let me know your final decision."

I went back to the house I had rented. There I met my housemaid. I was restless. What should I do? The feeling of security I drew from obedience had disappeared. This time no one was giving me orders; I was torn in this and that direction and waited nervously for my husband's phone call. As usual, he would tell me what to do. Finally, late in the night, his call came through: "Here everything's going fine. Come to Berlin whenever you wish. But your film will be a huge success; don't give up the studio."

I went to bed and immediately fell asleep, something that had not happened for a long time.

Why had the audience left the movie house on that memorable evening? First of all because they had been disappointed by Gary Cooper—who up to then had played only cowboy roles—and his new style. In *Morocco* he was never seen on a horse. Besides, it was time to light the stoves on the orange plantations of Pomona. The artistic merits of *Morocco* were not the issue. Meanwhile, previews have been given up, this stupid custom that has angered many great directors and whose passing nobody mourns.

ACTORS' STYLES

1. John Barrymore was a master in every way. When I came to America, he was the most famous actor of all time. His name exercised a great magic even on us Europeans. I heard Barrymore on the radio and saw him on stage. He was superb. Years later when I made a radio broadcast with him, he was no longer the same, and we had to support him throughout the performance. He thanked us, aware of his weaknesses. When he left the studio, we all had tears in our eyes.

2. The "hm" actors. Those who don't at all deserve to be called actors, since to "act" doesn't mean simply to say "hm" or to utter one-word lines or incomprehensible sounds.

3. After the "hm" actors come the "mumbling" actors. They attach great importance to the fact that nobody, not even the director, not to mention the sound man, understands what they're saying (the script girls gave up a long time ago and pray to heaven that the lines of the "mumblers" coincide with the script). For many years these "mumbling" actors were the finest of the finest. They were considered geniuses because no one understood a word of what they were "saying." Sometimes their partners would try to outdo them by murmuring their dialogue even more indistinctly. The result was ludicrous.

4. After that there was a reverse tendency, actors again spoke correctly. That was before the "What's happened to my other shoe?" period. James Stewart was the inventor of this original style. Even when he visibly made an effort to play a love scene, he always gave the impression he was wearing only one shoe and looking for the other while he slowly droned his lines.

One day I told him about these ruminations of mine, and he answered: "How's that?" Obviously, his sense of humor was poorly developed. He performed this way throughout his life and became very rich and very famous. Now he no longer had to look for his other shoe. My American partners had a peanut where other humans have a brain. I'm not saying there were no intelligent actors in Hollywood. There were, of course, but truth to tell I didn't get along with them.

The only really admirable actor with whom I worked was Spencer Tracy; unfortunately my role in *Judgment at Nuremberg* was a small one. We laughed a lot together since his sense of humor was like mine. European actors are quite different from their American counterparts. Robert Donat was magnificent, de Sica brilliant, comical, a director of genius.

Brian Aherne, my partner in *Song of Songs*, was very gifted and had a mordant English sense of humor I greatly appreciated. I never had the luck to work with David Niven. He was not only an actor but a writer as well, an amusing host, and listening to him was as pleasant as reading his books.

One time I thought luck was finally smiling upon me: I was scheduled to make a film with a friend, the great Polish actor Zbigniew Cybulski. But he died in an accident, all too early. You needed to have seen his face only once, with the eyes hidden behind sunglasses, for example, in *Ashes and Diamonds*, his best known film, and you would never forget it. I met Cybulski in Poland during one of my concerts. At that time he was making a film in Wroclaw (called Breslau before the war), and he would appear at my performance after a long and hard day's work. We were friends from the moment of our first encounter.

I had seen him on the screen. He, on the other hand, didn't know any of my films. He was astonished at my ability on the stage. He had assumed I was one of those superficial creatures out of Hollywood; he had fallen for the myth. Now he made it a point not to miss any of my appearances. On the last night he gave a party for the musicians and the technicians. I never knew any other man who could uncork a bottle of vodka by striking the bottom of the bottle with the flat of his hand. He repeated this trick several times to the great delight of all the guests as the bottles went from hand to hand around the long table.

I had to keep an eye on the clock because our train to Warsaw was leaving at midnight. Cybulski remained with us, saw to it that the whole troupe was properly accommodated in the sleeping car, bade us good-bye, visibly deeply moved, and promised to see us again as soon as he finished his film.

When the shooting was finally over, Cybulski, just like us, decided to take the midnight train. But he arrived too late. He tried to jump on the moving train, fell, and was run over.

To this day I am haunted by this shocking death of a great human being and a great artist. Never before had there been an actor who could perform without having to make use of his eyes, and I know there will never again be another. All the better! Cybulski is not forgotten—which cannot be said for most actors.

I also can't forget George Raft, my partner in *Manpower*. His unique, lovable kindness belied his appearance and his tough roles. We became good friends, in contrast to many actors with whom I was often together and with whom I worked. Shooting a film can take months that are not always marked by a spirit of harmony, but in spite of everything you get to like the other members of the team. Nevertheless, as soon as the last shot is "in the can," some actors just take off without the slightest nostalgia or the slightest feeling of having experienced a loss. That was never the case with me.

JEALOUSY

I've been an innocent victim of this passion, this disease that has pursued me relentlessly. Beginning with my chauffeur Bridges, whom I liked from my very first days in California and who helped me during the time of the kidnap scare and later in France, up to the manicurists, the hairdressers, the female personnel of the publicity department, the photographers, and on to individual friends (I'm speaking of my *real* friends) and the directors (the great ones and the others like Tay Garnett, George Marshall)—all have caused me trouble with their jealousy.

All my musical directors, without exception, were jealous of Burt Bacharach since he was the only musician I blindly trusted, the only one upon whom I relied completely and with good reason. Jealousy accompanied me on all my tours, yet I didn't let it lead me astray. I've never reproached anybody for anything. I never said: "Burt would have done it differently" or "Burt would have done it this way." I always kept my mouth shut and worked. Or better still, I would open my mouth and sing as I had been instructed to. I alone know what I had lost with him, and I still feel the aching void he left behind.

Burt Bacharach always contested the claim that he had taught me everything in the way of music. He sought no fame, no honor. What kind of "honor" would it be anyway to be the director, musician, arranger and teacher of a movie actress now a songstress in the making. "Nil!" to use a favorite expression of his. Yet all those who came in contact with Burt Bacharach were jealous of him. They were jealous of my deference toward him; they couldn't admit that he had created what they had failed to achieve. Burt Bacharach had first attended the Music Academy in Montreal, later the Juilliard School of Music. He had studied composition. In addition to being a talented composer, he was just as talented a director, which explains the feelings of some of his less gifted "colleagues."

Jealousy has destroyed more than one life. Not mine, thank heaven. I've never been jealous of anyone. "Jealousy" is even a foreign word to me, yet it has left its imprint on my professional as well as on my private life.

Jacques Feyder, the great French director, displayed a violent jealousy of my other directors and took a devilish delight in tormenting me in the presence of my leading man, until one day (I was to be filmed naked with my hair swept upwards in an old bathtub) he broke down and asked repeatedly to be forgiven.

Frank Borzage was the only one unaffected by the "galloping jealousy" virus. I was very fond of him. He directed *Desire*, whose direction has been wrongly attributed to Ernst Lubitsch; Lubitsch wrote the script, but he didn't direct the film.

Then there was also the jealousy of the cameramen, who claimed to have invented the lighting techniques von Sternberg had developed, and the false statements of the dentists, who swore on the Bible they had extracted my molars and thus formed the face that was to enthuse the entire world. Thank God, jealousy had no dominion over my family and over those close to me. My husband, my daughter, and my friends were too smart and reasonable to let themselves be infected. As for myself, I developed real defense mechanisms to protect myself against all arrows shot at me.

My life was by no means easy. I began to work at the age of seventeen. I've paid my taxes, and, I confess, I've helped many needy persons. To me that seems a normal thing to do—the most banal of imperatives: If you have money, you give; if you don't, you can't give as much as you'd like. It's that simple.

It always distresses me to deny financial help to the thousands who ask me to pay for their mortgages, for the education of their children, for their hospital bills, etc. I would like to have enough money to alleviate their needs. That should be the task of the rich, but I no longer belong to that class.

I really admired Aristotle Onassis. Unlike most rich people, he wasn't boring. He sparkled with *joie de vivre* and possessed a generosity from which everybody profited. I met him when I was shooting a film with Vittorio de Sica, and found him to be not only a real friend but also a man who taught me a lot of things. Unfortunately, I couldn't follow his advice: You need money to make more. He had a sense of humor very rare among the rich. We understood each other perfectly, but our friendship was brief because I had to go to Rome and finish shooting my film. He left behind with me an inextinguishable impression of an extraordinary human being.

GIANTS

CHARLIE CHAPLIN

We became friends when he was in the middle of one of his many divorce suits, and we spent many evenings together—which didn't drag on for very long because we both had to get up early and go to the studio.

Above all, our sentimentality brought us close together. Not to be confused with "feeling." The music Chaplin composed was "sentimental" (schmaltzy, one would say today), but it was balm for my soul. My German disposition and his English roots fit magnificently together. But there were times when I didn't agree with him . . . for example, when I discovered that he was suffering from a terrible ailment called "Hitler." He was making preparations for *The Great Dictator*, so it was normal that he should be fascinated by his model. But he went beyond the person, and this "obsession" often aroused my anger and led to violent verbal exchanges. Apart from that, I was in complete agreement with his bold convictions and granted that it must have been difficult for so arrogant a person as himself to get along with so stubborn a German as I. My fame left him cold, although he sought the company of prominent people—for which I'm not reproaching him. Stars, if they are to draw the attention of millions to themselves, must tower above the mass of actors, and Chaplin was driven by curiosity. He wanted to bring their secret thoughts to light, by constantly pretending, playing jokes, looking for a public and applause.

I liked his arrogance, his vanity. Arrogance is a privilege of men of his caliber. Not so with women. Arrogant women are a plague.

Chaplin and I met for the last time in Paris during a benefit performance at the Comédie Française. At that time he was both an actor and a producer and had little time.

I cannot add to all that which has already been written on this great man. All I can say is that in a world of corrupt politicians, his so-called "sentimentality" was a great trump card. And he could put them all in his vest pocket.

ALFRED HITCHCOCK

I made only one film with him, *Stage Fright*. What most impressed me about Hitchcock was his calm authority, his ability to give orders without being taken for a dictator.

Hitchcock, effortlessly, never failed to captivate, to explain, to rule, to teach, to enchant. Yet, at bottom, he was reserved.

Hitchcock filmed *Stage Fright* in London when food was still strictly rationed. He solved the problem by having steaks and roasts flown in from America and delivered to the best restaurant in London, and then after work, he would invite Jane Wyman and me to a princely dinner. "Ladies must be well fed," he would say, as we gratefully polished off the delicacies. These dinners were the only contact we had with him outside the studio. He kept us at a distance. Like many geniuses he didn't like being idolized.

I loved his English sense of humor; he constantly joked with us without ever playing up his fame or seeking our applause. A German slogan says: "Often copied and never matched"—so it was with Hitchcock.

RAIMU

Raimu was also one of my "heroes."

I revered him, knew all his films by heart. *La Femme du Boulanger* (*The Baker's Wife*) was my favorite film. I was in France shortly after it was shown in the movie houses.

One evening as I was having dinner in a restaurant, a powerful manly figure suddenly bent over me and in a voice that I knew all too well, said: "My name is Raimu."

I got up from my chair, speechless. How should you react when you're suddenly standing before your idol? I stammered something or other, he was very charming.

Nobody has been able to replace him. No actor could hold a candle to him.

RICHARD BURTON

This man was not only a great actor but also a man who made hearts beat faster—the perfect seducer, the man for whom the word "charisma" could have been invented, the ideal of whom all young girls and women dream, the perfection for which they would like to exchange their days spent in silence and hard work.

He always astonished us—as actor and as human being. I was completely under his spell from way back, but unfortunately, I met him when he was deeply in love with another woman, so there was nothing I could do. I admired his writing talent just as much as his theatrical achievement.

Publishers and the public considerably underestimated his talent in this area. Read his *Christmas Tale* someday, and you will fall in love with him—unless you've already done so. He certainly could have written a love story featuring his country, forebears, and the people he knew so well, the Welsh—a people dear to me.

Richard Burton apparently gave up the theater to dedicate himself entirely to the movies, to which I never go. But if he had

Marlene Dietrich with her parents, 1906

The relatives: Uncle Hermann, Aunt Ida, and Max Dietrich

Marlene Dietrich as Shanghai Lily in the film *Shanghai Express*, 1932

Marlene Dietrich and Josef von Sternberg, 1930

In the garden of her house in Beverly Hills, early thirties

Marlene Dietrich as Catherine II in the film *The Scarlet Empress*, 1934

Marlene Dietrich as a Spanish dancer in the film *The Devil Is a Woman*, 1935

Marlene Dietrich in the Selznick film *The Garden of Allah*, 1936

Marlene Dietrich under the direction of William Dieterle in the film
Kismet, 1944

Marlene Dietrich and Orson Welles as magicians in the film *Follow the Boys*, 1944

returned to the stage before his death, I would gladly have flown to London to applaud him, as would many of his admirers. You so rarely saw actors of his generation who towered above the greatest.

I've seen Laurence Olivier on a British stage, but afterwards he began to do commercials.

A great actor who does commercials shows that he needs money. I know, of course, that an actor too must feed his children, but I'm an old-fashioned woman and regret such a decision because it inevitably destroys the image. You can't be King Lear and be selling some kind of product a minute later. John Wayne once filmed a commercial in which, dressed as cowboy from head to foot, he praised the effectiveness of a headache remedy. I think it's the most ludicrous thing I've ever seen on TV: a "he-man of the great outdoors," on horseback with his hat and all the other trappings of a real cowboy on, praising the effect of a headache tablet. Too funny for words!

Burton never did anything of this kind. He was head and shoulders above all the other members of his guild. Moreover, he never found it necessary to earn money in this way.

He set his own rules and stuck to them.

I loved him; I revered him more than I could say or write.

SIR ALEXANDER FLEMING

Almost the greatest of my "heroes"!

When I was making a film in London, my dear friends Mr. and Mrs. Spoliansky offered to introduce me to Fleming. I didn't want to make his acquaintance at all, I just wanted to have a look at him, if only from a distance. But they assured me it would be easy for me to meet him. A relative of theirs, Dr. Hindle, who became famous through his researches on the yellow fever virus, could arrange a dinner at their place if I would prepare the menu. I trembled with anxiety, wired Erich Maria Remarque in New York and asked him which wine I should serve with the dinner, and he answered me promptly. Why all this excitement? Because Alexander Fleming had the reputation of being an excellent connoisseur of wine and London's greatest gourmet to boot.

What a challenge! I got permission to leave the studio early, and I was at my friends' at the right time for the banquet I had thought up and believed I could prepare. At eight on the dot Alexander Fleming was at the door, accompanied by Dr. Hindle.

I took his coat, a simple gesture that almost moved me to tears because the little chain on the collar (that was supposed to serve as hanger) was torn. I knew Fleming was a widower. My friends and I had decided in advance that penicillin was never to be mentioned during our table talk since I was convinced he no longer wanted to hear anything about it.

We sat down at the table. I observed Fleming, who ate as though there was nothing and nobody around him. I was quiet. But my table companion, Dr. Hindle, heartily helped himself, praised the dishes, the wine, the tastiness of each course. I thought he was doing that just to calm and reassure me. I uncorked one bottle of wine after the other (those Remarque had recommended), and finally the dinner was over. Dr. Hindle had been the "gourmet" of the evening. I felt uneasy because Fleming had not uttered a word. I wondered if it was due to a suspicion of admirers, male and female, something I would have understood only too well. Finally, we rose from the table and made our way to the living room.

Again silence, again embarrassment on my part. Would my friends keep their promise?

They did. We spoke about the great success of Mischa Spoliansky's "Tell Me Tonight" ("Be Mine Tonight"), about all the songs he had written. Fleming hummed some bars from "Tonight or Never" and, here and there, proudly sang a few words.

Suddenly Fleming placed a hand in the pocket of his jacket. An angel streaked through the room.

From his pocket he produced a tiny object, which he handed me across the table. "I've brought you something." I touched his hand and took the object. It was a little, round glass jar. "That's the only thing I thought I could give you," he said. "It's the first penicillin culture."

We were on the verge of tears (except Dr. Hindle, of course), and the evening ended with kisses and the vow never to lose sight of each other. Upon my return to America I regularly sent Fleming eggs and other groceries at that time lacking in England. He married again and didn't have to spend his last years in loneliness.

Again a lonely human being, again a genius. That's what they all have in common—loneliness.

Monuments have been erected to the honor of pop singers, but I have never seen one to the glory of Sir Alexander Fleming. Perhaps there is one somewhere. He deserves it.

ORSON WELLES

I admired Orson Welles before we met.

Fletcher Markle, one of his pupils, made many radio broadcasts with me. I'm indebted to him for the opportunity to dedicate myself to roles as different as Anna Karenina and Camille, and to occupy myself with the modern repertoire, things never offered to me in films.

Orson Welles was already inaccessible then, and we became close friends only when I substituted for Rita Hayworth in a magic act that had been organized in Hollywood for GIs.

At that time Rita was filming for Columbia Pictures and Harry Cohn, the tyrant, had forbidden her to appear before ordinary GIs. So, Orson Welles urgently needed a new, popular actress.

I rushed to his assistance, of course. This work, which required that I show up every evening at seven o'clock, was lots of fun. Orson Welles had rented a lot in Hollywood on which a huge tent had been erected. The actress Agnes Moorehead arranged the guest appearances, and we took care of the regular act. We financed the actual performance. Tickets for the first three rows were sold at a high price so that Orson Welles could pay the extras. He had learned a thousand and one magic tricks, but for him that was still not enough. He performed the tricks other magicians conventionally demonstrate in a reverse sequence, beginning at the end and finishing at the beginning. Evening after evening I would watch him, before and after my own entrance, but I never succeeded in seeing through the tricks. Later, however, when I organized performances for the army and needed different numbers, he let me in on some of them. In particular he taught me mind reading. Welles was extremely generous. Like all great talents his inner richness protected him from pettiness, and he let others share in his ideas, his experiences, and his dreams. He made it so easy to love him.

When I was discharged from the army, I was penniless. Welles offered me his house. I settled down in it and worked with him on the radio until the war in the Pacific came to an end. We spent most of our time in the studio in front of a microphone at which he was much better than I was.

We worked together until we were told one day that our services were no longer needed. We didn't kiss each other or fall into each other's arms. That wasn't Orson Welles's style, nor mine. We continued as though nothing had happened, cleared out of the studio, and then went home.

Later I worked together one more time with Orson Welles, in *Touch of Evil*. The budget Universal had granted him was pitiful. A handout to a beggar. So Welles had to drum up his friends, among others Mercedes McCambridge and me . . .

Today *Touch of Evil* is an international classic. But in 1958 Universal was very indifferent to this film; they treated Welles in a shabby, shocking way.

Many years later, when Orson Welles received an Oscar for the film, the hypocrisy of the Universal bosses was unendurable. I would have liked to have put a bomb under them—or better still to have dispatched them to hell.

Back to the shooting of *Touch of Evil*. Following von Sternberg's methods, Welles asked me to prepare my own costumes and to appear on the set on the scheduled date. We were to meet at eight o'clock in the evening in Santa Monica where he had discovered and restored a rundown bungalow. He had even installed a pianola. "In the film you're running a Mexican whorehouse," he explained to me, "so dress accordingly and be punctual." On the fixed date I appeared for the shooting in my costume. I had ransacked the dressing rooms of all the costume designers I knew and decked myself out in dresses, jackets, earrings, wigs, etc., so that Welles would have some choice. As usual I had arrived in Santa Monica earlier than expected and—hoping for a sign of approval—I went up to him. He just wandered off, but then he suddenly turned around and gave a shout since he had not recognized me at first sight. His reaction surpassed my boldest expectations. He took me in his arms and shouted for joy.

I worked with him for only one long evening. I don't think I've ever performed so well as on that day. To hell with modesty!

In *Touch of Evil* I play only a supporting role, but he was charmed by my outfit and that was enough for me. Nevertheless, I never worked with him again. Since both of us were always on the road in different countries, we didn't often see each other. Yet thanks to the telephone, we remained in touch, and each one knew where the other was hiding.

My "biographers" often list "Films of Marlene Dietrich" that are not at all mine. In some that were shot, I made a momentary guest appearance or simply performed, for friends, a scene so short that nobody can say whether I really am that person. In one of these productions, *Follow the Boys*, with Orson Welles, I repeated the magic act we had earlier performed for GIs in which he sawed me in two. In others, sometimes I can be seen for a little longer, as for example in Michael Todd's *Around the World in Eighty Days*, but in no way can these works be included in a list of the films of Marlene Dietrich. Another example is *Paris When It Sizzles*. I just happened to be in Paris when the film was being shot. The producer and the director thought it would be amusing to see me descend from a car and enter Christian Dior's well-known fashion salon. I obliged them, of course, but when I see this film on a list of my films I get angry. This is a fraud and, above all, very humiliating for the leading performers in this film.

Along with many other things Orson Welles also taught me something about love.

He sat on the windowsill in the room of my Paris hotel (the George V, or "the Fifth" as Americans call it) and admonished me: "Mark my words, you can't make the man you love happy *if you yourself are not happy.*"

Incredible, no? I had never understood that. I had always believed that one must just be nice and friendly and dutifully darn the socks of the chosen one in order to be happy. Naïve? I was and still am naïve in many respects. When you spend a well-sheltered childhood, youth, and life as a woman, you never learn what other women, who must manage without protective walls, learn. But my naïveté is a blessing. Perhaps it makes me boring, but those who were afraid of being bored have never remained with me for long.

Orson Welles shot *Ten Days' Wonder* in Alsace-Lorraine with Claude Chabrol. I flew there and spent several days with him "to recharge." His presence and his gaze resting on your face sufficed "to recharge the batteries."

During this visit in Ottrott-le-Haut, we would sit for hours next to each other whenever he had a free day or even a free afternoon—and the most beautiful phrases would effortlessly flow from his mouth.

When we saw each other, we never talked about our private lives or our problems. I never forced myself on him. I took pains to be a pleasant friend. At any rate, I have always been a loyal friend to him, and he would have certainly agreed if he had ever been asked.

Great writers and critics, primarily European, have described Orson Welles's tremendous talent. So I'll add nothing to that. In France, Welles is viewed as a savior who came down to earth to make films, but France is a civilized country. I think it would have been marvelous if Orson Welles had taught. I don't know whether that was of any interest to him, but I do know he was extremely gifted even in this area.

Europeans look down on the so-called American accent. This opinion is based on the films they see. Yet American can be a magnificent idiom—just as beautiful as British. To be sure, it must be correctly spoken, as, for example, Orson Welles did. He spoke what Germans perhaps would call "High American." Orson explained this to me one day when in my incorrigible naïveté I told him I found American dreadful, that all Americans seemed to have a hot potato in their mouth and worse. I had done my best to imitate this accent; however, I never succeeded, thank God.

Most Americans betray their origins by their accent. And many, for that matter, are very proud of it as, for example, the drawling Texas accent. But it is frequently the butt of jokes. When someone has an important position, it's infinitely better to speak a pure American, even if it requires some effort. There's nothing that one shouldn't learn.

All movie experts know that Orson Welles revolutionized photography by his use of the frog perspective, a perspective Eisenstein had used in his outdoor shots. Orson Welles employed it in indoor shots, and the set had to be cleared from one day to another because the camera was to be directed upwards. In the Hollywood of my time sets had no covering. Everywhere planks propped up the heavy spotlights, and the electricians almost suffocated in the hot air under the studio roof. Every time we took a break I'd bring these poor devils some refreshments. Their work at that height was dangerous. A fall was not out of the question.

Orson Welles had coverings attached over the set, and we didn't have to worry about the electricians anymore. He also rearranged the spotlights and photographed the area from below, handling the camera as nobody ever dared to do before him. You only need see *The Magnificent Ambersons* to be convinced of his brilliance.

Orson Welles was a master of the film art which he renewed from the bottom up. Unlike von Sternberg he didn't irritate his co-workers. He was always friendly and understanding. He didn't incur the hatred von Sternberg so easily aroused.

He was the first to use the hand camera—with a "swivel device" as the only aid—instead of the huge, bulky and unmovable cameras that had been the rule. Handheld cameras are much easier to use. Today they are customary, but that was not the case in the studios where I worked. The marvelous thing about Orson

Welles was his amazing camera angles. Teams of young camera-men crawled across the floor with their equipment, pursuing something new, something that had not yet been seen in a great film.

Orson Welles was satisfied at the end of every day in Santa Monica. An artist worthy of the name can never be more than satisfied. A true artist is never "fully satisfied." Unlike the lesser ones, he always has doubts about the end result. One day as I stood backstage with Sviatoslav Richter, the great pianist, he took me by the hand and said: "It wasn't perfect, it wasn't even good," while a storm of applause filled the concert hall, and he released my hand and went on stage to bow again before the enthusiastic audience. I saw Richter again later in Edinburgh and later in Paris. And each time we had a leisurely chat. He repeatedly voiced self-criticism and dissatisfaction, and I didn't know how to contradict him. He had seen me perform; he was enchanted by my roles, but he didn't listen when I expressed some special reservations about my own work.

One evening the audience sat around him on the stage. While he was playing a piece, a woman directly behind him collapsed and died on the spot. She was carried out of the hall. I was deeply impressed by this incident and thought to myself: "What an enviable fate, to die while Richter is playing! What a strong feeling for the music this woman must have had when she breathed out her life!" But Richter did not share this opinion; he was shaken.

Orson Welles had a thousand and one faults to find with his films! He would explain to the least detail how this or that should have been done, and as usual, he was right all along the line. Unsparingly and with a sharp look, he repeatedly called himself into question, fought like a lion for his ideas and, of course, for the right to cut the films as he pleased.

Once more I must come back to this phase of filmmaking: the cut. All directors who know their craft contractually stipulate that they themselves are to cut their film. On the other hand, those who know nothing about cutting leave this difficult task to others. The cutter then cuts the film according to the script. He keeps it lying in front of him and follows it word for word—here a close-up, there a long shot—a completely mechanical task.

The cutter has neither the knowledge, the talent, nor the requisite flair to edit a film as would a master or a creator. The result corresponds more or less to the mostly dry, initial shooting plan. This is foreseeable, as the scriptwriters are not around when the scenes are shot and, moreover, the scenes are often changed during the filming.

Orson Welles rejected the risk linked to such a method. He kept the helm firmly in hand like the captain of a ship making its way through churning seas, and he supervised his work from beginning to end. He took responsibility for everything upon himself: manuscript, takes, acting performance.

Although he was still young, at that time he worked without a script as many great directors had done earlier.

He will always remain the wunderkind of film.

I feel his absence, the absence of his friendship, of the strength he gave me, as a painful loss. I try in vain to reach him in my helpless dreams.

BILLY WILDER

When I had only two films a year to make, I would go by train and ship to Paris whenever I had the time and when my husband wasn't busy shooting films in other countries. In Paris we lived in hotels that nicely met our needs. One of them was the Trianon Palace. There I met my friend Billy Wilder again. Then, too, he was as witty, clever, and intelligent as today. I loved and admired him! Later, I worked for him in Hollywood—but that is already part of film history.

He has said the following about me: "At work [Marlene] Dietrich was like a soldier. Splendidly disciplined and helpful to everybody. If an electrician in his windy heights sneezed, she would run barefoot to her dressing room to fetch all possible kinds of medicine, which she always kept around, and on the next day she would inquire whether the electrician was feeling better.

When she was in Hollywood, she always lived with me. During the war she was right in the very front line with the ordinary GIs. In Paris I once asked her: 'Tell the truth, Marlene, have you slept with Eisenhower?' She replied: 'How could I? He was never that close to the front line!' "

But let's get serious again. Flexibility is an invaluable gift that all truly great men possess. They bubble over with imagination and overcome all obstacles standing in their path. They simply and skillfully replace one thing by another, their wealth of ideas is inexhaustible. Nothing, not even a technical problem can upset them. Since they command the secrets of their calling even in their sleep, even sceptical souls can do nothing but bow to their authority. At a time when self-censorship was widespread, I saw with my own eyes what talent can accomplish.

We were rehearsing a scene; camera movements, lighting, and everything else was ready when a representative of the producers appeared and told the director that the scene could not be filmed. It was impossible (and I'm not relating something from prehistoric times!) that a man and a woman should be seen together on a bed, not even if the coverlet were perfectly and properly smooth.

I remember such a scene in the film *A Foreign Affair*, which I made with Billy Wilder in 1947. The story takes place in bombed out Germany, in the room of a poor girl who can't afford a sofa, much less a living room. But it was expressly forbidden that two persons of different sex should sit on the same bed, even when it was properly covered.

Billy Wilder smiled over these remarks, nodded his head approvingly several times and promised to make all necessary changes. I remember that his assurances made me angry. I also loudly expressed my anger, whereupon Billy Wilder announced: "Lunch break! And all of you better be back here in an hour!"

Billy Wilder wasn't at all annoyed. He pondered the matter, gave his imagination free rein and solved the problem while we were eating lunch. The scenery was rearranged and he was ready to shoot, laughing and joking as always. Afterwards he told me that the studio's moral apostle had actually done him a service when he compelled him to restructure the scene.

"I've got more than one trick up my sleeve," he would often say. As a writer and director he never ran out of ideas, and he loved challenges that gave him an occasion to outdo himself. Billy Wilder was a master builder who knew his toolbox and used it in the best way possible to set up the framework on which he hung the garlands of his wit and wisdom.

I spent wonderful moments with him and Charles Laughton during the shooting of *Witness for the Prosecution*.

The producer had phoned me in New York and offered me the role. On the same evening I attended a stage performance of the play on Broadway. I was enthusiastic over the prospect of playing this role. Naturally, the part of "the other woman" made me uneasy, and I took all conceivable pains to transform myself into a person who would be as different as possible from the person I really was. Since the film would stand or fall on this transformation, I made the most extraordinary efforts to become an ugly, ordinary woman who succeeds in leading one of the greatest lawyers by the nose.

Despite my many attempts I was not satisfied. I applied makeup to my nose, made it broader with massages, and called on Orson Welles—the great nose specialist—for help. In the long shot in which I'm seen going along a railroad track, I have cushions around my hips and legs. I wrapped pieces of paper around my fingers to make them look as though they were deformed by arthritis. And to complete the picture I painted my nails with a dark lacquer. Billy Wilder made no comment, like all great directors he gave his performers a free hand in the matter of costumes.

Yet there was still a major obstacle to overcome: How was I to handle the cockney dialect that this woman, sprung from my imagination, spoke? The studio decided: we would be dubbed, but I was to recite the few lines prescribed in the script.

"Let's play a little trick on them," Charles Laughton said to me. "I'll teach you the dialect, and you will speak your lines in the

127

purest cockney. I'll vouch for its authenticity. Nobody in Hollywood understands anything about it anyway."

I went to his house with him. His wife, Elsa Lanchester, was
very nice to me. We sat around the swimming pool, and Charles
Laughton began his instruction. I made rapid progress since cockney with its nasal sounds and its constant grammatical inac-
curacies is quite similar to Berlinese.

But to perform in this dialect was something altogether
different. Charles Laughton would remain in the studio, although
his day's work was done and he could have gone home. He
watched over my performance and my diction like an eagle over
its prey. He assumed full responsibility for this sequence. Billy
Wilder, who was not an expert in this area, readily relied on
Laughton. But he also warned me: "You'll never get an Oscar for
this. People don't like to be made fools of."

This hint left me cold. To win an Oscar means nothing at all
to me. I have found that they've been handed to all and sundry
indiscriminately. The awarding of Oscars is one of the greatest
frauds of the century. The final decision is unanimously taken by
all the members of the so-called Academy. On this basis if a film
has engaged two thousand people, they will vote unanimously for
the film on which they have worked together. They would control
two thousand votes against, for example, a thousand votes cast for
a more modest film with fewer co-workers.

Whenever Charles Laughton gave any thought to the very
peculiar voting system of the Academy, he would uncontrollably
burst into his wonderful laughter. He was a splendid actor,
upright, pleasant without a trace of these shifting moods and
bouts of ill humor with which many good performers cause their
producers a lot of trouble. He was generous, indeed very generous
and very intelligent. "I like to play a blind man," he said. "All you
have to do is to close your eyes, hold on to the bannisters and go
downstairs. The simplest thing in the world. You can be sure that
there will always be a stairway for roles of this kind and the trick
never fails."

Billy Wilder was right. I was never once nominated for an

Oscar—and that was no accident, inasmuch as even a nomination would give you a high standing.

What must one do to receive an Oscar? Play biblical characters, priests, and victims of sad and tragic disabilities, such as blindness, deafness, muteness or different varieties thereof, or alcoholism, insanity, schizophrenia, and other mental disorders, which have already been seen in successful films. The more tragic the disability, the greater the chance of grabbing an Oscar.

The juries of the Academy are of the opinion that to portray a disabled person is a brilliant feat. That's not so. Since these figures are more dramatic, they have a greater impact on the audience. Yet in view of the fact that only experts award these Oscars, it is incomprehensible that they can confuse an actor with his or her role. The audience, of course, constantly muddles the two, which is understandable. But there are also some critics who simply can't keep apart roles and acting ability and that's inexcusable. If the Oscars were to be awarded in a serious way, as is done, for example, with the New York Theater Critics Award, perhaps now and then an actor or actress who has played a brilliant role in a not too successful film might be rewarded with an Oscar. A further reason for this masquerade—the people who award the Oscar are swayed by friendship, envy.

For some time now a new prize has been added to the Oscars: the "Deathbed Award." It isn't a distinction at all. Either the lucky winner has performed for the first time or has not been chosen for a prize by the Academy until the last moment; at any rate, he or she has never succeeded in winning the real Oscar.

The aim of the "Deathbed Award" is to salve the conscience of the jury and to save face before the public. The Academy tastelessly awards this prize to a star who is completely overwhelmed by his or her emotion, so that everybody may understand why this distinction is being so hastily bestowed. Lucky the actor or actress who is too ill to watch this ceremony on TV!

With my own eyes I saw James Stewart, on such an occasion, sob into the microphone: "Hold out, Coop, I'm coming." At that moment I knew that Gary Cooper was dying. What a circus! In the film world conscience is always stirred too late, which does not exclude—to the extent that those in power are aware of what is going on—a sincere reparation for past mistakes. I have also seen an actress (who would have been better off if on that day she had been hoarse) rush up to the stage and thank everybody from the washroom lady to the director for their help "without which I could never have done it, etc." I for once would like to hear an actor or actress say: "I did it all by myself. I don't feel I owe thanks to anyone. I earned my Oscar a thousand times over." And then, without embracing anyone and with an expressionless face, walk off the stage leaving the trophy behind for the audience to behold. That really would make me happy.

I confess that my patience with ham actors, hypocrites, and charlatans wears thin very quickly. But I can't say I have any desire to be patient with them.

When I arrived in Hollywood, a new tax law had come into force affecting those in the higher brackets. Hollywood stars had been able to accumulate those giant fortunes because, up to then, they had paid almost no taxes. They bought villas, had twelve automobiles, lived in incredible luxury. But we, the latest to arrive in Hollywood, had to pay taxes. And as if that weren't enough, tax officials dogged and pestered us and spoke of sums of money never received.

These harassments didn't bother me—I was still innocent about life. I still went along the path traced out for me by von Sternberg and what the studio considered the right path for me. I busied myself with my household chores, took care of my daughter, and waited to be summoned to a reading. But the telephone never rang for another reason.

From my very first days in Hollywood, von Sternberg made it clear to reporters that I was not to be bothered. I've never liked being talked about, and I have remained loyal to this principle.

Reporters in those days were much friendlier than they are today. They had respect for others. And yet what pests they were!

I was young and inexperienced, but I knew that the reporters had no power over the success or failure of a film. If it was good, the most disparaging articles couldn't harm it. And if the opposite was the case, the most beautiful phrases wouldn't lure the public to the box offices. Metro-Goldwyn-Mayer had come up with the bright idea of forbidding Garbo to grant even the briefest of interviews. I envied her because from the outset I was exposed to a lot of stupid questions that no one could answer—such as, for example, "Do you like America?" the moment I descended from the train that had brought me to California. "I don't know America," I answered, "I've only just arrived." And the headlines in the next day's newspapers read: "Miss Dietrich doesn't know America!"

Von Sternberg constantly comforted me, as I was the victim of a series of injustices, which, moreover, continue. Any injustice can bring tears to my eyes to this very day. Aside from that, the atmosphere in the studio was calm and relaxed. It became my second home. That's the way it was in all the dressing rooms I've occupied since. Those I had in Hollywood at that time consisted of two small rooms furnished with a refrigerator and a hot plate. The beautiful and comfortable living room was painted white. In the adjoining room, lit by electric bulbs, a charming hairdresser was at my disposal. I was dumbfounded by this luxury. The other dressing rooms I had known were dark and depressingly dirty. My dressing room in Hollywood would have made a charming country house. The administration brought me my meals when I had time to eat.

We always worked until late at night. There were no unions that would have prevented us from doing so. The studios paid the members of the camera team overtime and nothing stopped us from working late. The electricians and the stagehands liked this. Often we were at our best after dinner when everything was quiet. Close-ups of my face were taken almost up to the finish; my skin didn't wither, the makeup was not absorbed, and it withstood the long hours in the hot light of the reflector. I looked just as fresh, no, even fresher than I had in the morning. Oddly, the men seemed to be more susceptible to fatigue. Toward eleven o'clock in the evening they would complain of weariness and look exhausted. Actors are tender creatures. Anyone who has never looked behind movie sets may take them for tough guys, but they're more fragile than actresses. The acting profession, moreover, is not worthy of a man. This life of false appearance and of illusion is only for those with great talent, for those who, moreover, are determined to endow this calling, formerly compared to the antics of circus people, with a loftier reputation. For a man this is a demeaning occupation.

Jean Gabin understood that. He always said that you could earn money more easily in this profession, and that is why he practiced it. He never believed in his "talent."

STILL ANOTHER GENIUS: JEAN GABIN

I got to know Jean Gabin when he came to Hollywood. He had fled from occupied France. As always in such cases, I was asked to help him get used to his new life. My task was to speak French, translate, and to hunt around for some French coffee and French bread. I had done all this for René Clair as well. But Gabin was supposed to perform in English. And he wanted to accept the challenge. So I taught him English.

He would hide in the underbrush of the garden that surrounded his home in Brentwood to escape his teacher—me.

He was shooting an idiotic film, the title of which I've forgotten, but he spoke correct English—I personally saw to that! I would cook native French dishes for the many French friends he had brought with him. One of them was Jean Renoir. Renoir loved stuffed cabbage, had an enormous appetite, and left almost immediately after the meal. At that time I was known in Hollywood for not taking offense at such behavior: You could come dine with me and leave when you pleased. No fuss, no fawning; Renoir greatly appreciated that. He was a frequent guest, and I made stuffed cabbage for him each time.

For me it was a lot of fun to cook for all these uprooted

Frenchmen. I had been "bent over a kitchen stove" ever since we—my daughter, her governess, my dressing room assistant, and I—found ourselves in an unknown land. During the first months of our stay in the United States, we took our meals in drugstores. At the thought of having to eat surrounded by such unsuitable articles as sanitary napkins, deodorants, and other items, I had to force myself to overcome an involuntary aversion. I always ordered hamburgers, since you didn't have to wait too long for them, but, my God, how bad and tasteless they were! I had the impression that other customers around us were gulping down the same stuff; following which, they poured down countless cups of coffee. My daughter, on the other hand, was so fascinated by the lively doings in the drugstore she even forgot the dreadful taste of the hamburger served in a rubbery roll—at that time I knew nothing of the delicious Italian bread that could be bought in some specialty shops in Hollywood.

Since German cooking is not famous, I asked my mother-in-law to send me a book with Austrian recipes, and I tried my luck. I was immediately enthused over my new occupation. It was a kind of therapy for me and filled out the many idle hours in my California paradise. Sometimes I made only one film a year, and at that time shooting schedules were shorter than today. I learned everything, even baking, from this cookbook, and soon—also with the help of French cookbooks—my reputation as an excellent cook spread in Hollywood. I think I was prouder of this fame than of the "legendary image" so zealously created by the studio.

Cooking is an art. You must have a gift for it. And, as with everything else, practice makes perfect. But talent comes first! You don't have to "measure" spoon by spoon, cup by cup—the eye is a good measuring cup. Let yourself be guided by your eye, your mouth, your hand. Imagination is always a help when available. If you find no pleasure in cooking, it's better to leave it alone!

Apart from the Swedish, I love Russian cooking most of all. Both are very superior to French cooking, so highly praised in all the world. But after all, how often does the truth find its way into print? Other countries have their famous specialties, but that doesn't mean that all their recipes are good.

German cooking is, of course, the worst of all. It must not be confused with the Austrian, which has far more to offer than Wiener schnitzel, and most of whose other dishes are very good.

I don't know whether Russian cookbooks are available now. But I advise you, if you see one, buy it. And use dill, lots of dill! Dill is the most important of all herbs. Without it fish is simply boring—but other dishes also require dill.

In the twenties Berlin was overrun by Russians. It was the time when I learned to cook. I've preserved my knowledge through the long years in America and refreshed it later in Paris where I had Russian friends. The only thing I never managed to do to perfection were the piroshki, but otherwise I don't do too badly with most Russian dishes.

I cook well only over an open gas flame. The baking oven isn't exactly my dearest friend. Probably because I can't look deeply inside it, instead having to depend on calculation. And I abhor calculation as such. *Ya lioublu tebya,* I love you and good cooking!

According to statistics, millions of American women buy cookbooks, but there is still no applause. It's not their fault. They were not created to be cooks. They have too many different interests, too many pressing demands, too many great ambitions—in many areas, but not in cooking. They read cookbooks, but their hearts are not in it when they try out the recipes. The result: Nowhere else in the world is there more snacking, double and triple hamburgers (the German city of Hamburg has nothing to do with these aberrations), cheeseburgers, etc., as well as Coca-Cola to wash down the hamburgers. And sweets are almost a must according to the unwritten laws of these fast food places. Millions of doctors and dentists in America profit from all this folly while the taste buds of potential female cooks atrophy. I can only hope they have other pleasures. It goes without saying that I'm not speaking of the rural areas of the United States or of dark-skinned women—who are by nature highly imaginative.

Patience was my greatest forte, and perfection, my aim; I was very well equipped for my new tasks. And I continue to learn, even to this day. Actually, my culinary skills are limited to very simple dishes. It's more a "country" than an "urban" style of cooking.

My *pot-au-feu* is a delicious winter meal, as my satisfied French "customers" have assured me. I have a special fondness for stews. I'm not an expert of roast because you need a man for carving, and I don't like to make my guests work. One of these days I'll learn that. Anyway, I've always found cooking even greater fun ever since I prepared my first meals for my French friends in Hollywood.

Helpless, Gabin clung to me like an orphan to his foster mother, and I loved to mother him day and night.

I took care of his contracts and his house. He had fled to Spain from France, and from there, with a friend, he had come to the United States. We furnished his house according to his taste, with all the French objects we were able to dig up in the flea markets or in the Beverly Hills shops. We wanted to make him feel as comfortable as possible.

His adventure in Hollywood didn't please him at all. But he had to swallow the bitter pill, since work in films was the only way for him to earn a living. This uncomplicated man simply swallowed his annoyance. I helped him to overcome all obstacles; I loved him very much.

Naturally, the French I had learned in early childhood strengthened my love for France and also my relationship to Gabin. I took all the uprooted and desperate French into my house, spoke their language and was mother, cook, counselor and interpreter to them.

Besides Gabin and Renoir there was also René Clair—not exactly one of the friendliest of men—the charming Marcel Dalio, and many other French refugees who had wound up in America. The language problem stood in the way of most of them, except for the directors and writers who could resort to the help of interpreters. But actors must speak the language of the country. Apart from Gabin only a few could do that. Almost all of them changed professions.

* * *

The fate of these actors was tragic. In addition, the French didn't understand the American way of life. Everything here astonished, disturbed them. I spent my evenings explaining America to them. I acted very cleverly, lavish with advice, and as much as I could, I broadened their knowledge and set aright their judgments. This apparently pleased them because they would return on the next day and question me further. A real ritual, a discussion followed the dinner in which they made me privy to all their physical and spiritual sufferings—a group of likeable young people for whom I was, above all, a friend and advisor. I took on all the tasks they entrusted to me. I soothed their lover's grief and sometimes spoke with their sweethearts. They were utterly dumbfounded when call girls would come up to the steering wheel of their car and ask: "Should we have coffee now or afterwards?" But they managed to cope with the situation as the French have always done. "*On se démerde*," as they put it. I hugely enjoyed my role. I, the German anti-Nazi, was taking care of these men who had escaped Hitler's troops. There were no women among them. Where were they? So I took care of them. As soon as they knew some English, enough to carry on a simple conversation, they bought cars and began to do battle with the studios. I was very proud to be their "good fairy."

They have all remained very dear friends. Naturally, we don't see each other every day the way we used to, but we haven't lost sight of each other. Friendships like these are indestructible. We respect each other and are always ready to help an old friend if one needs us.

We fought together, shoulder to shoulder. Gabin made films, complied with his contract, and then decided to join the Free French forces. He wanted to fight. I understood this wish very well. I was his mother, his sister, his friend—and more still.

I accompanied him to a secret port near New York where he embarked on a destroyer bound for Morocco. We swore an eternal friendship to each other like little children, and I remained alone on the wharf, a poor, forsaken little girl. The destroyer was sunk somewhere between the United States and Morocco, and I heard nothing more about him. I enlisted in the U.S. Army, was ordered to New York, and was dispatched from one port to another . . . but I'll talk about this episode of my life later. Gabin survived the sinking of his ship and landed in Casablanca, as I learned later. My lonely "child" had lost all contact with me. I was terribly worried. Where was he? I knew he needed me, and I could sense this longing from the other side of the ocean.

Everybody knows Gabin's acting talent. No word need be spent on this subject. What is not known, on the contrary, is his sensitivity. The tough-guy façade and the macho stance were put-ons. He was the most sensitive man I knew, a little baby who liked best of all to curl up in his mother's lap and be loved, cradled, and pampered. That's the image I have of him.

We were all expatriates in America: We were living in a foreign country; we had to speak a foreign language and adjust ourselves to unknown customs and ideas. Although we were film stars, we felt lost. Gabin, quintessentially French, protected him-self against every foreign influence in his modest home. I had to cook French and speak French with him, and we socialized only with French actors and directors. This life pleased me enormously. I really felt at home only in the company of French friends. In my innermost being I felt a kind of frustration, yearning, a dream for a homeland that had originated in my youth and drew me to the French.

Gabin was *the* man, the superman, the "man for life." He was the ideal all women seek. Nothing in him was false. Everything was clear and transparent. He was good and outdid those who vainly tried to do the same for him. But he was stubborn, extremely possessive, and jealous. I liked all these qualities about him, and we never seriously quarreled.

Gabin knew how to adroitly resist the siren songs of the new French regime under Marshal Henri-Philippe Pétain. He wanted to join Charles de Gaulle. Sacha de Manzierly, who at that time directed the de Gaulle office in New York, helped him.

The heroic deeds Gabin performed during the war are well known; less well known is his enlistment in General Jacques Leclerc's armored tank division. For him it was as dangerous as a plunge into a snake pit.

Jean Gabin had a deep aversion to anything relating to electricity. It was useless to ask him to change a light bulb or to repair an electric iron. And he had the same phobia about fire. Now it often happened that tank crews perished in the flames of their burning vehicles. Gabin was certainly aware of this danger, but he didn't shirk it and came out of it without a scratch as always. He enlisted with the Second Tank Division and got as far as Berchtesgaden. He brought back no souvenirs from Hitler's hiding place. I regretted that, but he had none to show me upon his return.

In France nobody knew anything about Gabin's attitude—all people think actors concern themselves exclusively with films and never allow themselves to confront reality, especially if it's dangerous. Once again I was enraged; he wasn't. He remained calm and went looking for a place where he could live and store his belongings. That was in 1945, after May 8, the day that marked the end of the war in Europe.

The soldiers returned home, except for the Americans. I continued to work for the troops stationed in France, troops who were jittery because they might be sent to fight in the Pacific where the war continued. I, too, was afraid. I longed for the end of the war, and I was not alone. After the bloodbath we had experienced in Europe, we impatiently awaited peace. We didn't, above all, want to be sent to another front where everything would begin all over again.

Jean Gabin had left the army after the end of the war and resumed his work in a Paris that was no longer the one he had known. He didn't like his new life. Winter arrived. It began to snow. He grumbled about the slush everywhere in the streets. He still felt himself to be an actor, but in the presence of Parisian crowds, the rich, untroubled by the ubiquitous mire, he didn't dare complain.

Gabin could never stand the bourgeoisie. At that time he was very impulsive. He had patience only with his friends. He was very nice to us, but easily infuriated when he encountered an injustice. For then it seemed to him that he had fought in vain; all soldiers feel that way, but Jean Gabin didn't have enough sympathy or patience to accept this contradiction.

It was easy for us civilians to show understanding. But when you've nearly lost your life, things look different. Jean Gabin understood that. He had voluntarily thrown himself into combat; he didn't want to be "in a safe haven" like many other stars who, when summoned by their consulates, always found an excuse to avoid enlistment. He went there and stared reality in the face unflinchingly. A benign fate alone had preserved him from death and annihilation, physically and spiritually.

His strength helped him to look disaster straight in the eye and survive. One of the fascinating aspects of his personality is this rare mixture of courage and tenderness. On the night of May 8, 1945, we both wept when we heard de Gaulle's speech, and we understood what there remained for us to do. He in his way, I in mine.

I also remember the winter of 1944. We were close to the front at the time of Bastogne, but we didn't know our exact position. That was also unimportant. We obeyed orders. After Bastogne our destination was changed, and we were sent to the south. Again the rumor that the front would be strengthened by the "Free French Forces" and the Second Tank Division was making the rounds. One afternoon my performance was dropped; I asked an officer to get me a jeep, and I set out on a search for Gabin. Finally I found his division. Evening descended on a great number of tanks standing in a field. I began to walk and look for gray hair under the caps of the "fusilier marines." Most of the soldiers looked almost like young boys; they sat around, relaxed, and watched the oncoming twilight. Suddenly I saw him from the rear. I called out his name; he turned around and said: "Merde!" That was all. He jumped out of his tank and locked me in his arms. I had hardly regained my breath when the signal sounded for the tanks to line up in formation. He climbed into his vehicle again, and soon all you could see was a cloud of dust and all you could hear was the growling of motors.

I returned to America. We often would phone each other.

Things were not going smoothly with him, but I couldn't help him. When a war is over, soldiers are always sad. It's a very peculiar sadness. There is no egocentricity about it, and it affects those who have fought and killed, those who can no longer find peace— a feeling I know all too well. Each one must define the word *kill* for himself. Once you've received an order to kill, that's legal. Nevertheless, it means to kill, no matter how you look at it. You put an end to another person's life only because you have been ordered to do so. *And then you also get a medal for it.* But if you dispose of someone who has really harmed you or your family, you're thrown in jail. Such are the rules, and they're difficult to understand. Neither Gabin nor I ever accepted them.

We met again after the war. He had no work, neither did I. Regularly I would be told in reproachful tones, "You haven't been on the screen for a long time." Gabin and I responded to this dig in the same way: "Damn civilians!" we would intone in unison. All these people who had sat comfortably behind their big desks, whom the war had not so much as touched, were imposing their laws on us.

But what was to be done? We were at their mercy for better or worse. We were completely broke, of course. How could we have earned money during the war? Now, as we could have predicted, we were penniless. We had only our medals. And you can't eat medals.

My decorations hang on the wall, but they're here only for the children. Normally, fathers receive medals, not mothers. The French medals are the only ones that really mean something to me. No, I shouldn't say "the only ones" because the Medal of Freedom that America awarded me is very precious to me. The French medals "Knight of the Legion of Honor," "Officer of the Legion of Honor," filled me with great joy. France, the beloved country, honored me, a simple American soldier, a simple woman who had loved France since childhood.

In 1946, I returned to France to make a film, *Martin Roumagnac*, with Gabin. It wasn't a very good film, although we had all been enchanted with the script. It dealt with the immediate postwar period: Electricity, fuel and groceries were rationed. Nothing new to us. Since I played the role of a provincial beauty, I had a permanent wave and wore ridiculous, supposedly fashionable, clothes.

Gabin taught me to contract my words, since I was not allowed to speak cultivated French. He sat near the camera and corrected me with infinite patience. Since Georges Lacombe, the director, expressed himself only in incomprehensible sounds, Gabin took over the job of telling me what I had to do. He took on an enormous responsibility.

It should have been an easy task to be a much-desired woman, "to live on air and love," and to be envied by all other women because I had drawn the first prize—Jean Gabin. But it wasn't so at all. Nobody believed in my sincerity, no doubt because of my own fault or the fault of the "image" people had of me.

Jacques Prévert (he had written "Dead Leaves," a song I was supposed to sing in another film, and was furious when I declined to play the role) wrote a very bad, disparaging review of the film.

Martin Roumagnac was a disaster. The names Jean Gabin and Marlene Dietrich were not enough to lure moviegoers. I was crushed as always when I felt I had failed to come up to expectations. Gabin remained calm: "Let's wait awhile," he said. But I couldn't do that. My financial problems forced me to return to Hollywood to make a film under Mitchell Leisen's direction, Golden Earrings. The money I was paid was half of what it had been before the war. That, too, was a bad film, but when you need money, you're ready to do anything.

Nobody knowingly decides to make a bad film. At the beginning everything was going along fine. Even the dressing room attendants who fixed my clothes and whose fingers could hardly hold the needle because of the cold, believed that Martin Roumagnac would be a good film.

In retrospect, I find that Gabin and I had a rather easy life in the United States. It was a miracle, but I don't know how it was wrought. The fact is that things seemed very easy. The house I had found for him with its garden and fence looked like a small rectory. Gabin felt well there, loved every tree and every shrub, strolled around and regaled me with stories about France. However, he never said that France was better than America.

Besides, he loved America. That's amazing for a Frenchman. Gabin judged simply, intelligently, and directly as only few foreigners do. He accepted America and Hollywood in his own way. And he decided to love them without analyzing them, without putting them under a microscope. This in no way means that he found everything commendable. He liked to joke with me about some of his reservations.

I was there to protect him. He did not notice. He considered me his peer. He had never experienced anything of this kind. I loved him as my child—indeed, for a certain period of time he took the place of my daughter who was no longer a child. He was gentle, tender, and had all the traits a woman looks for in a man.

An ideal being, the kind that appears in our dreams.

I lost him as you lose all your ideals, but only very much later. By the time he was again living in France, I had become to him merely a companion whom you lovingly take in your arms for the last time. My love for him has remained strong, unfading. He never asked me to prove it. Gabin was that way.

ON FRIENDSHIP

Very few understand the meaning of this word. Hemingway understood it; Fleming understood it, and Robert Oppenheimer, to cite a few names.

Friendship is related to maternal love, sibling love, eternal love, the love that is pure, dreamed of and yearned for. It is not love under the pretext of love, but, rather, a pure feeling, never demanding and therefore eternal.

Friendship has united more people than love. It is precious and it is sacred. It unites soldiers in combat, strengthens resistance; it encompasses us all even when our intentions are obscure.

For me, friendship is the most precious possession.

Anyone who renounces a friendship sees himself or herself excluded, forgotten, forever pushed out of the circle of friends.

That's how simple it is. Friends who deceive each other are condemned to death, if I may say so, and they will always wonder why they no longer find any acceptance. I despise them. They are the lowest of the low. The moment you experience the blessing of a friendship you have the sacred duty to obey its laws. Regardless of the consequences that may ensue. The rules of friendship must always be observed in silence or in words.

This is not an easy task, and at times it requires superhuman effort. But friendship is the most important human relationship, of far greater importance than love. Love is inconstant. Love, save for maternal love, is unfaithful and always finds good reasons for it. Friendship is genuine, or it's simply not present, and it's easy to make the distinction.

As soon as friendship has you in its grip, it carries you along at full sail. You can't go wrong about the person. A promise among friends, sealed with a handshake, is an inextinguishable vow.

There is a group of people who never experience what friendship can be—the escapists. They steer clear of difficulties, theirs and those of others; they don't want to relate. Woody Allen has defined them: "They close their eyes before all problems—they go shopping instead." I agree 100 percent with that definition. I'm surrounded by them, and I wage a futile battle to restore them to reality. They try not only to run away but also to shift the blame onto others. A pitiful lot.

All efforts are in vain. They escape.

WRITERS

HEMINGWAY, OF COURSE!

Our friendship naturally gave rise to much gossip and gabble. It's about time the truth was told. I was aboard a ship sailing from Europe to America. When? I've forgotten. At any rate, I'm sure it was after the Spanish Civil War. Ann Warner, the wife of the all-powerful Jack Warner, gave a dinner on board to which I was invited. When I came, I immediately noticed that twelve guests were seated around the table.

"Please excuse me," I said, "but I can't sit here, we'll be thirteen, and I'm superstitious." (I was standing at that moment.) Nobody made an attempt to get up, so I remained standing. Suddenly a giant leaned over me. "Sit down," he said. "I'll be the fourteenth." I looked up at the giant, saw Hemingway, and asked, "Who are you?" This shows how ignorant I was.

Order was restored. We were now fourteen around the table aboard this ship bound for New York. The dinner—just as at Maxim's—began, and my gigantic table companion took me by the arm each time he wanted to make a point. At the close, he escorted me back to my cabin.

I loved him from that very first evening.

I have never stopped loving him.

It was a Platonic love.

I say this because the love that Ernest Hemingway and I felt for each other—pure, absolute—was a most extraordinary love in the world in which we lived. Beyond all doubt, this was a boundless love beyond death—even though I know very well that it doesn't exist. At any rate our "amorous feelings" lasted many years when no hope, no longing, no wish for fulfillment remained to either of us—a period during which Hemingway felt only a deep despair, just as I did when I thought of him. We never lived together, but perhaps that might have solved certain problems. I respected Mary, his wife, the only one of his wives whom I knew. Like her, I was jealous of his former wives. I was only his friend and remained that in the years that followed. I have preserved all his letters, and I'm not willing to entrust them to a museum or to a collector. Not because I think I can take them with me in the Beyond, but because I don't want a stranger to lay his hands on them. They belong to me. He wrote them for me, and nobody will earn a penny from them. I shall do everything possible to prevent this.

He was my "Rock of Gibraltar"—a nickname he loved. The years without him have gone, one more painful than the other. "Time heals all wounds," it is said. A very optimistic but, unfortunately, false maxim, which I very much deplore. The void Hemingway has left in us and in the world will never close again. He was a writer but also a man who—without weighing the consequences of his action—decided to leave us. But after all, that was his decision.

We regularly wrote to each other when he was in Cuba. He would answer me "by return mail," as he put it. We talked on the phone for hours, during which time he gave me good advice, and never once told me to hang up and stop bothering him. He sent me his manuscripts, and once he said the following about me: "She loves literature and is an intelligent and conscientious critic. When I have written something that I find good, she reads it and tells me that it pleases her, then I am perfectly happy. Since she is well versed in things I write about—people, countries, life and death, questions of honor and conduct—I pay more attention to her judgment than to that of the professors. Since I believe that she understands more about love than anybody else." An extremely generous judgment, as was typical of him.

I shall never understand why he loved me "so intensely" as he said. The fact is our love even survived the war. Occasionally, I would meet him during this period—he always beamed with pride, had a thousand plans in his head, whereas I would be pale and sick, but I would pull myself together to cut a good figure. He had written a poem about the war that he made me read aloud. "Take this whore death as your lawful wife . . ." "Read further," he said, when I faltered. He actually called me "kraut," a word used by GI's to designate Germans. To me it seemed ridiculous to call him "Papa" as did many of his friends. I believe I called him "You." "Tell me, You," I would interpose, since this was the only expression I could find—"tell, tell me," like the little lost girl that I was in his and my own eyes.

He was an anchor, a sage, the decisionmaker, the best adviser, the pope of my personal church. How did I survive his death? To this question I have no answer. Whoever has lost a father or a brother, will understand me. You deny the fact quite simply, until the dreadful pain disappears from the heart. Then you keep on living as though you might meet the one who no longer exists any time of the day or night. You continue along your way despite your awareness of the fact that he will never come back. You get used to the sorrow.

Here I would like to cite some excerpts from his letters, some of Hemingway's sentences so that one can better understand the intensity of the feelings that united me with this great man, and also his sense of humor which so delighted me:

"Prudence is fatal for the imprudent—you and me."

"This letter is sadder than Switzerland and Liechtenstein put together."

"It [life] was easier in the Hürtgen Forest."

"Sometimes I forget you, the way I forget my heartbeats."

Grief does not diminish, it just becomes a habit.

For me habit is a good thing. Most people consider it something bad. But in regard to grief I find it really desirable. Hemingway also was of this opinion. He explained it to me at a point in
time when, compared to his, my problems were trifling. He taught
me everything about life. I knew only maternal love (which made
him laugh—his characteristic bittersweet laugh) and normal,
everyday love. He didn't teach me anything new, but his approval
confirmed my most secret thoughts, converted them into powerful truths, and gave them the appearance of something new.

He taught me writing and warned me against using too many
adjectives. At that time I was writing articles for *The Ladies Home
Journal,* and he would call me twice a day and ask: "Have you
defrosted your ice box?" And he knew all the little weaknesses of
aspiring writers, also the classic pretext "Maybe, it would be better
if I were doing something else."

I miss him terribly. If there were a life after death, he would
speak with me in my long sleepless nights, but there is no life after
death. He has left us forever; no grief can bring him back again,
and my yearning will remain forever unfulfilled. With time you
learn "to carry on," to make the best of things; that is, you accept
what before you couldn't endure—a kind of "diminished" life
Hemingway always detested (as I do) throughout the time he was
among us and could talk about it.

Anger is not a good antidote against grief. The anger you feel
when you have been abandoned is like a demand for alimony
(both are futile). Nevertheless, I was angry—against whom, I
don't know. But how could I prevent it? So beautiful a life extin-
guished forever for so stupid a reason.

On the day after his death I was in a rage, which was my way
of fighting grief. Hemingway had sworn that he would never leave
me—but what was I compared to all those whom he had left
behind, his children, his wife, to those who needed him? I was the
fifth wheel on the wagon. He didn't think of that. Like all of us, he
lived with the conviction that his days were not numbered. Nevertheless, he put an end to his life long before his appointed time.
That's how he wanted it. I respect his decision. But I still weep.

I never go to funerals. So I didn't attend Hemingway's burial.

"She wasn't there," the newspapers wrote. I haven't participated in any funeral ceremony since my mother's burial. That day was more than enough for me. I don't feel the slightest desire to experience anything of this kind again. I love the living and do what I can to mitigate their distress and suffering. But I don't feel affected by their burial. I am powerless against the frightful destructive power that transforms us into dust again, that rises triumphant and walks off with the mortal remains of those we have loved.

When Hemingway took his life, he had no wish to hurt anyone of us. He loved Mary. He loved his sons. And he loved me intensely, very intensely. He loved me with all his enormous strength, and I was never able to do the same for him. Can such a love ever be reciprocated? I tried to—within the extent of my capacities. He knew it. Since we were physically separated, the telephone and letters were our only means of contact. Every day he would tell me about his blood pressure, as though that were of decisive importance. But he believed it was, and I would conscientiously write down the numbers he passed on to me. One morning he told me that he was staying "in the most fantastic place in the world, the Mayo Clinic." He trusted the diagnosis of his doctors. I didn't. But who was I to contradict him?

Once you've had any experience with American doctors, you begin to entertain some doubts. The surgeons are the best in the world. But if they can't cut you up and look inside, they are completely helpless. In Europe, doctors are more qualified. They have an exceptional knowledge. Naturally, no miracle is to be expected from them either, but you die in a shorter time and with greater dignity than in the United States. In America, they are not finicky with the dying. There is no place for death (except in the earth). And that is probably also the reason why Americans attach such importance to burial services. Unlike Europeans, they do not show respect for the dying. For them you're only a "corpse under the knife."

Yes, Hemingway knew what he was doing. And I have never reproached him for his decisions, although my attitude toward life is, of course, quite different, and I don't let myself be as driven as he was. I'm an average woman, and incapable of committing so radical a deed. I would have fought like a lioness for him if I had had an inkling of his intention. But he was much stronger than any of us, so he would have promptly knocked me out on the floor.

I would now like to tell about how I met Mary Welsh, Hemingway's last wife. I had been sent to Paris to "decompress myself" as they used to say at that time during the war, and I was living in Chatou, a Parisian suburb. When I learned that Hemingway was in Paris, I drove there in a jeep to see him. He told me I could take a shower and then "report" to him. He also told me that he had met a "pocket Venus" whom he wanted to seduce at all costs. He confessed that she had rejected his first advances, that she considered him a "pitiful lover," and that only I could help him out of this fix by having a talk with the girl.

It is impossible to explain why a man desires a particular woman. Mary Welsh was stiff, formal, and not very desirable. Like most women of her sort, she probably would have gone on living sadly and joylessly if she hadn't found a Hemingway along the way, who, for a long time, had had no romantic affairs or sexual adventures. I know that on this day I didn't render him any special good service. But I followed his instructions. Mary Welsh didn't love Hemingway, of this I am sure. Yet this modest, inconspicuous woman war correspondent had nothing to lose. Fighting against my intuition, I accomplished my mission. I met Mary Welsh and talked with her. "But I don't want him," this charming little woman confessed to me. Stubbornly, I pressed Hemingway's suit, but she turned a deaf ear. Finally, I listed all the advantages of a relationship with him, and advised her to compare her present life with what she could expect at his side—since I was there to make her a "promise of marriage." My efforts bore fruit. At lunchtime her resistance began to slacken.

Lunch at the Ritz is always a decisive moment. At this time of the day, women are ready to make concessions and to think over their plans. Mary Welsh, the "pocket Venus," was no exception. Finally, she told me that she would "consider the proposal."

I had to face Hemingway and make my report, and I was trembling all over when evening arrived. But Mary Welsh showed up wearing a radiant smile and accepted his offer, in the presence of a single witness. Namely, me.

I have never seen anybody as happy as Hemingway. He could be happier than all of us. And, what is more important, he could also show it. His huge body seemed to emit sparks whose light fell on us and was reflected in our eyes. Shortly thereafter, I returned to the front and didn't see him or Mary again during the whole war.

His capacity to be happy was in astonishing contrast to his public stance of desperation and to his tragic decision. As a realist, I can't understand this contradiction. Like myself, he had a very strong sense of responsibility, and that doesn't accord with his suicide. We would talk a lot about responsibility and very often we were in agreement. Perhaps he sensed that his grown children no longer needed him; perhaps he was simply "fed up." Who knows . . . ? When the body no longer reacts as it once did, when the brain no longer functions as smoothly as usual, then it's time to muster your courage (if you can) and blow out the candle yourself. Till now, no one has been able to explain the reasons for Hemingway's suicide.

I think that it was a rash act, rather than a conscious decision. Did Hemingway perhaps act in a somnambulant state? I cling to this hypothesis. At any rate, I'm convinced that his act was not dictated by his father's example, that it had nothing to do with the weight of his remembrances. When he pressed the trigger, perhaps something distant in his memory flashed and suddenly forced itself on him . . . but I'm rationalizing too much. I know that he was very unhappy. Everything that his "biographers," or those who pass themselves off as such, have written about him is, to me, nothing but a pile of "shit," to use his own word. Up until now I haven't yet read his wife's book, which, I'm sure, corrects all this silly nonsense, but I doubt she has succeeded in capturing and rendering Hemingway's extraordinarily complex personality. The relations I've had with different great men may be difficult to understand, and I don't intend to explain them. Tough luck if you haven't understood. If you're only interested in physical love, then you can immediately close the book, since I won't be expressing any opinions on such matters. And for a very simple reason: I hardly know myself in this area. Throughout my whole life, physical love was a part of love itself, and only of love—for which reason I've never known "fleeting happiness." My love for Hemingway was not a flash in the pan. We simply weren't together long enough in the same city, and nothing ever happened. Either he was together with a pretty girl, or I was busy elsewhere when he was free, and when I was free, he wasn't.

I detest unclear situations, and I've always remained true to my principle of respecting "the other woman." Thus, I've met many wonderful men like ships that pass in the night. But I believe that their love would have been more constant had I dropped anchor in their port.

ERICH MARIA REMARQUE

Erich Maria Remarque, who became famous for *All Quiet on the Western Front, The Road Back, Three Comrades*, etc., was a sensitive man with a delicate soul and was endowed with a subtle talent about which he always had doubts.

We were bound by a very special feeling. First, we are both Germans—or were, rather—because we spoke the same language and loved it. One's mother tongue is very important, much more important than some famous writers have said or written. German was our principal bond.

I met Erich Maria Remarque on the Lido in Venice. I had come to visit Josef von Sternberg. Remarque came to our table and introduced himself. I almost fainted, something that still happens today when I meet famous people. I probably will never get used to seeing them "incarnate" before me.

Next morning on the beach, I met him again. I had a book by Rainer Maria Rilke under my arm and was looking for a sunny spot where I could sit down and read. Remarque came over to me. He saw the book's title and said rather sarcastically, "I see you read good authors."

Just as ironically, I retorted, "Shall I recite a couple of poems to you?"

His perpetually sceptical eyes were riveted on me. He didn't believe it possible. A movie actress who reads? He was dumbfounded when I recited "The Panther," "Leda," "Autumn Day," "Serious Hour," "Childhood." "Let's go somewhere else, and let's have a talk," he said. I followed him. I followed him as far as Paris, and I listened to him from then on. All that happened before the war.

In Paris there was a nightclub that he loved and that had the best wines, which he, as an expert, knew how to appraise. This also explains why I never learned anything in this area. I was always in the company of men well versed in the matter of wines who would order a bottle without consulting me, leaving me in a state of ignorance. Remarque was an outstanding authority on wines from all over the world. He enjoyed having his connoisseurship tested. Based on the taste alone, without having seen the bottle, he could give the name and the year of a *grand cru*.

Remarque had great difficulty with writing. He worked hard and would spend hours trying to construct a sentence. Throughout his life, he was stamped by the success of his first book, *All Quiet on the Western Front*, and convinced that he could not repeat, much less surpass that miracle.

His melancholy and sensitivity bordered on the pathological. I was deeply moved by this trait of his personality. Our special relationship all too often, unfortunately, gave me an opportunity to witness his despair.

When war broke out in the summer of 1939 I, my husband, my daughter, and he were together in Antibes.

I've forgotten to mention Remarque's passion for sports cars. He had a Lancia he was crazy about. Whenever we passed the car, he gave the body a light, gentle pat. He took my daughter to Paris, driving against the stream of refugees fleeing the war. My husband drove back to Paris in a Packard, and took as many people as possible to the capital, mostly Americans who had landed in southern France.

I had left our small group behind in the joyful and peaceful setting of Antibes to make a film in California. My husband, Maria, and Remarque first got back to Paris, and then boarded the *Queen Mary*, the last ship to sail from a French port.

During the crossing, there was no radio contact. Trembling with anxiety, I would be singing "See What the Boys in the Back Room Will Have." I received the phone call in the studio in which I was working. They were in New York!

I had been told that the *Queen Mary*, a British ship, had steered for a Canadian port. So I dispatched lawyers and a private plane to meet them on their arrival and bring them to America before the outbreak of hostilities. But, to everyone's surprise, the *Queen Mary* arrived at a pier in New York.

Remarque, whose books the Nazis had burned in a gigantic bonfire, had managed to purchase a Panamanian passport. My husband still had his German passport.

When America entered the war, my husband became an "enemy alien," and Remarque, who had settled in California, was "interned." For the duration of hostilities, he couldn't leave his hotel between six in the evening and six in the morning.

In New York the regulations were less drastic. My husband could move freely outside the hotel, but he had a "pink card" and couldn't work. It was all very sad, and I felt for them with all my heart. Yet the fact that they were safely in America moved me in a way beyond my ability to express it in words. Remarque became one of the first refugees who benefited from my protection. My husband had brought our child to Hollywood and helped us to settle down, but the California laws forced him to return to New York. He didn't want to be "interned" and hoped, despite everything, to be able to earn a living in New York.

I found a house for Remarque, although he liked living in the hotel, above all, because he could meet people during the time he was prohibited from being outdoors.

His paradoxical situation drove him to despair. Hitler had burned his books, and America had placed him under house arrest. We Germans are very sensitive to injustice. We can't come to terms with it. Over and over again, we brood on it, rebel against it, rack our brains over it, to no avail. But we don't accept it. We must drink the cup to the dregs—the bitter cup full of tears. We can't do otherwise.

Remarque was a wise, clearheaded man. But his wisdom could not spare him from suffering. As soon as he learned that the travel restrictions applying to interned aliens had been lifted, he settled for a brief period in New York and then left for Switzerland to live in exile. He left the United States regretfully, deeply affected by the terrible years that had plunged the entire world into chaos. He believed that he had shirked his responsibility, that he had not sufficiently struggled against Nazism, and often he would say, "Talk is easy, action is much more difficult."

We had a talk with each other before his death. And my daughter, whom he called "The Cat," also chatted once again with him. A friend told me that he had a fear of death. I can understand that only too well. To fear death, you must have lots of imagination, and imagination was his forte.

As a young girl, I was enthusiastic about Knut Hamsun. Today, I still know whole passages by heart from *Victoria, Hunger,* and *Pan* and many of his other books. If I rightly recall, it was the first time I was disloyal to Goethe. I was bitterly disappointed when Hamsun sided with the Nazis. But at that time I was already grown up and used to disappointments. I can't say that I liked to read novels. The great exception is *Job* by Joseph Roth. I would take this book with me everywhere, but I've lost it as I've lost things that mean something to me. Perhaps when I emigrated, perhaps later, during my journeys. Today, that book is not to be found. I've asked all the book dealers I know to inform me if they ever come upon it somewhere. Material possessions have absolutely no value when you emigrate. You learn to content yourself with essentials. That doesn't especially please me, but I can make a relatively easy adjustment.

Once, by chance, I was reading the novel *The Telegram,* by Konstantin Paustovsky, in a bilingual edition—on one side was the Russian text, and on the other, the English translation. This novel made so great an impression on me that I could no more forget it than I could the name of the author, of whom I had never heard before. Since I couldn't get any other novels of this great writer, I bided my time. When I went to Russia, immediately upon my arrival I asked about Paustovsky. Hundreds of journalists assisted me. They didn't ask me the stupid questions I was used to. I talked with them for over an hour, and was able to gather lots of information about Paustovsky.

I met him in Leningrad where we performed before writers, artists, and actors. Sometimes we gave four performances a day. Each performance took place in the theater or the hall of the sponsor group. On that afternoon, my beautiful interpreter Nora came to Burt Bacharach and me backstage to announce that Paustovsky was in the audience. He had been hospitalized shortly before, following a heart attack, as I had learned upon my arrival at the airport.

I said, "That's impossible." But Nora assured me it was so, that he and his wife were there.

I sang, and, oddly enough, Burt Bacharach afterward said I had been splendid. That's amazing, for when you overexert yourself, the effect is the very opposite most of the time.

After the performance, I was asked to remain on stage. All Russian theaters have stairs leading up to the stage, and soon I saw a man making his way toward me. It was Paustovsky. I was so overcome I was unable to utter a single word. I could express my admiration for him only by sinking to my knees before him. Just imagine that!

His wife calmed me down and explained, "That was good for him," for I—a nurse concerned about the health of one of her favorite authors—wanted him to return immediately to the hospital. When I consider the great pains that he had taken to see me!

Paustovsky died shortly after this evening, but I still have his books, his short stories, and this memory. He writes in a romantic, but not mannered style. His portrayals recall something of Hamsun. Yet, above all, he is the best Russian writer I know. I regret that I didn't meet him earlier. I would also have liked very much to have seen Rainer Maria Rilke, but the opportunity never arose. Perhaps at that time he might not have noticed a then unknown admirer.

Later, as a "star," it was easier to come in contact with particular people. My name was an "Open, Sesame." I have played that game only on behalf of others, never for myself. Thank heavens my fame was not utterly worthless.

Perhaps it may be surprising that I don't have more favorite authors than Goethe, Rilke, Hamsun, Hemingway, Remarque, and Paustovsky. I greatly admired Heinrich Böll, but he doesn't carry me away like the others. He writes a sober, splendid German. I love him very much because he has restored to the German language its original beauty, which it had lost through the silly Anglo-American expressions so beloved by Germans.

Naturally, I've read John Steinbeck, William Faulkner, and Erskine Caldwell with great pleasure. English writers also fascinate me—I'm not speaking here of the classics I had read in my early youth. But no other books have had the same impact on me as those of my "heroes," so beautiful and rewarding. Books and poems that you can always read over and over again.

Strange to say, I find no great pleasure in modern poetry, though I am interested in "modern" poets. Perhaps I'm too old to understand the allusions and hidden meanings of new works? After Rilke, there is no lyric poetry that rings in my ear, that touches my soul, and remains in my memory. Except, perhaps, for W. H. Auden, the poet whom I love the most, after Rilke.

Toward the end of our lives, we tend to remember the pleasures of youth; only the joys one has felt by reading great writers can match them. I'm not speaking here of Dickens, or Baudelaire, or of Rimbaud, to mention only a few of those who have given me joy. I'm speaking of Hemingway, Faulkner, Caldwell, Böll, Auden. And I'm speaking of *all* their books, not only some pieces here and there. I'm not a specialist in what is called "light reading," but I know John MacDonald, Rex Stout, Ed McBain, and other authors who make us forget our daily cares. We all need that. And I often admire their formulations, their narrative talent. They are uncontested masters in their field. How many sleepless nights I've spent with them! I'm grateful to them for this.

My nights are long, with or without sleeping pills. I like Dick Francis best of all. Since I love horses and horse races, he has become a good friend, although I've never met him. I browse in bookstores, looking for his newest books, and when I find one of them, I go peacefully to bed with Dick Francis.

Spy novels, on the other hand, don't interest me. The same goes for science fiction. But, of course, I also read best sellers— Erica Jong, for example, although I don't like descriptions of sexual intercourse. In my opinion, they are bad. You can endlessly express your opinion regarding what and how and why this person did this or that with this or that other person. But that has nothing to do with the real story. The great writers never found it necessary to describe sex scenes. They were refined enough to let us share in their nights of love without talking of "f——" or dwelling on the coming and going of the phallus. I'm strictly against pornographic literature, but it seems to sell. Today, perhaps. But weren't books also sold in earlier times? Those books will certainly not last. Their authors will be forgotten in ten years, and they will have deserved their fate. They make a fortune in a jiffy, and stash it away. Not even in their dreams do they think of working for posterity. Mediocre people. Mediocre writers. After one, or at best, two books, it's all over with them. The fount of inspiration is sealed off—if there ever was one.

NOEL COWARD—A "LOVING FRIENDSHIP"

We attended to each other like two lovers. Each of us was sensitive to the slightest change of mood in the other, the slightest wish. No quarrels, perfect harmony. No attempt to press the other into the mold of one's own ideas. We walked "on tiptoe," so to speak.

I saw the film *The Scoundrel* in Hollywood. I act with an incredible swiftness once my feelings are involved. I phoned Noel Coward at his country home in England and gave my name. He immediately hung up. The telephone operator dialed the number again, and I quickly said a few words about his film to him. I quoted a part of the dialogue. Thereupon, he explained the situation. He was afraid of being victimized by a certain kind of joker and had believed that someone, using my name, wanted to play a dirty trick on him. We talked for a long time and were friends from then on. Our relationship repeatedly astonished me because my interests were completely different from his. I was neither brilliant nor especially witty, so I didn't like invitations to soirées. I didn't belong to his milieu. I had other habits, shunned the limelight, and didn't view the world as he did. Despite all that, we were inseparable.

He brought me over to London to sing in the Café de Paris— something I would have never dreamed possible. On the first night, he introduced me with a poem he had written for the occasion. Then, enveloped in a radiant aura of fame, I descended the famous staircase and walked right up to his outstretched hand, after which he handed the microphone over to me. After that, great English stage actors followed his example and wrote introductions to my performances. Every night one of them would introduce me in the nightclub where I was scheduled to sing. For a long time I could hardly understand just what was going on. When Alec Guinness phoned me at the Dorchester Hotel to ask for my approval of the text he was to read that same night, I thought it was a prank of some kind. But Guinness himself came to the hotel, showed me his text and said, "Can you dig up a revolver for me somewhere?" He needed one for a parody on Westerns he was to perform before my concert.

No more seats were available in the auditorium, because of me and my magnificent costume, of course (I didn't sing very well at that time), but also because of all the actors present. The whole performance so pleased me that I accepted the offer to give another one next year. This time, instead of actors, there were actresses attired in tuxedos and evening gowns, and women politicians like Mrs. Bessie Braddock, who appeared before the spectators in a simple costume with a hammer and sickle on the lapels. She scored a big hit in this outfit.

We became friends. Later during a tour through England, she

made it a habit to take me along with her on her visits to hospitals and old-age homes, and then drop me off at the theater.

Noel Coward observed these undertakings with a pleased, triumphant look. Sometime after the Braddock episode when I was getting ready for a television show in London, I suddenly learned on the night before the recording that the words of a famous song I wanted to sing had been found objectionable. Noel Coward rushed to my help. We had submitted Cole Porter's "I Get a Kick out of You" to the producers, and everything seemed to be all right. Or at least so we thought. Not at all—the second stanza reads: "I get no kick from cocaine." I don't know in what year Cole Porter wrote this song, but I certainly know that all the great stars of show business had sung it just as it was. Cole Porter was no longer there when the TV bosses explained to me that the word "cocaine" was taboo. True to my slogan "Stay out of trouble," I tried to find a word with the same number of syllables and the same rhyme; but, after all, I'm no poet.

After exhausting my resources, I phoned Switzerland and explained my problem to Noel Coward. He said, "Wait, I'll call you back." So I waited and informed the TV directors that the old word would be replaced by a new one. Thereupon, they pointed out to me that Cole Porter's heirs would have to approve the change. Such were the many obstacles in the preparation of my first TV appearance, scheduled to be taped in a remarkable, splendid theater, still in the process of construction. Well, great premieres have taken place in the most unbelievable dumps, but artists are optimistic; they are born so they can be saved by unexpected miracles.

Noel Coward phoned me again twenty minutes later: "They say that smoking's insane." Rhyme and meter squared. As always, no problem for him.

He had often asked me to move into his beautiful house above Montreux, but I could never stay more than a few days. During my visits when I went to see him, I always bought tobacco in the village. His butler and I would roll our own cigarettes, but Noel thought they had an awful taste. One day, he said, "Bet you can't stop smoking."

"Of course I can," I answered, and then and there put out my cigarette. He did the same. For me it was easy, because I had no reason to smoke. But it was more difficult for him. I kept my word and never smoked again, a further proof of my stupidity. He continued smoking to the end of his days.

When I was still smoking, I slept the sleep of the just. From the time I stopped—since that conversation with Noel Coward— I could never sleep well again. I returned to Paris. Sleepless nights. I followed all possible and imaginable advice. I lay down in bed with my feet pointing North, South and West—never, however, East. Funny, I was just a bundle of nerves. But I wanted to keep my word at all costs. To my great regret, I finally had to resort to sleeping pills, since I had to work and needed sleep.

I don't believe in the stories circulated by scientists in the cancer research centers, claiming that smoking causes lung cancer. That's nonsense. My very good friend, the great tenor, Richard Tauber, never smoked a cigarette in his life, and died of lung cancer in Guy's Hospital in London. I remember it exactly because I wished to pay for his operation during the war, when all foreign assets, including mine, were blocked. You can die from too much aspirin, too much alcohol, or too many sleeping pills. Any substance can carry you off if you go beyond a certain dose. So why not write on Scotch or Bourbon bottles: "Surgeon General Warns That this Beverage Can Lead to Cirrhosis of the Liver"? The answer is simple: This sentence could mean the loss of millions of dollars. I think the cigarette manufacturers were ill advised when they bowed to the judgment of the universities and agreed to print this ominous phrase on packages of cigarettes.

When you stop smoking, you need a substitute. At the time when I was still smoking, I never drank anything, only at dinner, with friends. That was all. Strange as it may seem, people who quit smoking think they have made a pact with the devil and believe *they will never die.* In reality, they die from other illnesses: intestinal cancer, stomach cancer, cancer of the pancreas. Cancer forever gropes around for further victims. To make cigarettes responsible for all this is a great injustice.

Since I had to muster considerable strength to quit smoking,

I will certainly never start all over again, but that's the only reason. Smoking is not harmful—I would like to enjoy the taste of a cigarette again. Death is unavoidable. Why so much fuss over the way you die? Immoderation, of course, is harmful in all areas. But that's not everything. Noel Coward decided to smoke again, and he was right. His mother was dead; he had no children, and he was responsible only for himself, and therefore had the right to spend his last years as he pleased. He hated his "disability" as he called it, and we continually invented new games so that he forgot he could walk only with the greatest difficulty. One day in New York, we saw the play *Oh, Coward,* and Noel had to climb several steps in front of the audience. As usual, he turned the whole thing into a laughing matter. But the way he laughed broke my heart.

When he died in Jamaica, I was on tour in Chicago. At that time I was appearing in a kind of theater that he had always advised me to avoid. I learned the news by telephone together with Joe Davis—the great master of lighting who had prepared my first appearance at the Café de Paris—and broke into tears.

Suffering is selfish and muddles our thoughts. That's a fact; Noel Coward's sensitive egocentrism, with which I was so familiar, never prevented me from loving him with a certain detachment. He could live without me, and I could live without him. At least, we did just that. Today, after so many years, I still miss him. Nobody here below to "recharge my batteries." A total void in a bleak world. But this world didn't correspond with his ideas or inclinations. He left it without regrets.

PAINTERS
AND SCULPTORS

There are painters whose pictures instantaneously please me, and others whom I learned to appreciate in my youth. I like the Impressionists most. I idolize Paul Cézanne. He always gives free space to the imagination, in which it can take wing. He creates woods and trees with a light brush stroke, and suddenly you see the whole landscape through a painter's eyes. Almost no colors— although he puts on color with his brush.

I would also like to speak of a sculptor: Alberto Giacometti. One of his works is a dog I once saw at the Museum of Modern Art. I fell in love with this dog, although normally I don't like dogs.

One day, when I was in Paris, my friend, Alex Liberman, arranged a meeting between Giacometti and me. Both of us shun publicity, so we met in a bistro, out of the view of pestering photographers. As usual, I didn't open my mouth and just sat there like a mute. Giacometti took my face in his hands and said, "You're not at all hungry, right? Come, let's go have a talk in my studio."

At the time he was working on female statues so huge that he had to climb a ladder to work on their heads. The studio was cold and bare. He stood at the top of his ladder; I sat below, looked up at him, and waited for him to come down and say something to me.

Finally, he began to talk. But what he said was so sad, I would have cried if I could have cried at the right moment. When we were again at the same level, we embraced each other. He gave me a splendid *Figure of a Young Girl,* as he described it. He wrapped it in a newspaper. "Take it to America, and give it to your daughter," he said. I followed his instructions to the letter. I flew across the Atlantic with the small statue in my lap, knowing I would never see Giacometti again. He died all too soon from a cruel sickness. Like all great artists, he was a sad man. My admiration seemed to have touched him, but, although I would have liked to, I could not help him in his misfortune. We would go to the cafés in Montmartre, and to restaurants—he would watch me eat. His heart and his body were sick. Today I regret that I didn't accept all the treasures he offered me. I was, as usual, too well bred to accept such an abundance of gifts. But I didn't turn away his love—I hope the "professors" will keep their academic noses out of this! I can't say he enriched me. I tried to enrich him. But I had too little time. Too little time.

COMPOSERS

STRAVINSKY

I had admired him for a long time, but didn't think I would ever meet him. But I was lucky without any effort on my part, since I have never pursued my "heroes."

Igor Stravinsky sat next to me at a dinner given by the English actor Basil Rathbone. As calmly as possible, I told him about my admiration and said, "What I like very much is the part in *Rites of Spring* where the young girl runs away from the man and disappears in the woods, screaming."

He looked at me for a moment and said, "Such a scene doesn't exist anywhere in the music that I have composed, not even in my ballet music."

So I sang to him the very passage of which I had spoken. He waited patiently until I was finished. "If you believe that this music belongs to the scene you mentioned," he remarked, "that's fine with me, but I can only tell you again that there is no such scene in *The Rites of Spring*."

But I wasn't to be discouraged. Continuing to love his music as I understood it, I had no intention of changing my interpretation. Generous as he was, he later told me that he would have loved to have composed the scene I had described to him.

We saw each other again each time our paths crossed, and before he left forever. Unfortunately, these opportunities were very rare.

HAROLD ARLEN

How I loved him! How I love his music! How I loved his talent, his intelligence!!

He and his children were my good friends. Once he wrote one of his songs on the wall of my daughter's nursery. His generosity is limitless. When I finally had the courage to sing one of his songs, "One for My Baby, One More for the Road," in London, he crossed the Atlantic to hear me. I was half-dead from fear, but the song was well received and the results pleased him.

But that's not all. He also lent me money when I needed it.

He was very ill, and when I came back from Europe, I learned that he was hospitalized in New York. The doctors, who had diagnosed an ulcer after operating on him, had figured they could do nothing, and like good surgeons, they sewed him up again. I spent two terrible days at his bedside, while the famous doctors of the university enjoyed their peaceful weekends outside New York, where they could not be reached.

Since I wasn't related to Harold Arlen, it was difficult for me to make a decision, or to make any demands. I felt terribly useless. After his family, who had been waiting to see whether his condition would worsen, was informed, I called Dr. Blackmore, the great ulcer specialist, from a phone booth, and asked him to hold himself ready, which he did in keeping with professional ethics.

"If we can stop the bleeding in less than a quarter of an hour," he said, "he's saved." He succeeded and the bleeding stopped.

I didn't move from Harold's bedside. "Come back, Harold, don't go away, come back," I murmured into his ear. He heard me and soon was out of danger.

I became friendly with the nurse, a wonderful girl who

tended to his countless transfusions. At the end of the day, when it was no longer possible to find a taxi, we would walk home, arm in arm.

Harold Arlen, who owed his life to Dr. Blackmore's imaginative intervention, has since died. He was a great man, a great composer, unmatched and unmatchable.

ARTISTS

SINATRA

Frank Sinatra, the unchallenged King of Popular Song, is in contrast to what is generally said about him, a very charming man. That's understandable, since to sing as he does requires an extraordinary sensibility and a truly educated heart. The press has created his public "image." It absolutely does not fit him. I know him well. He doesn't need reporters. Nor has he ever needed them, these types who stick their noses in other people's private lives and falsify all information on command.

Sinatra has a great advantage over us women: He can physically defend himself against reporters. We would also like to do that, but it's much more difficult for us, although some women do have the requisite courage. Sinatra hits out only when he's forced to; yet his Italian temperament makes it difficult for him to conceal his anger.

Photographers act like wild beasts, particularly at airports. They try to take photos of people at the least favorable moments. I'll never forget the day when I had asked for a wheelchair because I didn't want to walk for miles to my plane. I was suffering from the effects of a serious accident and didn't want to exert myself unnecessarily. But after the assault of all the photographers and reporters who stormed the airport, I decided to walk and rid myself of this horde. My plan worked. The "gentlemen" had wanted to see me in a wheelchair. They were uninterested in pictures of me walking to my plane on foot, and disappeared, deeply disappointed.

Sinatra treats them the way they deserve to be treated, and he does that well, as in everything he undertakes. He tackles a song like a poet his text. His intonation, his breathing technique, his arrangements, are famous. His professionalism, his generosity, his loyalty—everything about him is famous. This brilliant genius can do without reporters.

NAT KING COLE

Nat King Cole was a shy, forthright man.

I got to know him in Las Vegas. At that time I was still new in the profession into which I had entered so suddenly.

Nat Cole was of the opinion that I shouldn't sing in that city; that I should perform in theaters, go abroad. And he advised me to begin with South America.

We met again when he sang at the Fairmont Hotel in San Francisco, and I had a contract with the Geary Theatre. I had come there from Texas and didn't know that so many musicals were being staged in the city while good musicians were really not available anymore.

Nat Cole visited me during an audition. He took me aside and gave me some advice: "You shouldn't be working with second-rate musicians because your arrangements are difficult. You should always consider two things. *Numero uno:* Fish around for the best musicians in every field. *Numero due:* Look for your impresario long in advance so that he can engage the best musicians, at the right time, for a definite date, in a definite city."

As his evening's performance at the Fairmont was drawing to a close, I hurried there to hear him sing "The Joe Turner Blues" again. He was holding the stage curtain in his hand while he sang the last refrain. Nat King Cole was a wonderful man who expressed his feelings with great reserve, but he was never shy when he had good advice to give. Without him, I probably would not have made the transition from nightclubs to theater. How unjust that he had to die so young! I believe that God loved him, even though it seems impossible that God loves those who die young.

MY FRIEND PIAF

Horrified, I looked on as she exhausted her energies and took on three lovers at once. It all made me feel like a country cousin. She didn't notice that at all. Around the clock she was concerned only with her feelings, her profession, her belief in all kinds of odd things, with her passion for the world in general and for certain people in particular.

In my eyes, she really was The Sparrow, the little bird whose name she bore. But she was also Jezebel, whose unquenchable thirst for love must have been due to a feeling of imperfection, her "ugliness," as she put it—her delicate, scrawny body, which she sent forth into combat like Circe, the Sirens and Lorelei, the temptress, who with her incomparable vitality promised all the pleasures of this world. She made me dizzy with all her lovers, whom I had to hide or lead to different rooms of her dwelling. I did what she demanded of me. I did many favors for her without ever understanding her enormous need for love.

She liked me; perhaps she loved me. But I believe she could only love men. Friendship was a vague feeling whose shadows sometimes scurried through her head and heart. She had no time to dedicate herself exclusively to friendship. And she was right, since her energies were not inexhaustible. I helped her dress at the theater and at the Versailles, the New York nightclub in which she sang. When the tragic accident occurred, I took over the practical problems of her life. We were to pick up Marcel Cerdan at the airport; she was sleeping when I heard that his plane had crashed over the Azores and that he was dead.

I had to wake her up at the scheduled time and tell her the news. Then came the doctors and the medications. I was sure she would cancel the appearance at the Versailles, but when I spoke to her about it in the afternoon, she said she had no intention of breaking her contract. I must add that she considered it absolutely necessary to ask the orchestra conductor for an intermission during the performance and to omit the "Hymne à l'amour" ("Hymn to Love"). Then, with the house electrician, I adjusted the spotlight to a softer light. I went to her dressing room again; she was calm and determined. She had decided to sing the "Hymne à l'amour."

All of us were afraid of one particular passage in this song: "*Si tu meurs, je mourrai aussi*" ("If you die, I shall die too"). But she stuck it out. She went through her repertoire as if nothing had happened. In fact, she didn't even seem to bow to that harsh law of show business, "The show must go on." She made use of her grief, of her mourning, so to speak, to sing even better than usual.

On succeeding evenings we sat in her dark hotel room and held hands across the table. She was inconsolable, and tried with all her will to bring Cerdan back. Suddenly she cried out: "There he is—don't you hear his voice?" I put her to bed, knowing that this lunatic despair would pass.

And it did pass. Long after these events, Edith Piaf announced that she was getting married. This storm, too, I let pass over me. The ceremony had to take place in a church in New York, and I was to be the witness to the marriage. Since I'm not a Catholic, Piaf procured a special dispensation for me. She returned to the land of remembrance and to her cherished superstitions, and on a dark New York morning I helped her dress. When I came to her room she was lying naked on the bed, as was her custom. The "custom," of course, was connected with her belief that in this way happiness would never abandon the young pair. Around her neck she was wearing a chain with a tiny emerald cross I had given her. She looked lost in this gloomy room, thousands of miles away from her country.

Afterward, she went back to France. We had a tender relationship, but it was not love. I have always respected her attitude and her decisions. Very much later, when she became a drug addict, I broke faith with her. It was more than I could bear. I knew my limits, even when I understood that she needed the drugs. To understand does not always mean to approve. What could I do? All my efforts to help Piaf ran into an unconquerable wall: drugs. I was inconsolable. Drugs, at that time, were not as dangerous as now—heroin was not as widespread, nor other similar atrocious substances. But anyhow, it was a matter of drugs, and I gave up helping her. My love for her remained constant, but it had become useless. She wasn't alone. As was to be expected, a devoted young man was at her side.

I gave Edith Piaf up like a lost daughter whom you forever mourn, whom you always shed tears over, whom I shall always carry in the depths of my heart.

RUDOLF NUREYEV

I've never known a vainer man. He certainly had good professional grounds for it. Perhaps one would have tolerated his attitude if he were not as conceited in private life as on the stage.

I got to know Nureyev through my friend, Margot Fonteyn. After their appearance, I would dry both of them off behind the giant, cold "wings"—if you can still call them "wings"—of the Parisian Sports Palace.

Nureyev is a loner, and, at the same time, an extrovert; an astonishing mélange that surprises anyone who comes in contact with him. But that is precisely his intention.

I often saw Nureyev in London, since we were neighbors. He constantly complained about his legs, which he considered "too short." My job was to assure him that this was not the case, that he was perfect on stage. The great dancer Erik Bruhn was his guru. Bruhn never left Nureyev's loge, and only the approving nods of his head could satisfy Nureyev. Since I had never seen Bruhn dance, I can say nothing about his talent, and must rely on

Nureyev's judgment. He must have been the greatest, although he in no way looked like a dancer. He looked very serious, and seemed to be alien to the theater and to the dance.

When I see Mikhail Baryshnikov, I always think of Nureyev and his fixation about having legs that are too short. Baryshnikov didn't have to worry about such things. He has beautiful, long legs, and the face of a young god. He didn't have any inferiority complex. I think he owes this remarkable balance to the fact that he loves women. He's not a loner, not even in his art. He's healthy, thank God!

ELISABETH BERGNER

Elisabeth was the idol of millions of people and, even before *The Blue Angel*, the idol of my youth. As I've said earlier, she was very kind to beginners. But I was afraid of her.

Each time you stand opposite an important personage, you're seized with fear. That's always the case with me. It has often happened to me. And when the person concerned is also a great actress, the fright increases tenfold. As always, in the late twenties, Elisabeth Bergner was a sensation on the stages of Europe. She was the queen of the theater, often imitated but never matched.

She was an impressive phenomenon, neither man nor woman. She was Bergner. She had a wholly special way of speaking German, with an unusual accentuation of the syllables. The lock of hair that fell on her forehead, the "Bergner lock," was the *ne plus ultra* of fashion. She also began to wear her hair short when young German girls were still letting their hair grow down to their shoulders. Elisabeth Bergner fascinated her audience, enchanted them like a sorceress. We became friends many years later in Hollywood and in England.

AFTER
THE DEVIL IS A
WOMAN

Josef von Sternberg's decision, against my will, to terminate our collaboration—to which the studio executives probably also contributed—marked for me the beginning of a long series of mediocre films. "If you leave Hollywood now," said von Sternberg, "the whole world will believe you have done so only because of pressure from me. You must continue to work here."

I made the films that followed without great conviction, to put it mildly.

Rouben Mamoulian was a very good friend and took me as I was. Others, too. The only film I need not be ashamed of is *Desire*, directed by Frank Borzage and based on a script by Ernst Lubitsch. I found Gary Cooper a little less monosyllabic than before. He was finally rid of Lupe Velez, who had been at his heels constantly throughout the shooting of *Morocco*.

Desire became a good film and, moreover, also proved to be a

box office success. The script was excellent, the roles superb—
one more proof that these elements are more important than
actors. But even before *Desire* became a hit at the box office, we
made another film (that's how it is in the film business), one that
was not so good: *Angel*. Ernst Lubitsch was responsible for the
script *and* was the director. Our morale was restored when *Desire*
was shown in movie houses all over the world.

THE GARDEN OF ALLAH

In 1936, when I was still under contract to Paramount, David O.
Selznick wanted to make a color film based on Robert Hichens's
successful novel. He negotiated with Paramount and borrowed me
for the duration of the shooting. David Selznick's situation in
Hollywood was quite unique. Through his extraordinary knowledge of the mechanics of power and his skill at achieving his aims
by listening attentively to his interlocutors, he had created his
own empire in which his every word was a command. I liked
working for him very much, since I knew exactly what he wanted
from me. Naturally, he wasn't infallible. But he could generously
make up for his mistakes, and he was also very liberal with money
for his own productions.

Selznick and I had the same views. Like me, he detested
garish or too powerful colors. Since he always knew what he was
about, he let Ernest Dryden design my costumes. That was a
tough job for Dryden. My role was that of a woman at once
mysterious and convincingly real. The action took place in the
desert, and Selznick didn't want an Amazon running around in
pants and boots. He was pleased with the idea of keeping the
costumes in sandy colors, and we began to try different materials
while Dryden continued to sketch. Despite all the stories that
have been told about this film, and although Josh Logan and his
anecdotes became the center of attention of quite a few parties,
The Garden of Allah remains the most beautiful color film ever made.

Charles Boyer played a monk who has broken his vows, and I,
an odd creature whose reactions are unforeseeable. I bore a ridicu-

lous name, Domini Enfilden, and I was supposedly seeking "peace of mind" in the desert. I found it exciting to be participating in the first great color film. Selznick attached great importance to the real-life character of my role, and he would listen to me with infinite patience when I explained my ideas regarding the costumes to him. I had decided to choose shades of color that would harmonize with the desert sand.

Dryden, a very talented costume designer, agreed with me, and we created some wonderful outfits. Pastel tones were used for the first time in the history of color film, and the takes were superb—which is saying a lot, since up until then, the great cameramen of black and white films had never been concerned with the special problems of color.

A young man, Joshua Logan, arrived from New York (at that time he had the job of "dialogue director"). Later, he wrote a book on our experiences, and scores of people at parties were entertained by his anecdotes of the shooting of *The Garden of Allah*. Although these stories do not always correspond to the truth, they are quite amusing.

We went to the Arizona desert, where we camped in tents with countless scorpions. The heat was awful. The makeup ran down our cheeks, but the greatest disaster was Charles Boyer's toupee.

In the early afternoon when the light of the still-scorching sun was already changing color, we hurried to complete the scene before the yellow rays could no longer be photographed, and the light no longer corresponded to the shadings of the morning. At that time nobody paid special attention to Boyer's toupee.

One day, when we were shooting the great love scene of the film, Boyer bent over me to kiss me when suddenly his toupee loosened. The sweat that had accumulated under it poured all over my face. General panic. Makeup artists and hairdressers ran around frantically. The sun sank lower and lower, and became more yellow than ever. The cameraman shouted: "That's it for today!"

Selznick sent the whole team back to Hollywood, where we were to await further instructions. In the meantime, the desert was recreated in a giant studio. Trucks brought sand from the shores of the Pacific. Huge ventilators were installed to simulate light breezes. The production company spent a real fortune.

Finally, we had to reshoot the scene ruined by the temperamental toupee, as well as the scenes following them.

At that time, it took several days before you could see the results of all such efforts on the screen. Again a disaster. The verdict read: "Wrong sand color." And, in fact, the sand from the Pacific beaches does have a different color from that in Arizona.

We were sent home again. While we were waiting, the "wrong sand" was removed and replaced by the "right" sand from Arizona. (Selznick was the greatest perfectionist I have ever known.) Yet, despite all the changes in the script, he could not save this film, even though it remains one of the most beautiful color films from those pioneer days. To our great regret, *The Garden of Allah* is no more than that. We all gave it our best to ensure its success. But the miracle was not wrought. Nobody can foresee what will please the critics. Every artistic activity is, and always will be, a poker game.

COSTUMES

Anyone with a modicum of knowledge of photography knows that there is a great difference between the human eye and the lens of a camera. The great artists who designed the costumes of film stars knew the technique of photography from the ground up. They knew the value of color and the effect of every material, even before the costumes took form in the tailor shops. Nevertheless, costume and makeup tests always took place before the beginning of the actual shooting. The tests showed the cameraman what problems he had to cope with, so that he could position the lighting accordingly.

I've already mentioned Travis Benton, who was responsible for all my costumes at Paramount. At Metro-Goldwyn-Mayer, there were Adrian, Irene, and Karinska. They had such practiced eyes that after the costume tests only rarely did major changes have to be made. At the time of black and white films, you had to be very sure all the material was tested in front of the camera because the costumes were commissioned; despite everything, color was of crucial importance. Pastel tones replaced pure white; tea-colored material appeared natural white.

Black (and above all, black velvet) was absolutely unusable. Josef von Sternberg had to muster all his skills to photograph the black clothing I so much liked to wear.

The advent of color films upset all these ground rules. The studios were under the draconian supervision of a woman named Madame Natalie Kalmus, the former head of Technicolor. Madame Kalmus was so proud of the new procedure that she demanded glaring colors for scenery and costumes. All the actors began to scream, just as they had when sound invaded the world of silent films. Naturally, I too was asked to take a color test. I chose a white dress, but before anyone could intervene, Madame Kalmus sneaked onto the set and placed a vase of red tulips near me. The colors were strong. The blue colors were so intense that, just like the sky, they had to be avoided during the takes. The sky could be photographed again only when the color technique improved. But the "hoopla over color" continued, as with a child who has just discovered a new toy. The studios established new departments, conducted endless tests, and finally black, too, was released from quarantine. New makeups were invented and tested, reassembled and tested anew. Even lipsticks were subjected to creative inspiration. The made-up actors looked like puppets. But no one could halt the ultimate triumph of color; all previous experience and knowledge now seemed antediluvian.

The best cameramen were ignorant of these new techniques. Second-rate cameramen had been able to study color photography in their free time, and now they used their knowledge to push their way back on the scene. A violent war broke out, but a solution was finally worked out: The cameramen experienced in color would handle the cameras and install the spotlights, while the aces of the black and white era would concentrate on angle shots and regulate the lighting, in particular on the faces of the stars. This compromise produced rather scanty results, but it was still better than leaving important shooting to inexperienced cameramen merely because they were knowledgeable about color. The spotlights blinded the actors, to whom it was explained that this glaring light was absolutely necessary. The first films made under these conditions were mediocre. They owed their commercial success only to the appeal of the new technique. Thank God I was spared this cup, and I had the fortune never to have to make a color film for Paramount. I had only been "lent" to David O. Selznick for *The Garden of Allah*.

Stage costumes present problems completely different from those of costumes for film. They are meant only for the human eye. That ought to simplify the matter. But unfortunately, here too, there are many difficulties to overcome. The fact that you face the audience directly is a considerable advantage and, at the same time, a considerable risk. Distance is the first problem. Only a few fortunate people sit in the first rows, which are already quite far from the actors. Consequently, clear and distinct accents must be placed. Accessories like rings and earrings are simply not visible, and on this point all efforts to recreate historical fidelity are useless.

Stage lighting that can change colors and forms also presents a problem. Unlike cinema, there are no close-ups. Everything is seen as a "long shot" and, consequently, the silhouette is of crucial importance. The actor's movements must be harmonious, since a "second take" is impossible.

Libraries and bookstores in every large city offer many works on this subject. The best way, however, is to draw inspiration from the actual play in order to find out what works best. "Historical" costumes are less problematic than modern ones, which should not strictly reflect current fashion, since clothes style quickly becomes passé. Since I was never really a stage actress, my opinion is based on the many plays I've seen in Europe, England, and America.

At all my performances I wore costumes that were works of art. Since I didn't have to hide behind an imaginary person, Jean Louis and I were able to devise dreamlike creations without, at the same time, being subject to the usual stage restrictions.

Jean Louis' creations metamorphosed me into a perfect, ethereal being, the most seductive there was. I have preserved some of his costumes—each one more magnificent than the other.

I am often asked where my preference for white tails and bow tie comes from, which I first wore at a performance in the fifties. It doesn't seem to be known that this is a very old idea. In 1900, an actress called Vesta Tilly—followed in 1910 by Ella Shields, particularly when she sang the song "Burlington Burty"—wore men's clothes. Other female artists of the British music hall imitated them. But that's not the only reason. If I have often appeared in tails, it was also for the reason that the best songs are written for men. For example, I absolutely wanted to sing Harold Arlen's "One for My Baby, One More for the Road." But it's impossible for a woman to stay in a barroom until a quarter to three in the morning. On the other hand, it's no problem for a man. That's the reason why I changed my costume with lightning speed and exchanged my dress for a tuxedo. I didn't want the audience to wait more than one or two minutes. That was an extremely hazardous undertaking. But it succeeded.

From that day on, I had a wide choice of cheerful, amusing, and sad songs at my disposal. I have carefully preserved a letter from Alan Jay Lerner, in which he assures me that in his opinion, I sing "Accustomed to Her Face" better than anyone else.

At the end of the performance, I would dance in the midst of a row of girls. But in some theaters, I had to give this up, since with the inclusion of the dance, the whole performance was changed from the category "recital" into "variety," which entailed considerably higher taxes for the owners of the auditorium. If they insisted on this point, I dropped the dance. This also made my life easier, for it meant extra work for my musicians, my electricians and sound engineers, plus the twelve dancers and two dressing-room assistants who traveled with me. Nevertheless, I often regretted the omission of this number. The girls wore black "sexy" panties, black stockings, white vests and top hats—a magnificent contrast to my black tuxedo. On the stage, everything was black, even most of the scenery.

I traveled with my own pink stage curtain, which was lowered directly behind me for certain numbers, and lit up by colored spotlights. All my stage clothes were made of flesh-colored material, and easy to light, since that eliminated any disturbing interference from other colors. Whether in films or on stage, I have always preferred neutral colors to pure colors, and the experts with whom I worked always agreed that I was right.

PHOTOGRAPHERS

One of the most important persons in the making of a film is the studio photographer. His job is to take publicity photos of the shooting and of the stars. Most of the photos in circulation are made in the studio.

"Marlene Dietrich was one of the persons I liked most to photograph," Davis Boulton has written about me. "She's a real expert. She knows photography as well as I do. She insists that only one spotlight be installed above her so as to highlight her hollow cheeks. Stars, as is well known, generally don't like to be photographed."

In my opinion, the photographer's greatest talent lies in his ability to relax the person in front of the camera by replacing embarrassment with euphoria and by letting the person "pose" correctly and change expression—in short to create a living session, even if it takes soft background music to meet his purpose. The photographer enjoys a great advantage over the filmmaker; his model doesn't move, doesn't even breathe. No complicated lighting to follow all the actor's movements.

In addition, there is the delicate work of developing and retouching. The latter is an art in itself. I've been able to familiarize myself with it, thanks to a young Japanese man at Paramount. I would watch him for hours at his worktable, as he searched for the least imperfection, which he then corrected with his brush. Normally, young assistants take care of the display and other technical problems.

A great photographer tries, above all, to preserve the image that he has in mind, taking, of course, public taste into account. He also has the advantage of taking many photographs (film doesn't cost much), choosing the best among them, and sending them all over the world, where they can be reproduced for years and increase his fame. So, it's not surprising that these photographers are the embodiment of politeness and charm, and that none of them has the slightest scruple when it's a question of achieving his or her goal. They all are ready to sell their photographic souls for a flawless negative.

But I love them without exception, and envy them for more than one reason.

My favorite photographers are Cecil Beaton, Edward Steichen, Anthony Armstrong-Jones, Richard Avedon and Milton H. Greene.

I was scheduled to make a film for Paramount. I had committed myself to Columbia to perform in a film on George Sand under the direction of Frank Capra. Suddenly came a stab in the back.

An owner of a chain of movie houses published an advertisement in all American newspapers: "The following actors and actresses are declared *undesirable at the box office.*" Printed in bold letters were the names: Garbo, Hepburn, Crawford, Dietrich, etc. That was a death sentence.

The studios at that time, it must be understood, pursued a strict business policy: Each time a distributor wanted a film, for example, one with Garbo or Dietrich, he was forced to buy six mediocre films (or even downright bad films) as part of the deal.

This public announcement shook the film industry. Metro-Goldwyn-Mayer remained loyal to its stars, and continued to pay them, but it no longer wished to invest money in their films. Paramount wasn't so generous; they fired me, and Columbia withdrew the George Sand project. Why run a risk with a star "undesirable at the box office"?

I didn't know any of the great actresses on this black list, nor did I know how I should react.

I packed my belongings and returned to Europe to my husband and my friends. To say I was desperate would be an exaggeration. At bottom, Hollywood meant absolutely nothing to me. I was helpless, needed some good advice, someone who would give me a helping hand. And I was lucky enough to find what I was looking for.

First, I went to Paris, where my husband was working, and I spent two weeks at the Hotel Plaza Athenée. We settled all our problems, abundantly enjoyed the French cuisine, and then decided to travel south as soon as my husband got a vacation.

We flew to Antibes. Here all my troubles were quickly forgotten. With friends, and the Chris-Craft, we lay in the sun, bathed in the sea, laughed over everything and nothing; no annoyance, no more headaches, total freedom. We had already spent several summers in this peaceful haven. But the summer of 1939 was not like those of the past.

Surrounded by my husband, my daughter, Erich Maria Remarque, Josef von Sternberg, and some other friends, I constantly would ask myself: "To which world do I belong? Am I a bad star, a has-been star, or simply a zero?" "Undesirable at the box office" the sentence of those gentlemen in Hollywood had read. But I had the same feeling as at the beginning of my career: What if I were to be a disappointment to others?

Von Sternberg had not been guiding my "career" for a long time. I was left to my own devices.

We spent a splendid vacation. The Kennedy family was there, and we really lived in a paradise. My daughter swam with Jack Kennedy to a nearby island; they held their clothes above the water so that they could dress for luncheon on the island.

From the shore, I didn't let these excellent swimmers (which I've never been) out of my sight and prayed to heaven they would not drown. They always arrived safe and sound. And they were always back in time for dinner—happy, soaked, radiant with joy. What a summer! We didn't know that it would be the last one, that it would suddenly come to an end with tears and threatening danger. We danced; there were two tables: one for the young people and the other for us grown-ups. Sometimes we changed places; one evening Jack Kennedy invited me to dance. I loved all the Kennedy children, and this love has never ceased.

During the course of the summer of 1939, I received a call from the Hollywood producer Joe Pasternak. "In spite of everything, I'm taking the risk of making a film with you," he said. "Jimmy Stewart has already agreed, and I would like to have you as his co-star in the Western, *Destry Rides Again.*" I answered, "Not for anything in the world." But Josef von Sternberg advised me to accept the offer. So I left Antibes and set out for Hollywood.

CHANGING STUDIOS

It was fun to make the film, and we were all delighted with its great success. Joe Pasternak was especially happy, since he had challenged the film industry and saw that his efforts had been rewarded.

After *Destry Rides Again*, he made several other films with me. *Seven Sinners* (1940), *The Spoilers* (1942) and *Pittsburgh* (1942) brought lots of money into Universal Studio's coffers.

Joe Pasternak had a talent for making everybody happy. We also had the support of directors like George Marshall and Tay Garnett. The actors, on the other hand, were not very helpful. Unpleasant people, actors.

First of all, John Wayne. Unknown, penniless, he begged me to help him. I did so. I phoned my agent, Charlie Feldman, who told me that he wasn't interested in beginners. But finally, he gave in to my arguments.

At that time, John Wayne earned about four hundred dollars a week, on which he had to live with his wife and child. I did my best to interest Feldman, inventing the most incredible "talents" for my protégé. John Wayne wasn't exactly brilliant, but neither was he bad, and he needed money. Through Charlie Feldman he got a contract with Universal, and I made some films with him. I can't really say he was my "partner," since his performance was kept within very strict bounds—he spoke his lines and that was all. I helped as best I could. Wayne was not a bright or exciting type. He confessed to me that he never read books. But that didn't prevent him from accumulating a nice pile of money over the years. It proves that you don't have to be terribly brilliant to become a great film star.

In 1942, when we were working together in *The Spoilers*, he had become a little more sure of himself but had not increased his talent. Randolph Scott, also a member of the cast, concerned himself with the "quality" of the acting. He performed the same function in *Pittsburgh*, which we made shortly thereafter. Later John Wayne became a veritable Croesus, and exerted an enormous influence in Hollywood. He didn't need my help any more. He had made it, without opening the pages of a single book.

Nevertheless, don't follow his example! Read!

I've already mentioned that all our friends who had fled Europe had too much self-respect to want to remain in America without working. We helped them find work to the best of our abilities, and Pasternak also did his part.

It was his idea that I should make a film with René Clair. At first, I resisted the idea, but finally out of loyalty to my old principle, that doing your duty was all that mattered, I yielded. So, in my date book, I wrote: *The Flame of New Orleans*, under the direction of René Clair, with Bruce Cabot.

Cabot was an awfully stupid actor, unable to remember his lines or cues. Nor could René Clair, who didn't speak a word of English, lend him a helping hand. Besides, Bruce Cabot, in contrast to John Wayne, was very conceited. He wouldn't accept any help. I finally resigned myself to paying for his lessons, so that he would at least know his lines during the shooting.

The team loathed René Clair (surely because of the language barrier) to such an extent that the technicians almost pushed me off the set the moment they heard the order: "Pack up your things." *The Flame of New Orleans* was a flop. I played a double role (two sisters) and, as always, wore lavish costumes, but that wasn't enough.

I didn't particularly like René Clair, but I didn't hate him as much as the rest of the team did. Fritz Lang was the director I detested most. I became conscious of my feelings toward him in 1952, when we filmed *Rancho Notorious*. In order to be able to work with Lang, I had to repress all the hatred and aversion he aroused in me. If Mel Ferrer had not been there, I probably would have walked off the set in the middle of shooting. But Mel was always near and helped to see me through those troublesome days. Fritz Lang belongs to the "Brotherhood of Sadists." He despised my reverence for Josef von Sternberg, and tried to replace this genius in my heart and in my mind. I know that because he confessed it to me.

The Teutonic arrogance he expressed deeply angered me. Only my professional honor prevented me from breaking the contract and walking off the job. Before the order: "Everybody on the set" resounded, Fritz Lang would spend hours marking our positions on the ground. At the same time, we were not allowed to look down at the ground. In this way he was trying to prevent, at all costs, the actors from being quicker than himself, and he seemed to take a diabolical delight in making us endlessly repeat our movements.

Fritz Lang simply laid out each step, each breath, with a sadistic exactness of which Hitler would have been proud. To be sure, Fritz Lang, as a Jew, had fled to America to escape Nazism. But here he behaved like a tyrant. He would not have hesitated— we could testify to this—to walk over corpses. He was tall, and took long steps, so that we could follow him only with the greatest effort. Mel Ferrer, an elegant man, but much shorter than Lang, took great pains to respect the markings and not step beyond them. Despite my height, I was unable to do the same. But that didn't bother Lang one bit. "Do it again," he would scream, and have me repeat the same gesture a hundred times.

Often, I could have choked him on the spot; he would give instructions that made no sense at all. He tried everything to make me responsible for the time lost placing the reflectors in my new positions, but I defended myself like a lioness. Since I had worked with great directors, I knew that this need to control an actor's movements, even before the actor could study his role, was a sign of pure dilettantism. But in Fritz Lang's case it had more to do with sadism.

Fritz Lang had made some successful films in Germany and in the United States without, however, achieving the international fame he coveted. I wouldn't shed a single tear for him. I felt no friendship for this man, hence no tears. *Rancho Notorious*, the film I made with him, was and remains a very mediocre work.

After that, I made *Manpower* with George Raft and Edward G. Robinson. Raft was simply wonderful throughout the shooting. Raoul Walsh loved each and everyone of us, and we thanked him. The film was a success. A stroke of luck for us all.

Long before, I had reflected on what I would do if America entered the war. I was well informed, and knew my duty. I needed money, of course, as always, and even more than usual. I still had time to make another film and also did that. But, in the meantime, I had been preparing for my departure, and for a long stay abroad—for as long as the war would last.

The "Hollywood Committee," which had been founded when the Nazis seized power, was all ready for action on the day of the mobilization. Its chief organizers were Ernst Lubitsch and Billy Wilder.

We sent sums of money to a contact man in Switzerland, a certain "Engel," for the purpose of liberating hundreds of prisoners from the German concentration camps and bringing them to America. I never got to know this Mr. Engel, but he must have been a wonderful person. He undertook this service to humanity regardless of the risks such activity involved. At the beginning, when the concentration camps were being set up, it was still possible to help prisoners escape and to bring them into Switzerland in secrecy, dressed as monks or nuns, thanks to a secret organization that functioned perfectly. They were given clothes and cared for, and as soon as they had recovered, they were flown to Los Angeles.

I remember a great popular composer, Rudolf Katcher, who was very ill at the time of his liberation and who died shortly thereafter. He had written the song "Madonna," known all over the world.

But most of our wards recovered quickly. Our task was to teach them English and then find jobs for them. Lubitsch and Wilder tried to offer these men and women a new chance in America, and often they were successful.

The most difficult to help were the theater people. They were still imbued with a sense of their former importance. They didn't like us Americans. Nevertheless, they settled down in the United States, and we did whatever we could to find them work.

I remember the day when Rudolf Forster had been summoned to the Warner Studios for a screen test (arranged by Lubitsch), for the role of a king. He came up to me and said that he didn't like the throne, and he refused to take the screen tests.

Lubitsch had infinite patience. Nevertheless, Forster, after a time, decided to return to Hitler's Germany. His departure discouraged us, since we had tried hard to make his exile less painful. We had done everything humanly possible to find roles for him, but this egocentric person wanted to remain the star he had been in Germany.

I don't know what became of him after he returned to his homeland. Since he wasn't a Jew, he probably overcame his disappointment at not having found a throne to his taste in America.

Thank God we didn't have many failures of this kind. We had even set up a fund from which we could help some war victims for several years. Some of them had suffered so severely, physically and psychologically, that it was difficult for them to adjust to a foreign language and a foreign country. These refugees could not work like the others. Nevertheless, they deserved a comfortable life.

With time, the number of refugees was reduced. The tightening of security measures in the concentration camps made escape almost impossible. Only men with a great capacity for resistance, who had to help load new victims on the freight cars, could escape when they were outside the camps and not too far from the Swiss border. There they arrived on foot, hiding by day and continuing the trek by night.

The Swiss arrested those refugees without identification papers, and stuck them in "camps." But these bore no similarity to the horror camps which they had left behind. Mr. Engel would free them, one after the other, and send them to America—a long and tiring procedure.

Our aim was to rescue some of these unfortunate souls, and it gave us the feeling of being useful. The organization continued its activity when the United States entered the war in 1941. Army training camps were quickly set up. All artists who could entertain and relax the newly enlisted soldiers were sent on tours through these camps. We traveled mostly in buses; the programs were hastily put together, but the enthusiasm of the artists helped to overcome a lot of the difficulties. Great comics like Jack Benny or George Jessel led groups and also performed themselves. The awareness of being on native ground gave them a feeling of security. This changed during the war. The next step consisted of selling "bonds," a kind of loan to the government to finance the war effort. On such tours, we were accompanied by a group of Treasury Department officials. Our tours were exhausting—six to eight hours a day, and sometimes also an evening performance. I had to go into factories and call upon workers to give a certain percentage of their salaries as a loan to the government. I gave speeches according to instructions, and even went so far as to pit one factory against another as rivals. This strategy proved very productive. All by myself, I raised a million dollars, which flowed into the Treasury Department coffers.

All that effort was supposed to contribute—at least in my eyes—to the ending of the war as quickly as possible.

I also worked in nightclubs in the evening. Spurred on by my bodyguards from the Treasury Department, I turned to the half-drunk audience with the zeal of a traveling salesman. I gratified every mood of the potential bond buyers.

The Treasury Department had entered into an agreement with American banks, which made it possible to have access to all current accounts, even in the middle of the night, in order to find out whether the checks I received were covered or not. During this procedure in the nightclub, I had to sit in the donor's lap and wait until I got a nod from the Treasury Department agent signaling that everything was in order—or that we had been hoaxed.

One evening in Washington, I was summoned to the White House. I arrived at about two o'clock in the morning. The Treasury Department officials remained in the car.

President Roosevelt was standing—yes, despite his polio he was standing—when I was ushered into the room. Then he sat himself down in his chair, looked at me with his bright eyes, and said, "I've heard all about what you are doing to sell bonds. We are very grateful to you for this. But I expressly forbid you to confuse acquisition with prostitution. From now on, you will no longer give any performances in these night spots. That's an order!"

"Fine, Mr. President," I said. I was sorry I couldn't stay there longer. If I had had to, I would have gladly slept on the floor.

I was brought back to my hotel, and from then on, I worked only during the day, which, however, didn't prevent me from giving performances on the streets. The "sales fever" continued for a long time.

I was too exhausted at that time to remember what happened later. I received a medal with the thanks of the secretary of the treasury and a magnificently printed document, and the matter was closed.

My zealous activity, however, did not prevent the same department from demanding belated tax payments from me at the end of the war, even though a law forbade taxing members of the Armed Forces.

I had hardly been discharged and landed at LaGuardia Airport when the gentlemen from the Treasury Department pounced on me.

It took years before I had paid off all my debts. I no longer had any money, but that didn't matter. The tax authorities have enormous power, against which it's useless to fight. They suck everything out of you, and you're completely helpless vis-à-vis these vampires. I can sing a song about it.

KISMET

I filmed *Kismet* before I enlisted in the army. Not many words need be wasted on my role in this film, but I needed money for my family to live on during my absence.

The great costume designer, Irene, and I spent hours pondering the costumes for the impossible person I was signed to portray.

Now, for the first time, I was working at Metro-Goldwyn-Mayer. For a long time we had envied the actresses who worked for this company, since they enjoyed special conditions: They were flattered and spoiled by the directors. I took lessons for the "exotic" dance I had to perform, half sitting on my heels, which made me laugh so much I lost the rhythm. Irene and I had an idea that was not very feasible, but which at first had struck us as something quite extraordinary.

The idea was to design a pair of trousers out of hundreds of tiny gold chains, which would jingle softly at every movement, and glitter under the spotlight. This had never been done before. I spent hours on my feet while two men tied the gold chainlets to my ankles and crouched between my legs with tweezers in order to fasten the single links to each other. They loved the work. I, on the other hand, was utterly exhausted with my legs so spread out.

In the studio, this extravagant idea was still a topic of conversation, and then came the day when, after I had tried all the dance steps, I appeared on the set. *The Rites of Spring*—take note!—was being played, and as prescribed, I took my first step. Suddenly all one heard was crack, crack, crack, the sound of the chainlets breaking, one after the other, then two, six at a time, until I stood there without pants . . .

General panic. I was shoved into a car and driven to my dressing room. Irene wept on my shoulders.

"We must find something else," I said to calm her, "and forget about the chains." But Irene turned a deaf ear.

I was sent home, and she was summoned to appear before the big boss, Louis B. Mayer.

Suddenly I had a brilliant idea, something perfectly safe,

something that would cause no complications. "Gold," I thought, "how is a golden effect achieved on the screen?"

It occurred to me to paint my legs with gold paint.

I wasn't particularly proud; I was simply in a big hurry to call Irene and to tell her that I found the solution to our problem and that we could set to work on the very next morning.

The next morning she was in my dressing room at six o'clock. Two makeup artists armed with brushes zealously painted my legs. The whole room reeked of paint; the floor was strewn with golden spots, but the effect was simply fabulous. Irene smiled again; at nine we had to be in the studio. Nobody had believed that we would be able to solve the problem in less than twenty-four hours.

At nine on the dot I climbed onto the set. The whole team cried "Ooh!" and "Ah!" The photographers bombarded me with the light of their flashbulbs. The director, William Dieterle, came, nodded approvingly, and the music began to play. I danced, this time without the slightest incident; the gilding held fast. An hour later, I suddenly became very cold, and trembled like a wounded bird. Heaters were brought in to warm me up—in vain. Nevertheless, I worked through the day, good girl that I was. The studio doctor examined me in my dressing room, while I tried to wash the color off my legs with alcohol. He told me that the studio was not covered by the insurance companies for something like "the present case." No one had thought of including an applicable clause in the contract in the event that the paint should permanently close the pores in the lower half of my body. (That was why I was so cold.)

I reassured the doctor. I didn't want to give up the paint. We already had one day's work behind us and simply had to go on (since a day in the studio cost a fortune). Meanwhile, my legs had turned green, and I hid behind chairs and curtains until the doctor left.

My experience with gilding went back to my first days at Paramount. Since I was supposed to appear blond on the screen, and refused to have my hair bleached, I used gilding. Not, of course, a liquid one, as with my *Kismet* legs, but a simple powder I had bought in a specialty store. After my hairdo was fixed, I sprinkled it over my hair. Suddenly it looked bright, and acquired a brilliance unachievable any other way.

I still hear the objections of the cameramen: "You'll see! The color will fall on your face! You'll see!" And I imagine Gary Cooper in front of me drawing himself up after a passionate kiss with a gilded nose! Well, you couldn't see it on the screen, but Cooper, nice young fellow that he was, did have to "dust off" his nose several times during the day.

When you're a pro and understand something about photography, you can always find ways and means to overcome difficulties. Most actresses let others concern themselves with things that do not expressly belong to their "sphere of competence." Not me.

On the day after the great premiere of the "gilded legs," the rushes arrived at MGM and everybody was relieved and congratulated me.

Ronald Colman was the star of this masterpiece entitled *Kismet*. I didn't really get to know him. He was rather cool and tight-lipped. And here I don't mean "English reserve." That I know and appreciate. We simply didn't suit each other.

Before I went into the army—directly after this film—I got all the requisite inoculations so that I could go overseas without risk. My swollen arm hurt me, and I hid it from the camera so as not to disturb the beauty of the cinematic creation. Ronald Colman shrunk from any bodily contact with his partner, in this case me. The studio even changed directors during the shooting in order to persuade him to give expression to the love that was supposed to be burning in his heart. But when he finally roused himself to do so, he naturally grabbed my sore arm with its needle marks. I screamed in pain.

I don't think *Kismet* earned much money for the studio.

As soon as the shooting was over, I left the studio and my beloved Irene; I left the Hollywood I knew forever.

Contrary to what people believe, Hollywood was not a small familial community, where everybody knew everybody else. Here, one was hardly aware of the war. I broke the few bonds I had.

I left with a light heart, without any great fanfare, without a word of farewell. And that suited me fine.

PART TWO

THE WAR

"I once had a beautiful fatherland."

—Heinrich Heine

An ordinary house. I go there every day. I go there just as one goes to an office—in a hurry, so as not to be late.

I've drawn a line across all my own plans, across my wishes, all my yearnings, all my prospects for the future. I go down there and I sit down. I wait. Everybody waits. The people look worried; some sit, others pace up and down. The air is filled with smoke. Announcements come over the loudspeakers.

Numbers are called as in a lottery. Men get up and go out, and leave their chewing gum on the revolving doors.

Where are they going? No answer. Here one doesn't receive an answer to questions—but every question seems superfluous.

In short, I, too, am waiting to leave, but I'm not involved in the shoving and pushing now going on. The overheated room is emptied. Outside it's slowly growing dark. The day is coming to a close. I took a bath before coming to this house; I always bathe before coming here. At Number One. I've never known anyone in any city, on any street, who lived at a Number One address. But, here I am at Number One.

I, too, have a number. It has not yet been called. I'm here in case it should be called. Under no circumstances must I miss this moment. As soon as I'm called, someone will come to pick me up and bring me to a certain place, and all the plans and dreams that I've given up will remain behind. I'll no longer have any need to think or decide—neither for myself nor others. I'll be fed and taken care of if I run into trouble. Life will be simple. I sense this—as I sit here—I sense it. Lots of coffee and cigarettes. There's an automatic coffee machine in the hall; the paper cup melts under the heat. Did I perhaps not hear my number? It's already dark outside. "Go home now," someone announces. "That's all for today. Come again tomorrow."

The street is like another world. I go out. I move away from Number One. At home, I'll be asked the same questions as yesterday, and I'll give the same answers. I'll go to sleep, take a bath and go back to Number One again. That's my job.

The voice that rings me up every day is harsh: "Report to Number One. Number One." I've been instructed to repeat it.

The voice pronouncing this order is calm and sits behind a desk. It makes me jump and hurry through the city. Another bath. The last one. I've never bathed so often. I've never learned that in life you can't store pleasures. I constantly try to come to terms with this rule. Departure, embraces, kisses, again a bath. Once again, vows of love unto death and beyond in all eternity. I have a job to do and it makes me uneasy. I have laid down this law for myself, which explains why it's so difficult.

Hurry up and wait. Wait. But hurry up. Wait until you're called, as for an examination. We are children all over again. The same feeling. The same fear. But also the same determination to succeed. Why must I cry? But I'm not crying at all. I say good-bye. I tear myself away from the embrace of my family. A taxi. To Number One.

I almost have the feeling that I'm being driven home. I've

grown used to this place. The smoke, the people sitting around, no word addressed to anybody. We're waiting for orders. What a pleasant feeling, to wait for orders. Like when we were children and obeyed our mothers, our teachers. The Sunday School—fall in, move forward, halt, sing, fall in, in twos. No fear. You need only to obey orders. That's simple. Breathe!

Pay the taxi. Count your change for the last time. For the last time? Who knows? Perhaps tomorrow will be exactly the same as today. But you must count your money. It's dark. The taxi driver smiles. Leave him all the change you have.

It's raining. Here I am at Number One. Take me, Number One. I've already come so often; here I am again.

"When you come to the other side of the hill, you'll all be safe. One of our boys should be there, near a shed I think. But be careful; everything is camouflaged. If you go too far, you'll run into the Germans. Get going now, lower your heads."

The ride was rough—head kept low, knees bumped against the chin, teeth knocked against each other. The jeep drove headlong up the hill. Sudden bursts of speed made my head fall back. My bones cracked. I saw the sky, the low clouds, the treetops, the earth. And helmets, an irregular row of helmets. The enemy. Suddenly a hissing sound. The toe of a boot is in my back. "Take cover, stupid!" We went down the hill at breakneck speed. A jolt, screeching brakes, and something like a giant centipede seems to spring from heaven on the helmets, the shoulders, the backs.

"Crawl out! Open your eyes, dammit! Crawl out, get going, stay under the net. Head for the shed."

A thunderous din. The echo reverberates in the hills. Our hands sink in mud. If they should hit us now! What a way to die—on all fours! The door of the shed is half open. Inside, silence and darkness. I can hear breathing. I feel I'm being observed. After a while I can discern dark, dirty, bearded faces; fixed glares under pulled-down helmets, rifles like upright lances on which the light of a match is reflected.

Next to me, two crates, turned upside down. The stage. The men don't make a move. Uneasy men in combat dress. The roar of the cannon grows louder. Someone sticks a finger in my back. "Shall we begin?" "Yes," I say.

We have to begin. The orders are strict. "Begin the moment you're there. Make it brief. The shed's under sustained fire."

They don't want what we have to offer. "What idiot gave you this order, girlie?" "Fine," I say. "We'll drop it. We'll wait for a lull in the firing before leaving."

We talk in whispers and smoke. Our voices show where we're sitting in the darkness. A brief burst of laughter on one side. A soldier is telling a story. A note comes from the accordion. Hesitantly, I begin to sing softly. A saucy song that tells what's going on "in the next room." Heads turn around me. Other eyes meet mine. I continue singing in a soft voice. They listen; hold them, purr, coo, hook them, hold them. Ten minutes of distraction, that's all, girlie. That's all they want of you. Can you give it to them? Do you think you can do it?

"Good will alone is not enough," the general had said. "If you lose your nerve, if you break down, then this good will only harms me. But if you can swing it—then bravo. It'll do the soldiers good to know that you're at the front. They'll tell themselves the situation can't be so bad if Marlene Dietrich's there. If we were all going to be mowed down here, the old man certainly wouldn't expose her to such danger."

"False reasoning," he added. "But you must reduce the tension; they need that."

"I'm not afraid of dying, General, but I am afraid of being taken prisoner. I have a captain's rank. Why only captain? Why not general? Perhaps the Germans know that I'm in the European theater of operations? My rank will hardly impress them if they catch me. They'll shave off my hair, stone me, and have horses drag me through the streets. If they force me to talk on the radio, General, under no circumstances believe anything I say."

The general smiled, turned around and took a revolver out of his windbreaker. "Here, shoot rather than surrender! It's small, but it's effective."

"No love, no nothing until my baby comes home . . ." The earth quakes. A clap of thunder reverberates around us. The next time they'll surely get us with a direct hit. "No fun, with no one . . . plenty of sleep." What now? Orders. I'm a silly goose! They're right. Sitting here and singing stupid songs. "I'm lonesome, heaven knows."

The eyes of all the soldiers are riveted on me. It's becoming darker and darker. The thunderclaps now seem to be getting less frequent. I get the impression that I'm waiting impatiently for the storm to disperse, counting the seconds between the lightning flashes and the thunderclaps in order to determine the distance before I run out and fly kites.

Steps on the straw, flashlights. "Scram, get out of here, quickly."

I touch cold hands, moist shoulders, good-bye for now, see you again. Our voices sound like children's voices. See you soon! Outside only half-smothered curses, shoves in order to get rid of us before something happens. The motor is started.

A hullabaloo over the hills like a smoke signal. Maybe they won't waste their ammunition on a single jeep. Suddenly, hell breaks loose. They're taking aim at us—but they don't hit us. Quick, quick, behind the hilltop and we'll be safe. The soldier at the wheel groans under the strain, crouched over himself and muttering curses. Now we're moving along steadily, the wind is cold. It dries the sweat on our foreheads. Forest—the tires roll over tender leaves. Behind us, on either side of the hill, they're fighting.

Suddenly, the sound of a voice: "Stop!" Who's that? Nobody can be seen. Before we left, we had been warned about enemy infiltrators, paratroopers behind our lines who wear our uniforms.

"Step forward and identify yourselves." An American voice. But that doesn't mean anything. The Germans are very good at these games. "One of you come here and identify yourself." A rifle appears on our right. Hands push me out of the jeep.

"Get a move on."

Why me? Here I am, in a French forest near Pont-à-Mousson,

and I state the number of my regiment, our base, our names. The rifle is still pointed at us.

"The password?"

Heaven help me! What is the password? I haven't the slightest idea. None of us knows it. Useless to ponder over it—I've never known it.

"I don't know the password," I say.

Abraham Lincoln's birthdate? How many Presidents has the United States had?

The voice begins to ask; my answers will indicate whether or not I'm a real American. If I were a spy, I would certainly know all the answers. But I knew only three. The rifle is still pointed in my direction. Doubt is buzzing through the armed man's head like a bat.

"Why don't you know the password?"

"We left our quarters before dawn; the password had not been given yet. It wasn't communicated to us. Please, let me come nearer, you'll see that we're not lying. Or go over to the jeep; there's a guy from Oklahoma, the accordionist, and a girl from Texas in it."

"Show business people, huh? Then tell me which song was Number One on the 'Hit Parade' in the summer and fall of 1941, just before Pearl Harbor?"

My God, how was I to answer this question?

"What idiot sent you here? A paper tiger? A henpecked husband? A rocking horse general?"

"Ask the comedian then," I said. "Maybe he knows the answer."

"Don't move from the spot," the GI ordered.

Two rows of white teeth smile at me suddenly. Good white American teeth. Suddenly I don't care about the password. I'm tired. The scent of pines is in the air. I don't know whether the wind is blowing. The men are still talking it over. Did the comedian know the right answer? It seems he did, because I climb into the jeep, and we take off again.

It's too cold to talk. If you stick your nose in your scarf, the edge of your helmet touches the collar of your overcoat, and you breathe warmer air . . .

"Here we are." I open my eyes. Funny, very funny . . .

"Tomorrow early, six o'clock." Okay, Okay!

We're in Nancy. . . . It's darker than in a tunnel. Railroad artillery is pointed at us every night. There's no point in putting the lights out because they seek out their targets during the day. But, after all, it's war, and we must respect the blackout. These guns. You'd think they'd come out of another war. Their noise can drive you crazy. In the rooms, there are camp beds for our sleeping bags. That will be more comfortable than on the floor.

We drink Calvados; I vomit in the toilet.

I'll get used to it, despite the difficulties, because it's the best way to protect yourself against the cold and avoid a stay in the military hospital. So I continue to drink Calvados on an empty stomach. I would rather vomit than be hospitalized. Otherwise, what am I afraid of? I'm afraid, period. A funny feeling. Fear of failing. Fear of being unable to endure this way of living any longer. And everybody will say, smiling, "Of course, of course, that was an absurd idea in the first place." I can't confide my fear to anyone.

I must keep up the morale of my small troupe so that we, in turn, can keep up the GIs' morale.

"Hey, you, we've received orders for you. You're to report to Forward Six. The general wants to see you."

I'm in for a thorough chewing out. We're not allowed to arrive in Nancy after dark. But we can't help it. I've got a fierce headache. I walk behind my guide. His MP armband is wet because of the rain. He shows me how to get to the general. In the dark. I prefer that to any other kind of instruction. I'll manage to find him. My French is helpful when I run into natives—shadows darker than the night. I lose my way twice, but then I'm finally sitting on a low divan before General George Patton who is pacing back and forth; his boots crunch, his belt crunches. He looks like a tank too big for the village square. His remonstrances are not too severe; he even shows a certain forebearance. I'm to describe for him the problems we run into.

201

Patton never demanded that I visit hospitals. He knew that I was "needed on the front," as he put it. This decision suited me fine, as I'm utterly unfit to infuse courage or hope in others. I'm too tenderhearted. It's only with difficulty that I can keep back my tears, and the wounded notice that immediately. "It's not that your girl friend is not writing you; it takes a long time for the army post office personnel to locate the wounded." Lies of this kind stick in my throat.

It was different in the field hospitals. Here you could do something, be useful. I've too much respect for soldiers to tell them fairy tales, such as, "The war will soon be over" or "You're not as seriously wounded as it seems." I can't endure pain in the eyes of the bedridden, the despair in their voices, their frail arms around my neck. Perhaps Patton had sensed that. I remained at the front for as long as I was attached to the Third Army.

Sleepily, I look up at Patton.

"One more condition: You've got to be back at your quarters before dark." Although half asleep, I try to keep my eyes open. "I'll see to it that you get the password every morning before you leave the quarters."

He strides, rattling across the creaking floor, lifts me like a feather, and has me brought to my quarters in his command car.

I sleep deeply, almost until dawn. We have to be off. No password. Still, Patton had promised us one. Again we drive through the forest, the cold cuts into our faces. Hot coffee awaits us at our destination.

We give four performances a day, always under enemy fire. Some K rations and coffee, always coffee. Night falls. Still no password. What should we do? Drive through the forest back to Nancy? We're back to square one.

"One of you get out and identify yourself."

This time, it looks as though it's really all over for us. Once again, I am pushed out of the jeep.

The GI with the gun looks at me. "Oh, it's you. Everything's all right," he says.

It's beyond my understanding. He lets us through. We return to our quarters.

"The password?"

". . . ."

"If you don't know it, how did you get to Nancy?"

"And what is the password?"

"Right. As a matter of fact, I've got news for you. It's cheese-cake."

General Patton had kept his promise.

He had a great sense of humor and an understanding of the GIs' sense of humor. Patton was a great man. I was still with him when thousands of German soldiers surrendered, and there wasn't enough barbed wire to fence them in. They had voluntarily become prisoners, but they had to be put somewhere.

Patton was advancing so swiftly that nobody, not even an order from the General Staff, could stop him. Finally, it was decided to cut off his gasoline supplies.

"It seems," he said to me, "that an American-Russian agreement has established the borders where Americans and Russians are to meet."

General Patton was about to go beyond this border, which is quite understandable when you're close on the enemy's heels. It's difficult to stand still when you're going full speed, and the road ahead is all clear.

But he was forced to stay put. No more gasoline. He took me (as interpreter) with him to the foul smelling camps. German generals in uniform saluted him from twenty steps away. I shuttled between Patton and the generals, transmitting messages. Patton wanted to know all about troop movements, the number of soldiers, tanks engaged, equipment, etc.

Each time I left, he bade me good-bye very politely. Without him, the Third Army would not have been what it was.

I still have the revolver he gave me. After the war, I hid it when I arrived at LaGuardia Airport. We had to give up all the precious Lugers, all the weapons we had gathered during the war, but we did so reluctantly and under pressure.

* * *

We took off from New York during a hailstorm. We had received survival instructions in case we had to make an emergency landing on water on this unforgettable night, the most improbable of nights to take off, after all this waiting.

Huddled closely together in the damp fuselage we had set out for an unknown destination; our instructions were sealed. We were allowed to open them only after takeoff, and read: "CASABLANCA."

This word dispelled all our fears. It was really Europe, and not the Pacific. Although we had been almost sure that we were bound for Europe, we were relieved to read "Casablanca" in black and white. And we rose higher through the hailstorm.

I was in an airplane for the first time. I no longer know today whether this was also true for my fellow passengers. Fatigue overcame us; we fell asleep. From time to time, we would awaken and repeat the security instructions: "In the event of an emergency landing on water, the rubber raft is over there, the radio apparatus over here, the K rations here, the flares there," and so on.

The soldiers crammed together in the plane had not yet seen combat; they came fresh from the peaceful training camps. Up till now they had enjoyed typical American nourishment and slept on American soil in clean, soft beds. In the flames of the cigarette lighters, you could see the fear in their faces. Nobody spoke—all we heard was the throbbing of the motors.

Casablanca. I knew this city only from films. Mysterious, fantastic, like a picture in a book read a long time ago. During the flight, we—that is, the group to which I had been assigned— didn't get to know each other well, but later we were to become like a family. Danny Thomas, a young comedian "with a future" constantly cracked jokes, the tenor snored lightly in his sleep, the accordionist held his whisky bottle close to himself, and Lynn Mayberry, the Texan lady, was wide awake after a few hours of sleep. At that time, there were no jets, so the flight was a very long one.

Abe Lastfogel, who directed theatrical activities on the front, had lavished special care on our crowd, so as to assure "a good performance" on the stages, as he liked to emphasize. He worked day and night; he was fantastic. "Danny Thomas has made a very promising start in Chicago," he explained to me. "I think he'll be a star one day. But I would like to have him in your group for another reason; he's a swell guy. We, you and I, realize the importance of our jobs. So, no hams. For your sake, but also for the army's sake. You'll have to perform in Camp Meade before the censor, but once you get the green light, there'll be no further reviewing or rewriting."

Abe Lastfogel also told me that Danny Thomas had an engagement at a nightclub in the United States, and could stay with us for only six weeks. As for myself, I was prepared to stick it out until the end of the war. I saw no reason why I should return to America, once I was "on the spot." Many didn't believe me. They didn't think I would last for so long.

The program was flawless. Danny cracked his jokes; I sang a couple of songs; together we performed some sketches written for us by celebrities like Garson Kanin and Burgess Meredith. We also executed a mind-reading trick I had already performed with Orson Welles in front of GI recruits. The Texan Lynn Mayberry had her own number. We could perform on trucks or tanks, since we didn't need a stage. We gave four or five performances a day, and like nomads, we would go in a jeep from one unit to another. In fact, our accordionist was a *real* Gypsy. I've always loved the sound of the accordion, and unlike the tenor, I didn't miss the piano at all.

Abe Lastfogel always knew where we were. God only knows through what miracle he always managed to find us. He had taken on a formidable task. To organize hundreds of performances for the Armed Forces, to combine the different talents, to choose the artists, to prepare them for their acts, and in addition, he also had taken on the responsibility for the morale of the troupe. And he did all this with enormous generosity; he dedicated all his time and energies to this task. To this day, I say, "Bravo, Mr. Lastfogel!"

The performance was approved by the censorship authorities in Camp Meade, and the waiting began, since at first we had to remain in New York. We all had code names.

Finally, we landed in Casablanca. No lights on the runways. Today, since I'm slightly more familiar with flying, I'd be scared to death. But, at that time, with my incredible naïveté, I contented myself with following the example of my fellow passengers and fastened my seat belt.

The plane made a bumpy landing, and the motors came to a sudden stop. Soldiers stormed the cabin.

"Who are you? . . . To which unit do you belong?"

The men from the base didn't know what they were supposed to do with us. This disturbed them.

"Let's just wait here calmly," I said to Danny and the other members of the troupe. "After this long trip, we don't want to make trouble on our arrival."

Danny agreed. We waited. The night was cold, or perhaps it seemed colder because we were so tired. Finally a colonel showed up and said that nobody had been told of our arrival, but that he would look around for quarters for us.

We left the plane and climbed into a jeep. I wanted to see the French coast, the country that I loved and that was occupied by the enemy; the country that we would free when the time came. The driver made a slight detour, and I imagined I saw France. The others didn't understand my emotions, but they were quiet as I dried my tears.

We visited the bases in North Africa and finally arrived at Oran. Italy was the next step from there. Meanwhile, we had gotten to know each other well. Danny beat on his helmet as though it were a bongo drum and invented witty lyrics to familiar melodies, lyrics that related our experiences; we sang, laughed, slept, ate—and we took cover.

The first thing you learn during a raid is to hide. Everything else is simple. Three things count: eating, sleeping, taking cover. My shinbones are still scarred, souvenirs of all the GIs who, cursing, threw me on the ground. For a long time, I believed that the bullets fired from the enemy lines actually were coming from our own ranks. I learned about that. I was more afraid about my teeth than about my legs. Thank God there was always a GI nearby to give me a shove.

Of all the soldiers I met, the GIs were the bravest. Bravery is simple when you're defending your own country or hearth. But to be bundled off to a foreign country to fight for "God knows what," to lose your eyes, arms, legs, and return home a cripple—that's something quite different.

I've seen these men during a battle and afterward. Long after the war I saw them again—in their homes, hobbling around on their crutches, or seated, legless, happily surrounded by their wives and children.

I've seen them all. I've loved them all, long after the world forgot them. In this area, I have an excellent memory, and my memories are unextinguishable.

How often I've met veterans, taxi drivers who talk with me and remember: "We were happier then." Then I ask them to drive once more around Central Park, so that we can continue to conjure up remembrances of those years and feel our togetherness as before.

I regret above all that today we no longer know any real camaraderie, that mutual trust we once felt. But it seems that the best human qualities only appear in times of crisis. Today, there are no longer any "times of crisis." America is a country marked by great insecurity, incapable of recuperating from the alleged "shame" of the Nixon era. Politics is always dishonorable. For me, there is nothing special about the "moral crisis" that has overcome America. As though no one had ever behaved badly before!

Never talk with soldiers if you want to live a peaceful life without nightmares and bad consciences. Don't talk with us, because we don't need to hear your ridiculous complaints. We thought the Second World War would certainly mean the end of wars. When we returned to the United States at the end of the war, we were greeted with stupid remarks. We were not allowed in restaurants without wearing ties, no matter how many medals a paratrooper wore on his chest. I was in the Champagne Room of El Morocco when I saw men, who had defended civilians in a war that had seemed largely irrelevant to them, actually turned back and not allowed to enter. And those civilians who had never gone through a war or ever heard the roar of a gun, sat in front of their thick steaks, staring coldly at us, as though we were pariahs.

But I must confess this pleased us. With well-chosen words, we told them to go to hell.

The years of "re-integration," a beautiful phrase, followed. Personally, I needed a very long time before I "re-integrated" myself. I walked through the streets of New York and simply could not believe that the politicians were dishing out more and more lies. We would meet in the streets; I took care of the soldiers—pardon, the veterans—paid their hotel bills, and tried to alleviate their misfortunes. The government didn't give a damn. Contrary to what we entertainers had been told to promise the soldiers after each of our wartime performances in Europe, there was no work for them. The veterans trudged through the streets.

The bureaucracy—the eternal enemy in one's own country.

None of the promises were kept.

Why do I feel so responsible? During the tough battles in the Ardennes, I had assured the soldiers that jobs would await them on their return. I gave them the same hopes I gave to myself, and I convinced them—because I was told to.

Without noticing it, as often happens, my hands and feet froze in the terrible cold of the Ardennes. My hands swelled up like balloons. I was told to put a kind of jelly over them, which made the swollen fingers look like the paws of a rare animal. That didn't matter to me, since I'm an incorrigible optimist. I knew nothing about the later consequences of such frostbite. It was more difficult to treat my feet. But we wore wide, comfortable combat boots, which considerably lessened the pain.

To this day, my hands become a curious color when they get warm; and their skin is as delicate as a baby's bottom. Sometimes I notice that someone is watching me during dinner, and I realize that my hands on the table are not a very pretty sight. I quickly hide them.

During the war, of course, all that counted for little. What was important was to do your job—and to do it well. When I read books in which actors tell stories about their work and how they went on tour in the United States, in spite of a fever or a sore throat, I can't help but smile. What, after all, is so important about a "performance"? Actors are really strange people.

Not Danny Thomas! He's a great guy—open, bright. He's not only gifted but also a man and a gentleman at the same time—something so rare! He taught me all the secrets of his art.

As I've said earlier, we had rehearsed our performances, and I felt secure about my numbers, but in Italy, I was suddenly standing before thousands of soldiers, seated all over the hillsides and bombarding me with war whoops, whistles, and propositions of all kinds. This wasn't in the program, and I didn't know how to react.

Danny taught me how to keep my self-control, how to impose silence on the audience. He also taught me a flair for timing; how to get a laugh, and how to stop one, and how to handle all those desperate kids who wanted to humiliate anyone who hadn't been in combat. This hostility was the most difficult to overcome. And Danny could do it superbly. He even rescued our tenor, a very nice fellow who sang "Besame Mucho" beautifully, from their hostile mockery. He was booed by the GIs the moment he appeared onstage. For reasons unknown to us, Danny had escaped the draft.

Danny kept everyone's morale up, including mine. When he left us, we had to wait for his replacement, who couldn't hold a candle to him. It wasn't his successor's fault. For who could replace Danny Thomas? In my thoughts and in my heart—nobody. He left instructions behind, which we followed to the letter. Long after he was gone from the battlefront, we remembered his words and suggestions. We sorely missed his way of singing, and drumming on his helmet, but we carried on, often telling ourselves, "Now, Danny would have done it this way or that way," but we didn't have our hearts in it, and we missed him very much. I don't think he ever knew that.

A couple of times I tried to tell him, but there were too many people standing around, and I don't think he heard me. Will he hear me now? I wonder. Time changes things and people. He is happy and has a large family—God bless him. Danny was irre-

placeable, but we survived that terrible winter, and stayed in
Europe until the end of the war.

We were sleeping somewhere in a shed. Suddenly I felt
myself being shaken and I heard voices saying, "It's the eighty-
eights." That meant nothing to me, but I could tell something was
wrong.

"They're pretty close by; the eighty-eights are aimed at us—
clear out, clear out!"

We crawled out of our sleeping bags—thank God we were
fully dressed—and ran out of there. But where to? Someone
bellowed "Run!" So we ran.

A jeep, jump in, helmets bump against each other. For
heaven's sake, hurry up; the eighty-eights aimed at us; what's
happened? How did they break through the lines? The front
of the First Army was solid. Hurry up, get going. Destination
Rheims.

"Rheims?" I ask. "But that's way behind us."

"Anybody ask you for your opinion? No? Then, clear out, get
going."

So we started moving, after I had gathered our things and all
my costumes together. Had I known that enemy troops had
broken through our lines, I would never have dreamed of taking
my clothes with me, but we had no idea of what was going on. We
figured it was just another alert, like so many we had already gone
through.

We came through. The 77th Division, composed of green
kids fresh from America, was wiped out. Then General Anthony
McAuliffe appeared on the scene, with his famous "Nuts!" and
managed to drive the Germans back, and saved us—when I say
"us," I mean not only individuals, but whole nations, the Allies.

The 82nd Airborne Division, under the command of General
James Gavin, arrived, and everything was once more under control. But losses had been heavy. There were many wounded, many
amputations, and a flood of letters went across the Atlantic to the
families.

Since we had received no instructions in Rheims, we proceeded to our headquarters in Paris. After a few days, we were again sent out on tour.

The war continued. I no longer remember the places and towns which we passed through. But I do remember that one day, I was ordered to report to Forward Ten in the rear—Forward Ten was the code name for the commander in chief. A soldier is always reluctant to fall back. So I began to argue, and the only answer I got was, "Orders are orders!"

The meeting took place in the Hürtgen Forest. General Omar Bradley was seated in a mobile home, as if he were waiting for me. Maps hung from the walls; the general was very pale and looked tired.

"I guess I can trust you," he said.

"Thank you, General," I replied.

"Tomorrow we're going to enter Germany, and, for the time being, you belong to the unit that will be the first to set foot on German territory. I've discussed the problem with Eisenhower, and we've decided that it would be best if you stayed in the rear and, for example, visited hospitals. We don't want you to be seen in Germany. If anything happens to you, we couldn't assume any responsibility, and wouldn't know how to deal with the criticism that would inevitably arise."

I was dumbfounded. "And this is why you asked me to come here?" I asked.

"Yes," he said. "The situation is very serious. The Germans would just love to get their hands on you. That would be a disaster."

I spoke in angelic tones; I pleaded with him; I did everything conceivable to tug at his heartstrings.

Here I must mention one very important point: All generals are lonely. The GIs can disappear in the bushes with a local girl. Not so the generals. They are protected day and night; eyes follow every one of their movements. Never and nowhere can they kiss someone, or lay someone down on a haystack. They are hopelessly alone.

General Bradley finally allowed me to enter Germany. His

only conditions were that I had to have two bodyguards who were to protect me day and night. The two soldiers assigned to this detail were delighted. What luck! They had thought they would be putting their lives on the line, and now all they had to do for the duration of the war was to stick close to my heels.

We pushed into Germany, and surprisingly, we didn't feel at all threatened. Nor did we feel the slightest fear. The people on the street embraced me; they asked me to put in a good word for them with the Americans; they couldn't have been friendlier. They welcomed me into my country, even though they knew I was on the other side.

American Army regulations were different from those in the English and French armies. For example, Germans were forbidden to be in the vicinity of any American quarters, but the French and British permitted a certain coexistence.

We were billeted in a small German cottage, whose inhabitants asked me to help them. They couldn't find a place for their cow anywhere else; would they be allowed to come feed her? They thought I had miraculous powers and could solve all their problems. But we were pushing ahead very rapidly and had no time to worry about every peasant's cow.

Often I had to speak on village squares, to tell people to go home and close their shutters, and not clog the streets, so that our tanks could drive through. No interpreters were available, since the troops in the rear had not kept up with our progress. After each time I spoke, I would be asked, admiringly, what it was that I had said because the streets would be cleared instantly. I would answer, "Does it matter? They cleared out, didn't they?"

We had no problems in Aachen—most of the city had been destroyed (precisely the parts where we stayed). We didn't run into any problems as we pushed through the rest of Germany, and my two bodyguards had a marvelous time.

However, in Aachen we did get body lice. And don't let anybody tell you that crabs can be transmitted only by another person. And don't believe they can't crawl. I have seen them crawl.

One day, it was announced that showers would be installed,

Star portrait by Cecil Beaton

Star portrait by Edward Steichen

Guest performances throughout the world: Las Vegas, 1959

The Olympia, Paris, 1959

Germany, 1960

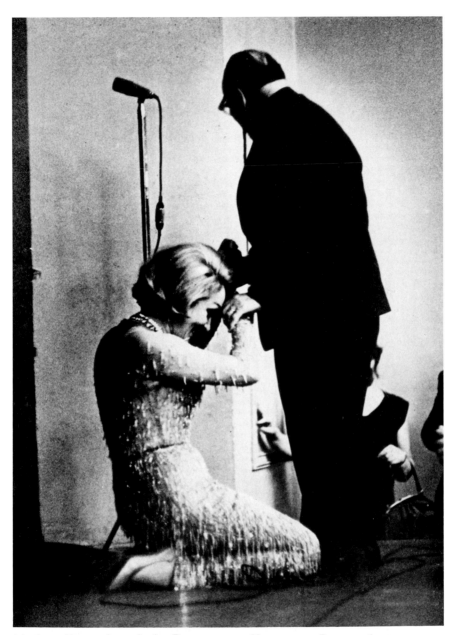

Marlene Dietrich with the Russian poet Konstantin Paustovsky in
Moscow, 1964

Jubilation in Moscow in front of
the Pushkin Theater, 1964

Jubilation in Sydney in front of
the theater

Final applause at close, Sydney

Marlene Dietrich with Erich Maria Remarque, late thirties

Marlene Dietrich and Jean Gabin, early forties, Paris and Hollywood

Marlene Dietrich with Charlie Chaplin at the Comédie Française, Paris

Marlene Dietrich and Noel Coward
at Café de Paris, London, 1954

Arrival in Paris: welcomed by
Gilbert Bécaud, 1959

With Edith Piaf in Melun, 1959

Marlene Dietrich and Jean Cocteau at the Théâtre de l'Etoile, Paris, 1959

Marlene Dietrich and Orson Welles at the Théâtre de l'Etoile, Paris, 1959

Marlene Dietrich with Burt Bacharach, the director and composer of her guest performances

Guest performance at the Prince of Wales Theatre, London, 1963

Guest performance at the Prince of Wales Theatre,
London, 1963

Guest performance, Malmö, 1963

Guest performance, Warsaw, 1964

Guest performance, Moscow, 1964

and that the women could use them in exchange for "some favors."
The "favors" were these: for two buckets of water, one look; for
three buckets of water, two looks; for four buckets of water (which
you needed if you wanted to wash your hair), some kisses and as
many looks as possible.

We were ready for anything. The prospect of some soap and
water after so long a time without was enough for us to forget all
shyness, all modesty.

It was on this occasion that we discovered our crabs. They
didn't make us itch or scratch. They were just there, obviously
content with their surroundings, and they didn't bother us. We
traced them. Dark spots. Easy to see. Lynn Mayberry, our dark-
haired Texan, ran to her tent, examined herself, came back and
said that she had some, too.

Our problem was to get rid of them. No doctor was available,
since we had advanced so quickly. After a few days, I had a
"brilliant idea." I think I have never had such a stupid idea.

"When I perform my mind-reading act and ask a GI to join
me on the truck, I'll ask him to come to my tent with me after the
performance." This was my idea. Nothing was more sensible than
asking a soldier, right?

If you want to know which person is suitable to be used in a
magic trick, you must first look for certain signs. Since this magic
act brought me rather close to the audience, as often as possible I
would pick a soldier wearing glasses. Men wearing glasses are not
as fresh as those who don't wear them. By that, I mean that when I
hung around the men, the fellows without glasses would rather
rudely grab me and not allow me to end my number in an orderly
way. Eyeglass wearers, on the other hand, were less aggressive,
decidedly more cooperative, and helped me to bring the performance to a proper close.

During one of our four daily performances, the moment
arrived when I had to pick an eyeglass wearer. But I couldn't see a
single pair of eyeglasses in the light of the setting sun.

I stoically endured my discomfort. Three days went by.

Finally, on the fourth day, I vaguely noticed something that looked like eyeglasses on the distant hillside. The sun was setting slowly, and I said, "You, there—no, not you—you. Yes, would you please come up here and help me with my act?"

The man who got up was very tall. He jumped on the tailgate of the truck, as though he were jumping over a step ten centimeters high. While talking to him loudly, I managed to whisper, in between, "Come to my tent behind the truck, after the performance." He didn't bat an eye.

I returned to my tent, told my guardian angels that I'd be having a visitor and waited. The tent lay in darkness. Only a ray of light penetrated between the entrance flaps.

I stood and observed the odd designs and images reflected onto the dirty fabric of my dress by the sequins that caught the light and changed with the rhythm of my breathing.

Suddenly a huge silhouette appeared at the entrance to the tent.

"Ma'am," said a voice.

The man had removed his glasses.

"Good evening," I said. "Thank you for coming."

He was silent. I mustered all my courage. "I don't know how to put this to you." Then I waited.

"You don't know where we could go?" he asked finally.

"No, that's not it. I just would like to tell you that I've got crabs."

Quick as lightning, he replied, "That doesn't bother me."

"You don't understand."

"So, what's it all about?"

"What can I do to get rid of them?"

"Is that all you wanted?"

"Yes."

Then he came toward me. Closer, he looked even taller. He was a Texan, and Texans are a breed unto themselves. The reflections of light from the sequins played on his face. He looked angry.

"Didn't they give you any de-lousing powder? You can get that anytime."

"I know, but I thought it was to be used only against ordinary lice."

And he, growing angrier, "Spray it over you and don't wash."
Silence.

"And if you want to know how they die," he erupted, "the powder paralyzes their jaws so they starve to death."

I remained rooted to the spot. He bowed low, turned around on his heel, and pushed the entrance flap aside. I had to give another performance, and hoped I would see him again, but he had disappeared forever. I'm sure he was furious. Texans certainly aren't used to that kind of conversation with a woman, especially not in the middle of a forest in Europe, while all of his buddies were certainly waiting to hear a detailed description of a most improbable conquest.

We stayed quite awhile in Aachen. We lived in a bombed-out house; bathtubs were suspended in midair, but at least there was a roof under which we could spread our sleeping bags. There's something reassuring about a roof.

The war in Europe was marked by endless rain. Mud was everywhere, moisture was everywhere, and crept into our clothing—and then there were the rats.

Rats have icy paws. You're lying on the bare floor in your sleeping bag, the blanket pulled up to your chin, and these creatures run over your face, their paws as cold as death; they give you the jitters.

Then the bombs—are they V-1s or V-2s—also scare the pants off you, and you don't know which way to turn.

The rats in Aachen gave us no peace. They came every night. I sprayed a kind of wall of de-lousing powder around me—in vain. This way, at least, I got rid of the crabs—and of my Texan friend.

There was a Texas division in the army. My God, how proud they were of their origins. When they took over a city, they would teach the children that the United States was part of Texas. But no matter how proud and arrogant they were, they did a damned good job during the war. There aren't men like this anywhere else. And nobody had better try to contradict me.

215

Once I said to a Texan soldier, "You're beautiful," and he answered me, "Ma'am, you should never say that to a man."

"And what should I say to a man?"

"In Texas," he replied, "the most you can tell a man is that his pants fit him well." Well, that's quite true; their pants do fit them well.

They are men who inspire trust and confidence; they are dynamic. Texas is an immense state. That explains why there were so many soldiers in the Texas division. Glory and honor to you all! I embrace them, and send them all my love, from far away, through space and time. I think there's a photo in which I appear with this Texas division, somewhere in Europe.

Back to the rats. Our stay in Aachen dragged on. The Red Cross nurses helped as well as they could. They had made doughnuts, and we helped distribute them to the liberated POWs and the survivors of the concentration camps.

Rats everywhere. Now we put wet towels over our faces so that these creatures would run off somewhere else. They didn't like "alien" coldness; they liked only their own cold paws in their own cold environment.

Apropos of rats, one day we were performing in a real movie house in Aachen. It was cold, as usual. The proprietor of the place came over to me and asked if I would like a cup of hot coffee.

All the others said, "Don't take it, it might be poisoned."

"No, they would never dare," I answered and drank the coffee.

Then I asked the man, "Why did you offer me the coffee? After all, you know I'm on the other side."

"Of course, I know that you're on the other side, but"—and he sighed—"but you are also the Blue Angel. . . ."

All that because of a film!

I was able to see the same reaction everywhere in Germany. Perhaps the Germans had not forgiven me, but they knew me, begged me to help with their problems, something for which they cannot be reproached.

I was born a German, and I shall always remain German, regardless of what has been said about me on this score. I had to change my citizenship when Hitler came to power. Otherwise, I never would have done it. America took me into her bosom when I no longer had a native country worthy of the name, and I'm thankful to her for it. I've lived in this country and have abided by its laws. I've become a good citizen, but in my heart I'm German.

German in my soul? Just where is this soul? German because of my education. That I can't deny, the traces cannot be over-looked. German philosophy and German poetry are my back-ground. I would never have believed that roots are important. Today I know they are. You can love your adopted country out of gratitude and also because you gradually let yourself be infused by the values of its people, by its true aims, its sense of humor, its feelings.

Thus, new roots are planted alongside the old ones.

We ended our tour in Aachen as planned and returned to our barracks to report that everything had proceeded according to plan. But the war was far from over. Since we were the fifth wheel on the wagon, we were shipped around here and there, like many others, civilian or soldier.

President Roosevelt died, and we had to comfort saddened soldiers who were as overwhelmed by this loss as we were our-selves.

The news was given to me in the middle of a performance. I was used to difficult jobs—when you've seen lots of men die, you become hard inside and out. We interrupted the performance, and I went up to the soldiers who sat quietly in front of me on the slope of a hill. We talked for a long time, until darkness fell, then scattered, to return to our duties.

We advanced as far as Holland, where many more V-1s and V-2s were being dropped than ever before. These rockets were somewhat different from ordinary bombs: They struck without warning. It was impossible to foresee them or to protect yourself from them. Only our optimism helped us survive. Only hope kept up our morale—hope and Calvados. It made life seem rosy, and it also helped us sleep.

In the north, we performed before British troops. We varied our jokes a bit since, in comparison to the Americans, the English are "rather dense," or so it was said. But they certainly weren't that way on the battlefield.

The Canadians were the liveliest of all. We met them a lot in Italy. Every time there was some kind of trouble and we heard that the Canadians were coming to help us, everybody was pleased, including the General Staff. They were dependable. They had a combination of the best American and British qualities. They exhibited a British stoicism when they were entrusted with an impossible mission. And they didn't swear as much as the Americans.

In 1944 we experienced a sad Christmas, as well as the return of the lice. But by now we were ready for them, and knew how to get rid of them. Nevertheless, we were sad. Because of Christmas *and* because of the lice. We all felt down, exhausted. It was becoming harder for us to perform with the same enthusiasm as before. Although I had learned a lot, I still wasn't as good as Danny Thomas. But we had to make the soldiers happy.

The German counteroffensive had been driven back, and we pushed on ahead. But how long would this war last?

Back in my early childhood, I had learned that God doesn't fight on any army's side. So there was little point in praying. Nonetheless, before every battle prayers were read, all kinds of incantations were recited, staged by all sorts of preachers.

We attended these ceremonies, and I saw how the soldiers stood in place, as though they couldn't believe their ears. "You will be fighting." I couldn't believe it either, but I counted for nothing.

The Jewish sermons were the most convincing, for the Old Testament says, "An eye for an eye, a tooth for a tooth." This is an appropriate farewell address for a man setting out for bloody combat. I have always wondered how Christians reconcile the injunction "Turn the other cheek" with war.

But they all went, with or without prayer.

Since then, I've given up any belief in God, in a "light" that leads us, or anything of this sort. Goethe has said, "If God created this world, then he should review his plan." Probably it's a matter of a botched plan.

The confusion continued to the day we won the war. Everything had come to an end; we slept in stables, tramped through villages. We waited for instructions that never came. Once again, as at the beginning of this whole thing, we waited. We were worn out, discouraged. All around us were dirty, pitiful figures waiting to be discharged and sent home. Some were sent home, others to the Pacific. The war continued there. As for us, we just sat around. We had our K rations, coffee, sleeping bags—and we waited for orders. We slept. Now we could sleep peacefully. We were sure that someone was on guard outside.

We had to be repatriated when the war in Europe came to an end. A large-scale organization was created for this purpose: Thousands of planes came to return thousands of soldiers to their homes, an air armada to bring back equipment, documents, etc.

We waited until it was our turn.

We listened to the radio—news from the Pacific—and spoke about our gloomy future. We stuck it out. The fact that we had to rely on ourselves was difficult to endure. No joking could banish our uneasiness. It was May, but our quarters in Chatou were ice cold. We were aware of our insignificance and didn't expect "orders" from anybody.

"Fall in, by twos!" Familiar sounds, then, finally: "Destination: LaGuardia Airport, New York. Group number so and so, get ready." God knows, we *were* ready.

We didn't say a word in the plane that brought us back to the United States. These men had won the war, but they couldn't celebrate it. The war in the Pacific lurked in the back of their minds. The plane was jam-packed; we hardly had room for our legs and feet. Nothing to eat. No laughter, none of the usual joking. We were all together for the last time, but already far from each other, like civilians.

The return flight was longer and more quiet than we thought it would be. The victors were returning to their homes, and, how ridiculous, our biggest worry was that nothing should go wrong on the flight. Yet, deep within, the men were happy, only they couldn't show it. They were thinking of the buddies they had left behind in simple graves; they were bitter. Americans are a naïve people. They have not experienced war on their own soil since the

Civil War. They know it only from history books. They react like children when they are in the presence of a real tragedy. Their naïveté makes them almost saintly.

We landed at LaGuardia. It was raining—of course! Nobody was there to welcome us. We dragged our baggage along, were searched from top to toe, and had to give up our precious war souvenirs. Then we found ourselves penniless at the taxi stand and didn't know where to go.

Anybody in the United States who has no money is really a nobody. The scum of the earth. We explained that we had just come back from the war—in vain. People didn't care. Nobody wanted to listen to us. "We're too busy, ask somebody else."

Finally, I talked a taxi driver into helping us, with the promise of the biggest tip of his life, if he would take us to the St. Regis.

The taxi driver believed me and drove us to the hotel.

"Good day, Miss Dietrich. Good day. Good day."

"Can you pay the taxi for me? I don't have a cent."

"Of course. All you have to do is sign a blank check. A big tip for the driver?"

"Yes, a big tip."

"A nice suite as usual?"

"Yes. And then I need some cash."

"Of course. Write out the check, and I'll have the money brought to your room."

There we stood with our dirty field packs at the elegant reception desk of the Hotel St. Regis. The war was not yet over, but here you got the impression that no one had ever heard of it.

Since the hotel employees didn't know my financial situation, they accepted the check I wrote out. I made it out for a hundred dollars. I don't know why I didn't make it out for more. I was really unable to act without someone telling me what to do, and I had been out of America for so long that a hundred dollars seemed like a fortune.

We went upstairs, and my buddies took baths, one after the other. I ordered food. Delicious American food that nourished my guests when they finished their baths. We decided to say good-bye before sunset, since everybody wanted to get home before dark.

The farewells were very sad, but there were no tears or sighs—we had experienced too much for that.

I remained behind, alone in my suite at the St. Regis and waited for the maid to clean the bathtub, so that I could take a bath, the first in many months. My God, how lonely I felt! Too early to phone California, and an inconvenient hour for the offices in New York.

And what would I tell them anyway? That I was back from the war? Who was interested in the war?

The telephone rang; it was my agent, Charlie Feldman. I had tried to reach him while the others were taking their baths.

"Please," he said, "don't write any checks. They won't be covered."

"I couldn't know that," I answered.

"Hang up, let me give it some thought; I'll call you back."

I took a bath. I lay in bed, stared at the ceiling and waited—for what? Suddenly I no longer had any roots! Where were they? In the war that had raged in Europe?

I was utterly confused. I had already accustomed myself to being a resident alien and then becoming an American citizen. Now I had to adjust and re-integrate myself all over again. What I mean is that I came back to America, a country that had not suffered in the war, a country that really didn't know what its soldiers had gone through over there on foreign soil. My hatred of "carefree" Americans dates from this time.

It shouldn't be difficult for anyone to imagine that I was not greatly loved in the fall and winter of 1945.

The more soldiers returned from the Pacific, the fewer jobs were available in the United States. We went through the streets, and everything revolted us. We no longer felt a sense of purpose. I'm not speaking of myself but of the sympathy I felt for these men. It was a difficult time for all of us. For us, who were completely with them in mind and heart.

The hospitals (to get to them, you had to travel all over New York as far as the suburbs) were filled with wounded soldiers, whom we patted and comforted, whom we read to, and once again promised that their wounds would heal. Again the same lies, the same dialogues of the "come dance with me . . ." kind. The worst cases were the amputees. It was absolutely senseless to say "soon we'll dance again," but they smiled.

Sad, sad experiences of the postwar period.

I needed a whole year to "re-integrate" myself; I, who had come through it unscathed, except for my frozen feet and hands. A whole year of despair and anger, a year in which I had to take insults, unintentional for the most part, but all the more shocking, because they came from well-fed citizens of the United States who didn't have the slightest notion of what was going on outside their borders. At that time I naïvely believed that every American had heard of bombs, destruction and death, but I was to discover that this was the case with only a few. Above all, they didn't want to be reminded of the existence of the war.

I'm not talking about the families of the soldiers who had fought at the front, but of people who had never experienced war, whose daily routines had never been shattered by the war, who had always preserved their inner peace.

This expression "inner peace" reminds me of an experience during the war. I was in Italy, in Naples to be exact, at the Hotel Parco.

A friend of mine, the actor Jean-Pierre Aumont, had contacted me through official channels, and I received permission to pay a visit to the French unit to which he belonged.

He had come to pick me up in his jeep on the previous day. He gave off a peculiar odor.

"I slept under a tank next to a dead Senegalese soldier," he explained to me. "You must excuse me."

We heated some water and brought it to my "room with bath" so he could take his first bath in weeks.

Jean-Pierre Aumont was a well brought up young man, very educated, with an extraordinary sense of humor.

We set out before dawn. He's a Capricorn, like myself, so we knew what we were doing. At least we thought we knew—Jean-Pierre Aumont didn't have a map at hand. Soon, after a few hours, we were stuck in the mud. The jeep wouldn't move forward or backward.

As the genuine Frenchman and soldier that he was, he said, "Let's leave it here." From the distance we could hear the rumble of guns.

So we left our bemired jeep and trudged in the direction of the river, which we had to cross to arrive at our destination. Before us stretched a long strip of land. White ribbons fluttered in the wind. Detached from their poles, they swayed like clothes on a line. We knew that this was a mine field and the only way to the river. As far as we could see, all the bridges were blown up. How were we to get across to the other bank?

"Listen, Jean-Pierre," I said to him. "You've got your whole life ahead of you. So, I'll go in front of you, as best I can, and you follow right in my footsteps. Then I'll be blown to bits before you set foot on these filthy contraptions."

You should have seen how we argued with each other in this no-man's land. For Jean-Pierre, of course, loved to argue. He said, "I'll go first, and *you* follow in *my* tracks." No sooner said than done. He showed me how to do it.

Looking back, the scene strikes me as very funny: a German and a Frenchman lost in Italy, who outdo each other in politeness in order to decide who will be the first to be blown to bits.

Naturally, he led the way. We crossed the mine field and then the river, leaping from rock to rock. We were soaked through and through when we got to the other bank. Artillery fire, a fantastic spectacle. We didn't know where we were. Still out of breath, we looked around us, and I said, "Stay behind me. If anyone comes I'll take care of him, friend or foe. Just leave it to me."

Dusk. The sudden sound of a motor. "Stay behind me," I said to Jean-Pierre, but he didn't listen.

To our left behind the curve of the road, the sound of the motor continued. It was impossible to identify who it was. We waited.

Suddenly we saw the signs on the jeep coming toward us. We waved and it came to a stop. Two GIs: "What do you want? Who are you?" And, turning to me, "Are you a nurse, or what?"

"I'm Marlene Dietrich," I said. "We're lost. Can you show us the way to Naples?"

"If you're Marlene Dietrich, then I'm General Eisenhower. Let's go, get in."

So we returned to Naples, and Jean-Pierre returned empty-handed to his unit.

We said no more about this incident. Since we both have a sense of humor, we can both laugh about it today. But many tragedies have soured our laughter.

Jean-Pierre is a man before he's an actor. If only all living actors were as good as he is! The actor's calling is not suitable for a man. Yet Jean-Pierre has ennobled it, now that the greats, Raimu and Gabin, are no more. Except for Jean-Pierre Aumont, I met no other great actors during the war.

Some American actors volunteered for service; we called them "Ninety-Day Wonders" because they immediately received officer's rank, without any training.

Most actors did not fight. Some did, but not very many. We often wondered what they would tell their children. Then we stopped wondering about it. Like everything else, it, too, went down the drain. Everything ended in the bitter disappointment of the warriors. No triumphal marches to welcome them home.

But the names of some men—George Patton, Anthony Mc-Auliffe, Maxwell Taylor, James Gavin (the "fighting generals"), and Omar Bradley (the brain who directed the war)—are now in the history books.

America wanted to champion peace and, so, made winning the war its goal in order to achieve this aim. No one can contest their success on this score. America lost its best men, but it defeated the Nazis. Americans fought them without really understanding why they were fighting; they simply did their duty. It mustn't be forgotten that most of them were drafted; therefore, they didn't want to fight but had to fight. And they were forcibly drawn into a war about which they knew nothing.

We traveled through countless German towns and villages. At the end of the war we ended up in Pilsen, in Czechoslovakia.

Everywhere we heard the same stories, the same suffering on

both sides, everywhere. And no prospect of salvation except through the "end of the war," for which everyone was waiting.

The war ended in general mourning. At the end of the First World War, I was still too young to be able to remember it. But I imagine it wasn't much different. The same despair, the same depression, the same dirge: "Tell me, oh tell me, why I marched off to war?"

The same tumult in the minds of all soldiers. The same fear of the future, the fear of returning home and discovering that wife and children have become strangers. The fear of being alone again, as before, of having no buddies, as before, of being unable to share the worries and tears of others. Becoming a head of a family again and being exposed to the harsh criticism of the women who resented their husbands but who had done every-thing—in this country that for so long had been spared the horrors of war—to "trap" the husband, whom they now reproach daily when the refrigerator or the heating system doesn't work.

How can the soldier, returning from war, speak to his wife and children when they are spending the whole day in front of the radio or TV?

So many marriages and engagements broke up as a result of the war. Absence doesn't make the heart grow fonder. To the contrary.

Many soldiers with whom I've spoken explained that they had married the first girl they could find, so that in case they were killed someone would get the government pension. So it's under-standable that the relationship between the married couple ceased to exist on the husband's return. And no sadness. This kind of marriage had no future, no hope.

That is all I have to say about the war. Nothing very impor-tant, in view of what has already been written. An ant's-eye view, as it were.

After my repatriation to the United States (I have already mentioned the painful circumstances of this return), I performed again in order to earn money. I was not the only one who suffered from postwar depression. But somehow, one way or another, I managed to get through it, thanks to the help of Mitchell Leisen (*Golden Earrings*), and Billy Wilder (*A Foreign Affair*). I recovered financially, and made some films—I hope they were not too bad. As always, I did what was expected of me. And even more, it seemed to me at the time.

Billy Wilder had come to Paris to persuade me to play the role of a Nazi woman. I refused. At that time, I didn't know that you can't refuse Billy Wilder.

The plot of *A Foreign Affair* closely followed the events of World War II. Wilder filmed in Berlin all the scenes in which the leading actors did not appear. Then he flew back to Paris, where I was living, to explain the project to me. Naturally, I couldn't resist him.

A NEW ADVENTURE

One day, in New York, my daughter asked me to help her in her charitable work and participate in a gala event that was to be held in Madison Square Garden.

Stars were going to ride elephants. That was not for me. Not that I have anything against elephants, but I wanted to do something different. So I undertook the role of Master of Ceremonies.

Brooks Company made all the costumes to order. I added little details here and there, and "invented" the short pants, later known as "hot pants." I looked wonderful, with my boots, my whip, and all the rest.

I learned my lines, I announced my numbers, and everything went beautifully.

The performance was the beginning of a new adventure for me: I now performed "in the flesh," no longer just on film. That pleased me immensely, and I've never regretted it.

I received my first offer from an extraordinary man, Bill Miller, who, at the time, was manager of the Sahara. Miller offered me such a huge salary that I couldn't refuse. I charmed Harry Cohn, the head of Columbia Pictures, and asked if I could use his studio's costume workshop.

Later on, all my costumes were designed by Jean Louis and by Elizabeth Courtney, a woman with very talented fingers. I followed their advice. I don't remember how many costumes we made. I have preserved them all, and I take those I still wear out of the trunk as carefully as I would take a baby out of a cradle.

I'm very attached to them. On tour, I myself did any sewing that was needed. The needles came from France (only there can you find needles of such fine quality) as did the thread, though often Elizabeth used one of my hairs for sewing. I had to stand perfectly still—sometimes as long as ten hours at a time—since most of the work was done while I was wearing the dress. Naturally, the zippers were also made in Paris. All my clothes have zippers. Don't believe the stories that say that I was sewn into my clothes every evening. That's nonsense, since the dress would have torn instantly. Anybody who knows anything about dressmaking knows that, and wouldn't believe such chatter. The fabric from which my gowns were made was called "souffle." Biancini manufactured it especially for us, and there is no such product today. This fabric had the delicacy its name suggested. It was exactly right for our purpose: I was dressed, yet I looked naked.

The embroidery, done by a beautiful Japanese woman called Mary, was a work of art in itself. We spent hours designing it and just as much time in a room where young girls embroidered on large frames. Each pearl, each sequin had its own specific place.

It's true that Jean Louis and I (with Elizabeth, who then would give her opinion) had endless discussions over where a diamond, a miniscule mirror, or a glass pearl should be placed. Elizabeth would mark the spot with a tiny red thread.

None of us, in all these years, has regretted the effort or the many hours we spent on these creations. We loved our work and were proud of the results. Many people have tried to imitate our work, but these attempts, as is so often true, fall far short of the original.

Elizabeth is no longer alive, and that is unjust. She was young, gifted, friendly, loving. Fate was unkind to her. She loved me as much as I loved her. She would fly to Las Vegas to help me dress. She would accompany me, teach me sewing and all the tricks of this trade, which is, in truth, an art.

After a few years, I was an excellent seamstress. I worked only by hand, never on a sewing machine—that mysterious apparatus that, frankly, I never found necessary to use.

My first tour in Las Vegas lasted four weeks, and I was swimming in happiness.

Up until now, I've spoken only of the costumes, and for a very good reason. In my eyes, my outward appearance was extremely important, since I had no illusions about my voice. I had, of course, sung in some earlier films, but that had all taken place in quiet recording studios, and when the actual shooting began the image counted for much more than the sound. The most important thing was to keep your eyes on the chalk markings on the floor, which is not at all as easy as it sounds. And that's not all. You not only have to keep your eye on the floor markings but also synchronize your lip movements with the lines of the song being played, which has been recorded in the sound studio a few days earlier. At first, you don't recognize your own voice in the deafening sound; then you tell yourself that you've certainly sung this song much better before. And, finally, you try to chase all these thoughts away so that you can concentrate and coordinate your lip movements with the roar coming from the loudspeakers.

Ordinarily, a person sits on a high stool, very close to where you have to walk. When the recording is finished, all heads turn toward the sound engineer to see whether or not he shakes his head—and whether everything has to be done over again. The sound engineer is responsible for "perfect synchronization." Since the smallest mistake is fatal, you have to start again from the beginning until the man on his perch nods approvingly.

When you're forced to pay attention to the markings on the floor, rivet your gaze on a particular point, and at the same time try to coordinate your lip movements with the sound (a real chore at the end of the twelfth take), you find yourself wondering why you don't just stay home instead of making films.

It's not difficult to understand that compared with these conditions it's a pleasure to be on stage. No floor markings, no "turn your head to the left, and your eyes to point number 31," no difficulties with lip synchronization.

Nevertheless, I continued to pay attention to lighting. Joe

Priveteer helped me. He would come from Las Vegas, and for many years he was responsible for the lighting at all my performances. My performance was not, however, the main feature. Actually, I wasn't supposed to stay "on the stage for more than twenty minutes, so the guests can go back to the gambling tables." So I sang approximately eight songs, all of them from my films— no more.

The audience would applaud madly, and, in my naïveté, I thought everything had gone perfectly. It was, I thought, a perfect performance. Year after year, I played Las Vegas. A splendid time. No worries. Lots of money. Happiness.

Then a man came into my life who took me to seventh heaven.

Since I have a "Russian soul" (which means that I easily give what is close to my heart), I suggested my arranger and director at that time, Peter Matz, to Noel Coward, who had just signed his first contract in Las Vegas, and who wished to substitute the usual orchestra with a piano.

I explained to him that his idea was sheer madness, and persuaded him to meet Peter Matz. Coward was delighted with him, snatched him away from me, and hired him on the spot.

Peter Matz gave me the news on the phone. I gulped first, and then I asked, "And how about me, what am I to do? I open in Las Vegas in two weeks."

"I can't leave Noel Coward in a lurch," he said. "You've got to understand that."

"I understand, I understand."

"I'll call you later," he said, and hung up.

I always have to be the understanding one. Everybody expects that of me. Why, I don't know. The understanding that I've shown has never helped me to solve my problems.

Peter called me back and said, "I know someone who's flying to Los Angeles. You're going there, too, aren't you?"

"Of course, I've got to sign a contract."

"If I can still catch this guy at the airport—I don't know when he's landing in Los Angeles—I'll tell him to get in touch with you." End of conversation.

I took my flight and registered at the Beverly Hills Hotel. Thank God I'm not the nail-biting or down-in-the-dumps type because otherwise I'd simply have given up at that point.

One day a handsome man knocked at my door. He introduced himself. "My name is Burt Bacharach. Peter Matz sent me."

I invited him in and sized him up. He was young, very young, and very handsome, and I have never seen such blue eyes. He went directly to the piano (there's always one in my suite), and said, "What song will you sing first?"

BURT BACHARACH

I stumbled over a chair, reached for my sheet music, hesitated, and turned toward him. "A song that Mitch Miller wrote for me, 'Look Me over Closely.'"

"Let me see it."

He leafed through the pages, and said, "You don't want this kind of arrangement to open with, do you?"

I felt very inexperienced, which I was at that time, especially when it came to arrangements.

I stammered, "How do you picture this song?"

"Like this," he answered.

And he began to play as though he had known the melody for a long time, but at a tempo that surprised me.

"Come, try it once."

I tried it. Bacharach had infinite patience. He said I should let myself "get carried away." Naturally, I didn't know what he meant, but I did my job as well as I could, while hiding my weaknesses as much as possible.

He played one song after another, sometimes making notes, and then said, "Tomorrow at ten, agreed?"

I nodded, and he left. I didn't even ask him where he lived, and wouldn't have known how to reach him if he hadn't shown up the next day. But I was sure he would come back—what I didn't know was that he was to become the most important man in my life after I decided to dedicate myself completely to the stage.

At that time, the name Burt Bacharach was not known to the public. Only the recording studios knew him. My request that his name appear in lights next to mine was refused at first. But after a while I was able to convince the director.

My work also began to please Bacharach—my highest goal until the day he left. The applause, the calls and demands for encores from audiences all over the world were not that important to me. Not even the number of times I was called back on stage (one evening, it was sixty-nine times). It was enough for me to watch for the look in his eyes, and I could see whether my performance had been good or just average. I had never given a bad performance—on this point I could trust him. But some evenings, he would take me in his arms and say, "Terrific, baby, absolutely terrific."

From then on, I lived only for the performances and for him.

That was the luckiest break in my professional life. I had been dropped into a world about which I knew nothing, and I had suddenly found a teacher. With the force of a volcano erupting, Bacharach had reshaped my songs and changed my act into a real show. Later, it was to become a first-class "one woman show."

We no longer performed in nightclubs, but in theaters all over the United States and in Latin America. We played in Canada and, finally, on Broadway. My One Woman Show on Broadway was a big challenge for him. He hired the best musicians in New York. My old British friends, White and Lovelle, also joined us. I managed to get work permits for them, because they knew us well and consequently didn't need much rehearsal—a critical point in the United States. The theatrical directors always want a perfect performance, but they are very stingy with rehearsal time.

Rehearsing with an orchestra of twenty-five musicians takes a lot of time—all the more so because Bacharach's arrangements were not simple. They have nothing in common with the usual orchestrations. The premiere took place at the Lunt-Fontanne Theatre. Since the house was sold out for the first fourteen days before we opened, we extended the show by two weeks.

We were a smash hit; we got splendid reviews. We were a

complete sellout for every performance. We had to close only because another show was waiting to open in our theater.

After our last performance, we stood in the dark halls of the theater. The trucks with the scenery for the next show were parked outside while the drivers ate. Sad farewell. Only actors know what it feels like to leave a theater, to pack up your things and to leave. It's not easy.

I wrapped my clothes in tissue paper, lots of it, packed them in boxes that were specially made, and put large rubber bands around them so they wouldn't open—and we moved on to the next theater.

Later, I performed again on Broadway, at the Mark Hellinger Theatre. If someone asks me today why I never went back after that, I always reply that I had such a splendid time then, and the good things in life should only be enjoyed in moderation.

I loved Broadway. Loved the audiences. I gave matinees twice a week, even though Noel Coward had advised me against it. I liked "the women who wear hats," as he called them. Perhaps they didn't understand his sophisticated patter, but they understand my simple songs very well.

Burt Bacharach did a beautiful arrangement of Pete Seeger's "Where Have all the Flowers Gone?" I heard it sung by a group, but it didn't impress me very much. But my daughter insisted on this song, and worked along with Bacharach on the arrangement. I sang it for the first time in Paris in 1959; in subsequent years I recorded it in French, English, and German.

I wrote the German lyrics with the help of Max Colpet, to whom I gave my author's rights. Since then, I have closed my performance with this song, after which I would always be called back on the stage again and again.

I sing the song differently than Seeger does; at the end, I repeat the first stanza, which I feel accentuates the tragic fate of the fallen. The passage about the graves also has a greater dramatic emphasis in my version. Bacharach's orchestration begins with a single guitar, then more instruments join in, one after the other, until the last stanza, which is once again accompanied by the guitar. Every time I praised him for this idea, he would smile and say that it had already been done by Beethoven.

We made long, extensive trips. Bacharach was enthusiastic, since he had not seen much of the world. I would wash his shirts and socks and have his tuxedo hung in the theater's boiler room. In short, I took care of him as though he were my savior. He accepted all this with good humor. But after every performance, he gave his objective judgment. He directed the orchestras that played for us with great patience, but he was also very strict. It was easy for him, because the musicians saw immediately how well he knew the score and all the instruments. The love they felt for him fused with mine.

Burt Bacharach possessed other assets that I think merit mentioning—his estimable knowledge of sound, for one. Tirelessly, he would run around the huge auditoriums in which we were performing, listen to the string instruments, dash back to the stage, position the microphones, and confer with the sound engineers (who also loved him) until he achieved the desired effect.

Moreover, he was clever enough to know when to stop. When he knew that nothing more could be drawn from an orchestra, he would say, "That's all for today." And we felt that he was satisfied.

I don't know how many years this dream lasted. I know only that he loved Russia and Poland because the violins there were "extraordinary" and artists were accorded very special attention. He also felt at home in Israel, where music was also much revered. He liked Edinburgh and Paris and had a special liking for the Nordic countries. I think it had something to do with the beautiful Scandinavian women, and I often kidded him about this.

He liked *all* our trips, without exception. Latin America, too, where we recorded one of my best albums, *Dietrich in Rio*. In the evenings, we would climb the hills around Rio to listen to the drumbeats that rose from the city. He was tireless when he observed, when he learned, mastered, and arranged, and could refresh his memory with the sounds of the countries in which we had traveled—sometimes only briefly.

He went to West Berlin for a recording session, but spent all his evenings at the East Berlin Opera, to listen to famous musicians. He had no fear. At that time very few Americans dared to go on the other side of the Wall.

Bacharach certainly didn't forget the exceptional days when he traveled down the Neva with one of the most beautiful girls of Leningrad and lived in a room in which Prokofiev had slept.

He certainly remembered the love and admiration of all those who accompanied us or the disappointment, especially in Germany, where everything could have been wonderful, but I was always disturbed by the love-hate relationship that I encountered there. In 1960, I was boycotted in the Rhineland, and someone spat in my face—nevertheless, I had to give my performance, and I got through it thanks to his help and my own Germanic stubbornness.

Most of the time while I was with Bacharach, I was in seventh heaven.

Up to now, I've spoken of the artist. Burt Bacharach, as a man, embodied everything a woman could wish for. He was considerate and tender, gallant and courageous, strong and sincere; but, above all, he was admirable, enormously delicate and loving. And he was reliable. His loyalty knew no bounds. How many such men are there? For me he was the only one.

I would like to relate an incident that happened during a recital in Wiesbaden. I sang "One for My Baby, One More for the Road," sitting astride a chair, in tails. Just a single spotlight lit my face. At the end of the piece, during the last bar of the song, I would make my way back to the wings, followed by the spotlight.

On that day, I was going offstage as usual, but I had misjudged the size of the stage. I went too far to the left, and fell off the stage. It's an eerie feeling when suddenly there is no floor beneath your feet. Since my left hand was stuck in my pants pocket, I hit the floor with my shoulder. I managed to get up and get back on the stage. I saw the chair where the stricken electrician had aimed his spotlight again, sat down, and heard a peculiar faint noise—drops of perspiration falling on my starched shirt-

235

front. I simply could not remember the opening of the next song I was supposed to sing.

Suddenly, there was the noise of a gong in my ears. I wondered where the noise was coming from. Gradually, I realized that it was Bacharach, who kept on striking the same note on the piano to bring me back to reality. He had instinctively sensed that I was about to sing the same song again! Which, of course, I also did. Then I sang two other songs as well as the finale, in which I danced with the twelve girls in the troupe. I still had not yet taken my left hand out of my pants pocket.

That same evening, I went out to dinner with Josef von Sternberg, who had arrived with his son. Only when I got back to my room did I realize that my painful "scratch" might be something more serious. I phoned my daughter in New York.

I must explain why I always call my daughter first whenever any problems arise. My daughter knows everything she wants to know or has to know. Beyond that, she's an excellent actress; she has four sons and a husband. She cooks, takes care of her household, and goes on long trips. I know of no one else who better fits the title of a "Mother Courage, Jr." A good Samaritan to those in need, a loving heart in which I take priority, together with her father, whom she took care of when I was working abroad.

Although she was in New York and I was in Wiesbaden, she advised me to go to the American Air Force Hospital in the city. Don't ask me how she knew about this clinic. For a long time I've given up wondering about her almost uncanny knowledge.

After a sleepless night, Bacharach and I drove to the hospital. The verdict was a fractured humerus, which made us burst into laughter. But Burt's laughter was forced. He was pale when he came out of the X-ray room with the doctor. The doctor, handsome as most Air Force doctors are, explained that it was very much like a "typical paratroop jump injury." I remembered the many times I had been right next to whole divisions of paratroopers and wondered why I had never seen a cast. So, I said, "I don't need a cast, right?"

"Well," answered the doctor, "during the war we had to be satisfied with tying the arm to the upper part of the body to set the fractured shoulder carefully in place. So the fracture had to heal completely on its own."

I had heard what I wanted to hear. I waited until the X rays were dry and left the room with a very hesitant Burt. We got into the car that was to take us to another city. Burt stood next to me as I tied the belt of my raincoat around my arm and the upper part of my body, and we took off. He was always at my side.

Never did he say, "Let's call off the tour." He knew that I didn't want to cancel any performances. He, no doubt, had his own thoughts about this, but he never expressed them to me.

He didn't pressure me to give up or try to change my decision. He was my "lord and master," a designation that probably displeased him, but that's just the way it was.

The first concert I gave with only one arm—the other hidden, tied firmly to my body with a bandage covered with sequins and rhinestones—was a disaster. A single outstretched arm has a dramatic effect, while two outstretched arms express utter abandonment—a plea for help and understanding. After that first failure, Burt and I discussed the problem, and with his help I found a solution. I learned to sing without using my arms and controlling the movements of the one arm. Everything went even better than I imagined it could. The fracture was healing well. If I bent forward, I could even do my hair with my forearm. But I couldn't move my shoulder yet.

Naturally, we were all insured. My producers as well as myself. But I didn't want to cancel the tour and collect the insurance.

I phoned my producer, Norman Grantz, who at the time was in Latin America with our beloved Ella Fitzgerald. He allowed me to cancel my tour whenever I wished but requested I forego any insurance claims. We continued to give our recitals, and closed with "thunderous applause" in Munich (the album *Wiedersehen mit Marlene* originated here).

I had to fly home, but without Burt, who remained a few days longer in Germany to supervise the recording. On the phone he told me that we had received sixty-four curtain calls and that the technicians had apologized for not having enough tapes to record them all.

We found that very amusing, since sixty-four curtain calls were certainly much too long for a record. But we were grateful to the Munich audience.

To the amazement of the specialists, my shoulder healed completely within three weeks. I was still somewhat limited in my movements, but my elbow could be moved enough for me to wash my hair.

You have to be a genius like Bacharach to find, after the musicians have gone home, the right relationship between the individual instruments and the recorded voice, all by yourself.

One day in Berlin, after a recording—the musicians had already gone—we were gathering the scores, and we suddenly discovered that we had forgotten to record one of the songs. We had not brought the orchestration along. Burt ran out of the studio, found some musicians who were still hanging around the halls, took them back with him, and improvised an orchestration on a sheet of paper, rehearsed it over and over again, and finally had the result recorded. It was a song of Friedrich Hollaender's, "Children, Tonight," witty, full of bounce and *joie de vivre*. We worked at it past midnight, until everyone was satisfied with it.

Finally, this memorable tour came to an end, and we wept in each other's arms. We went to Israel, where we were to be accorded great acclaim. Burt felt as much at home in this country as I did.

Israel, the big cities, the kibbutzim! How many the memories etched in my mind! Since some of my songs had German lyrics, I had to either drop them or ask permission to sing them.

At that time artists performing in Israel were forbidden to perform in German. I had prepared myself in advance to sing in French or Spanish. So I was surprised when the audience, on the grounds of my record against the Hitler regime, wanted to hear me sing in my native language. I sang old folk songs, hit tunes from the twenties, happy, sad, sentimental songs, and when I closed with a Hebrew song, the response of the audience was overwhelming.

I had learned this song in an airplane from one of the stewardesses, who had sung it to me over and over again on my way to Tel Aviv while Bacharach took notes. The Israeli orchestra surpassed all our expectations; above all, the strings were superb. We performed in the splendid Frederick Mann Auditorium as well as in the biggest theaters of Jerusalem and Haifa. In the kibbutzim, we had a piano, a percussion instrument, and a guitar at our disposal; we trudged through the trenches followed by crowds of children who had never known streets. When we arrived at the performance site, we would wait until evening and the fighting had stopped.

In the big cities, there was always a restaurant open late somewhere, so that we could eat after the show. Despite the difficult period the country was going through, we were welcomed with love everywhere.

The word "love" reminds me of Russia. Russians love, sing and drink like no other people. After the First World War, my native city, Berlin, was inundated by Russians who had left their country after the Revolution. After they had spent all their money, they opened shops—the women made hats, and we young girls were fascinated by their skill and their romantic, and to us, eccentric view of life.

By nature sentimental, I had close contact with the Russians whom I knew, sang their songs, learned a little of their language (the most difficult of all), and gained many Russian friends. Later, my husband, who spoke Russian fluently, reinforced my "Russian mania" as he called it.

Thanks to my new profession, Russia opened her doors to me. This country also had a fantastic and moving surprise in store for me.

I never, never let my sheet-music folders out of my sight. They held the scores for my recital and many other songs that I didn't always sing. I was as careful with them as I was with my costumes. I took them with me on the plane, slid them under my seat, or held them under the blankets on my lap—in short, my music and I were never apart. Their loss would have been a disaster for me.

So I felt myself the guardian of a treasure. I always saw to it that everything was in order, that the sheet music was placed on the music stands. That was my sacred duty, my personal responsibility.

Moscow. After many rehearsals we were finally ready. I stood in the wings, eager to go onstage. The curtain had not yet been raised. Bacharach was standing on the stage. He liked to talk with the musicians before the performance, and when he didn't know their language, he made himself understood through the music.

Suddenly, the lights in the orchestra went out. All the lights went out. The music stands were literally in the dark—the sign to raise the curtain had already been given. Burt hurried over to me and told me that I should have the curtain lowered again, because the musicians couldn't read a single note.

The first violin rushed over to me. In German, he said, "Don't have the curtain lowered; we know the score by heart. We don't need any light."

He quickly returned to his place, and I waved to Burt. The performance could begin.

The man had not lied; the musicians knew every note, and the orchestra was terrific. After the performance, we had vodka and caviar, and Burt and I embraced each one of them.

I always gave great dinners for my colleagues and invited their wives and relatives. Since you can't take money out of Russia, I happily gave everything to our Russian friends on the spot.

That was my first Russian tour. Others, just as delightful, followed.

The stage was paradise for me . . . naturally, because through my profession I got to know Joe Davis, who could transform the barest, dirtiest stage into a fairyland. Even when we performed in airport hangars, those gloomiest of sheds, Davis achieved a dreamlike effect, sometimes with a simple flashlight placed far from me on the floor. Joe Davis is the uncontested master of stage lighting. His wishes were always my commands. I endured all his moods and let him do as he pleased. He never gave up; he never compromised. The troupe's technicians adored him. At the end of a tour, when we had to split up, they always insisted on giving him a farewell party. I adored him and his friendship was very dear to me.

I have a sad memory of Poland when we were there in midwinter. The theaters were beautiful, but so many traces of war still remained—destroyed cities, desolation everywhere . . .

In Warsaw, we stayed in the only hotel still standing. Dressing rooms were prepared for us in each theater where we performed, so that we could change. It was bitterly cold, but the Poles were anything but. They loved our performances.

When I came out of my room, women were kneeling on the floor, kissing my hands, as well as my face. They said that they knew that I had fought on their side during the Hitler era and told me that even the prisoners in the concentration camps knew of my commitment, and that it had given them new hope. They so overwhelmed me with their memories and their kisses that I was moved to tears.

I visited the Memorial of the Warsaw Uprising and wept again. I had been full of hatred for so many years, and now, standing on the site of the former ghetto, I felt this hatred plunging the rest of the world into darkness. It brought a lump to my throat, and I felt the weight of guilt for the whole German nation more than I had during the Nazi rule, which had driven me from my homeland.

As for Burt Bacharach, when he became famous, he could no longer accompany me on tour around the world. I understood that very well and have never reproached him in any way.

From that fateful day on, I have worked like a robot, trying to recapture the wonderful woman he helped make out of me. I even succeeded in this effort for years, because I always thought of him, always longed for him, always looked for him in the wings, and always fought against self-pity. Whenever he had the time, he still worked on the arrangements for my songs, but as director and pianist, he had become so indispensible to me that, without him, I no longer took much joy in singing.

When he left me, I felt like giving everything up. I had lost my director, my support, my teacher, my maestro. I was not bitter, nor am I today, but I was wounded. I don't think he was ever aware

241

of how much I needed him. He was too modest for that. Our separation broke my heart; I can only hope that he didn't feel the same way. We were like a true small family, when we traveled together, and laughed at everything together. He misses that, perhaps.

Now, I again traveled alone and revisited the countries in which I had lived. I've often sung in Paris at the Olympia and at the Espace Pierre Cardin, where I received such a royal reception that I immediately signed for a second engagement. Under these circumstances, I could scarcely refuse! Of course, I have loved Paris for a long time, but I also loved Cardin, his organizational talent, and his generosity. He took good care of the people who worked for him.

In 1961, the director, Stanley Kramer, came to Las Vegas and asked me to play in *Judgment at Nuremberg*. After that film I never again set foot in a film studio. Since Hollywood thought I would dominate the whole film, I didn't have an evenly matched partner. The fact that Spencer Tracy's name was on the film credits certainly influenced my decision to take the role. At that time he was in poor health, and his working hours were adjusted to accommodate this—mornings between ten and twelve, and afternoons between two and three.

Spencer Tracy was a very lonely man, or so he seemed to me. I don't understand how a man can feel lonely when he shared such love and friendship with Katharine Hepburn, but . . . Perhaps he drew his strength from solitude. He was the consummate loner, long before this type became fashionable.

I can no more judge *Judgment at Nuremberg* today than I could when it was being filmed. But if the film was successful to some extent, it was due to Tracy. He was a stamp testifying to quality. A wonderful man, Spencer Tracy was a wonderful actor as well.

Undoubtedly he was a man who had suffered very much, and death must have been a relief for him. He deserved a more pleasant life, but egocentrics often do not have simple lives. And nobody was more egocentric than Spencer Tracy.

He terrified me. Compared to other men I have known, he had a very mordant sense of humor. With just a look or a single word, he could mortally wound one! I loved him for this reason, and because he knew how to command. He refused to stick to the studio's working hours. He worked when he pleased, and everyone—including me—waited patiently for the prescribed time like race horses at the starting gate. I found that he was perfectly right to claim that privilege. So I never raised an objection.

We performed together in a good scene, though it was not written with great skill, which revolved around a cup of coffee. I trembled when I had to speak my line, tense with fear that I might not get the right tone and the audience might laugh at the wrong time. But Tracy made the matter easier for us.

So, after *Judgment at Nuremberg*, I no longer wanted to do a film.

I was so busy with my career as a singer and with my commitments all over the world. But, above all, I hated the restrictions during the shooting of a film. I preferred the stage by far. The freedom to express yourself as you please, no cameras, no directors constantly looking over your shoulder. And, above all, no producers. In a word, I loved the stage, and I've been loyal to it.

A further advantage of the stage over movies—at least in my eyes! I come on without disguise or false appearance. I don't have to play a "woman of easy virtue," and for a long time this was my role on the screen. I alone choose my songs and sing what the words suggest to me.

When I told Gilbert Bécaud that I would like to sing, "Marie-Marie," he looked at me and laughed. "That's a song for a man," he said. "It wouldn't be the first time that I sang a 'man's song,'" I replied. Despite my answer, he wasn't really convinced that my idea was a good one, but he allowed me to include "Marie-Marie" in my repertoire.

When I visited him with Burt Bacharach, and he heard the band with Burt's arrangement, there were tears in his eyes. I sing this song in French, German, and English. It's one of my favorites. In advance, I explain, in the language of the country, that it's about a prisoner who writes to his girl. Then, everything is clear.

If I sing a lot of "men's songs," it's because the lyrics are more meaningful and dramatic than in songs written for women. Naturally, there are also "unisex" songs! But I sing "Makin' Whoopee," for example, only in tails. It would be unsuitable to wear a dress and sing that song. The same goes for "Let's Take It Nice and Easy." A splendid song for a man—but not wholly suited for a woman. Oddly, certain words sound out of place in a woman's mouth, but witty coming from a man.

When I give a performance without this quick-as-lightning change of costumes (my record time is thirty-two seconds), I have to give up some of the most beautiful songs in my repertoire. But to put on a tuxedo while the audience waits, and then run to the end of the stage and make a surprise entrance from the other side requires a lot of work and the help of experienced dressers. And this was not always possible, since in some theaters, the backstage area was too small to permit this kind of acrobatic change of costume.

Nonetheless, the performances I gave in women's costumes were also effective. I sang many simple sentimental songs, and these went over well.

I'm not a "mike eater," as opposed to most other variety singers, some of whom actually hide behind the microphone. The position of the mike stand is always carefully laid out. I check it before every performance to determine the distance and height are correct in relation to my face. Each time I take the microphone in my hand and walk around the stage, I always hold it rather low to make sure that it doesn't hide my face.

There's a French song that I especially love, and that I always sang standing near the piano, holding the microphone in my hand: "Je tire ma révérence." It's an old song that made a name for Jean Sablon. In America, where audiences supposedly don't care for this kind of song, people listened to it in rapt silence. I didn't translate the words but simply went with the original lyrics, and merely announced: "And now a farewell song."

FIRST STEPS IN TELEVISION

For a while, I left the true paradise the concert stage meant to me, since I had finally let myself be persuaded to make a TV special for an American producer and the firm that was financing my stage show.

All my wishes—all my technical requirements—were met. The production company was able to obtain a theater in London. It was still in the process of construction, but I liked it and preferred it to a New York studio.

Since I've always loved British audiences, and they seem to like me as well, I thought the mutual enthusiasm would carry over on TV.

But I didn't know that the law prohibited the filming or photographing of a paying audience. The audience must be "invited." So hundreds of admission tickets were distributed to the employees of different firms, who hadn't the slightest interest in my recital. And this was the audience before which I had to perform. Cameras had been set up in the auditorium to film the audience, which apparently was not displeased; women straightened their husbands' ties when they noticed the cameras were on them, and they touched up their hairdos to make the best impression.

In addition, I had my own difficulties on the stage. The orchestra and the conductor, Stan Freeman, who normally were behind me on the stage, were put backstage, so that we were no longer in close communication. Against his will, Stan had to wear earphones to hear me properly—he couldn't see me. Being a polite gentleman, he made no objections—unfortunately I didn't either. "Don't make waves," I had told myself.

I sang my songs in all the languages I knew, without pause. I tried only to salvage what was salvageable. Not that American television has such high standards. Generally, it's the worst. But that wasn't my problem. I just wanted to give a performance as good as those I had given on Broadway and all over the world. In vain. But it wasn't my fault alone. I do have a deeply ingrained sense of fairness, and I put the blame where it belongs. I also assume responsibility for my part.

I've never forgotten that show. They'll probably rebroadcast it again after my death. Prospects of a great success!

In all the years that I've performed on the stage as a singer, I've never cancelled any performance—no sore throat, no illness, no excuses. I was always there one or two hours before the performance. Until that disastrous evening, when I tripped over a cable backstage, and broke my thigh bone. That happened in Sydney, in 1976, in the last week of my Australian tour. I leaned on my producer's shoulder, and he helped me to my dressing room. He cancelled the performance. I managed to make it to my hotel room, and waited until the next morning when the X rays could be taken. Incorrigible optimist that I was, I didn't want to believe that I was seriously injured.

After an anxious night, I learned the next day that I had broken my left femur. After my leg was placed in a cast, I was flown to California to the hospital of UCLA. Since my husband was in California at the time, I wanted to see him. From there, I was shipped to New York. I say "shipped" because that's what it was. I lay on a stretcher, I could hardly move, and felt like a piece of furniture. But the shipping costs were considerably higher. Contrary to what has been reported in the press and in certain books, I did not undergo a hip operation. I was put into traction. A piece of metal was screwed into the bone just below the knee, and heavy weights were tied to the metal, with a rope hanging over both sides of the leg. This is what they call "traction." It's hellish! You lie on your back, condemned to immobility, and at the mercy of the nurses—some of whom you have to pay off—in addition to the astronomical cost of a shabby room in a New York hospital.

I'm sure that some hospitals are cleaner than others. But the one to which I was taken was so filthy that, due to my condition, I had to ask my really good friends to come clean my room.

The food was atrocious; I worried about patients who didn't have any family or friends in New York, and who had to eat what they were served: chunks of indigestible, half-frozen food that was all the same but given a different name each meal.

The patients around me, who were just as hungry as I was, all told the same stories. They sent me a few messages through the nurses, some of whom came from the Philippines and were quite charming. They really took care of us, as opposed to the Americans, who were utterly indifferent to their jobs and were keen on only two things: their "rights" and their salary. I spent several months in this hospital.

When the doctors decided to remove the traction, they put me in a cast that extended from my thorax to my injured leg. I spent the end of the year in this place, neglected by nurses who had no time for me. I used to wonder how sick people adjusted to Christmas and New Year's.

I had to do exercises every day with my healthy leg. The "therapist"—a girl so young, I wondered how she could have had time to receive her training and diploma—came every day. But on holidays she disappeared.

It was a terrible time, but it was my own fault! I should have put up a fuss, or stayed in Australia with the remarkable Dr. Roarty and the caring nurses. But I wanted to be close to my family and had insisted on leaving Australia.

That was a mistake, I realized later. But it wasn't the first mistake I made. I remember a guest performance in Washington, when my director, Stan Freeman, had to pull me out of the orchestra pit. This fall had caused no fractures, but half of my leg was torn. It was the first of a long series of accidents. I was alone in Washington, misjudged the severity of my injury, and waited twelve hours before calling a doctor who didn't help me. Why didn't I go to Walter Reed Hospital, where I would have been accepted, without question, as a veteran? A riddle! . . .

I continued my tour through other American cities and through Canada. My leg was bandaged, but the wound refused to heal despite daily treatment. When I sang in Dallas, I phoned my friend, Dr. Michael De Bakey, and asked if I could see him on Sunday, my day off. I was in Houston on the next Sunday morning. Dr. De Bakey was waiting for me at the door to his clinic.

He was very pleasant, examined my injury, and told me it could be closed with a skin graft. I told him that I still had three performances in Dallas but would come to Houston immediately afterwards. "Don't wait too long," he said.

In contrast to the disorder that reigned in the other hospitals where I had been a patient, De Bakey's clinic was wonderfully organized. Beautiful rooms, charming staff. De Bakey worked day and night, and visited me twice a day, sometimes even at eleven o'clock in the evening, to make sure that everything was all right, and that I and the other patients were being well cared for. Michael De Bakey is certainly one of the greatest doctors of his time. Like so many other former patients of his, I hold great admiration for him, and tremendous gratitude for his high ethics and the great compassion with which he ran his clinic.

Apropos of hospitals, next to Houston I would also recommend the University Clinic of Los Angeles. It is an excellent place, and the doctors there are tops. I spent only three days there in my giant cast, and the nursing care was superb. The nurses, pretty-as-a-picture Californians who were not only cheerful but also friendly and efficient, took excellent care of me. One of the nurses accompanied me when I was transported to New York. I was fastened to a stretcher, but my escort spent the entire night awake, in case I should need anything. A sweet, beautiful girl.

But, back to Houston. Before the operation, the staff didn't even remove my nail polish. "Don't touch her beautiful hands," De Bakey had ordered. The doctor who did the skin graft suffered a detached retina two days after he operated on me (I learned this later). But Dr. De Bakey supervised my whole case.

When I came out of the anesthesia, my leg lay in a cast. The surgeons had taken a broad strip of skin from my left hip. It was painful. A lamp was shining on the spot, so that the "scarlet" salve that had been applied over it would dry. The piece of skin was large, much larger, it seemed to me, than the wound on the leg. When I asked why so large a piece of skin had been cut, I was told, "If the graft doesn't take, we have another piece, in the refrigerator, so we can make another try." Naturally, I didn't expect the first graft to take. All my optimism had vanished after the months I had spent with the unhealed leg. A crew of doctors, young and old, examined me three times a day. Three weeks later I was told I could get up and slowly walk up and down the hospital corridor. Once, twice, then three times a day. Finally, Dr. De Bakey, after many hugs, escorted me to the car so carefully and solicitously that I was moved to tears.

I phoned him from Sydney later, when I broke the same leg. He spoke with the doctors there, was reassured that "only" the thigh bone was broken, not the skin itself, and gave me the name of the best orthopedic surgeon in America. Once again, he had placed a protective hand over me, and saved me from the mistakes I might have made. He made the decisions for me—my "hero," Dr. Michael De Bakey. His right hand, Sonia Farrell, was my guardian angel.

After my thigh was completely healed, I spent two months at home, still in a cumbersome cast. When it was finally removed, I could walk. I had become stiff, but I could walk, clumsily, with an iron will. My left leg is still stiff because of the traction, but I can walk.

Since then, I've read scores of reports of people who have endured the same torments and who tell me about their "immense affliction." That's very sad; I, on the other hand, don't feel particularly afflicted. I limp, of course, but that's not a disaster. I manage rather well. I limp only slightly, and those who really love me find my gait quite interesting. My hobbling will disappear with time, and I'll be like a "newborn" again. At any rate, that's what they've said. May God grant this grace!

Today, I live in Paris. Konstantin Paustovsky has written, "A man can die without having seen Paris—and yet he has seen it in his dreams and his imagination."

No one could better describe the charm of Paris. My own words seem feeble, but in accordance with Paustovsky's wish (it was he who inspired me to write), I will try to describe the unfathomable magic and fascination that Paris holds for me.

Its light melts even the hardest heart. The light of Paris is blue. By this, I don't mean to say that the sky is blue. That it is not! But the light is blue. It cannot be compared to any other light in the Western world. You have the impression that you're wearing blue-tinted glasses, which is much better than seeing everything through rose-colored glasses.

In this light, the Seine also has a magical effect, even if we know that sometimes it is very muddy. It has its own magic. The tiny, crooked streets, and the majestic boulevards—created by a taste that has disappeared from our world—have been beautifully preserved in Paris. The only other place I can think of that has this same feeling is, oddly, Buenos Aires, a city so similar to Paris that tears came to my eyes the first time I saw it.

The fascination that Paris holds is as difficult to describe as the love between a man and a woman. Spring, summer, autumn and winter are—as Alan Jay Lerner says—wonderful and peaceful seasons of incomparable beauty, in Paris and in all France. In Paris you can rest, and let the world pursue its own mad course. When someone dies, it's said that "angels carried him away." Here is a poem that can describe this city, this country which I love, better than I can.

DREAM AT TWILIGHT

White meadows in twilight gray
The sun sets slowly
The stars begin to shine.
Now I go to the most beautiful woman,
Far across the meadows in the twilight gray
Deep in a bush of jasmine.

I go slowly
Through twilight gray in the land of love,
I don't hurry.
A soft velvet ribbon
Draws me through twilight gray
In a gentle, blue light.

Otto Julius Bierbaum

EPILOGUE

As far as this book goes, everything is true, even though there are imperfections and certain things that have been left unspoken. Pain and sorrow are private matters.

I've done my duty. I've always assumed my responsibilities. That's all that counts for me.

It's well known that I've always had a great mistrust of reporters and other people who wanted to write about me.

Only I know the truth about myself. The truth about all the years spent on the stages of the world. The truth that some writer friends also wanted to express.

Hemingway:

"She's courageous, beautiful, loyal, charming, and generous. She's never boring. In the morning, in the shirt, trousers and boots of an American soldier, she looks as special as she does in the evening or on the screen. Her honesty as well as her sense of the comedy and tragedy of life are responsible for the fact that she can never truly be happy, except when she loves. She can also joke about love, but it's gallows humor. Even if she had nothing but her voice, she could break your heart with it. In addition, she has this beautiful body,

251

and the timeless beauty of her face. What if it does break your heart if she's there to put it together again?

"She's never cruel, but angry, yes, that she can be, and stupid people get on her nerves, and she makes no secret of it, unless the dunderhead happens to be in need. Whoever needs help, to some extent can count on her sympathies.

"Marlene sets her own rules, but the standards she sets for the manners and honesty of others are no less strict than the original ten commandments. That is one of the things that probably makes her so mysterious; that so beautiful and talented a woman, who can do what she pleases, does only what she considers absolutely right; that she was so clever and courageous to set up her own rules, which she follows.

"I know that I, myself, could never see Marlene without her moving me and making me happy. If that's what makes her mysterious, it's a beautiful mystery. It's a mystery of which we have known for a long time."

André Malraux:

"Marlene Dietrich is not an actress like Sarah Bernhardt; she is a myth like Phyrné."

Jean Cocteau:

"Marlene Dietrich . . . Your name begins with a caress, and ends with a whiplash. You wear feathers and furs that seem to belong on your body like the fur on animals and the feathers on birds. Your voice, your look, are those of a Lorelei. But Lorelei was dangerous. You, on the other hand, are not, since the secret of your beauty lies in your goodheartedness. This goodness of heart places you above elegance, above fashion, above style, even above your fame, your courage, your walk, your films and your songs.

"Your beauty is not to be overlooked, but there's no need to even mention it. So, I bow before your goodness. It illumines you from within that long wave of glory that you are. A transparent wave that comes from far away and generously deigns to roll in toward us. From the sequins in *The Blue Angel* to the tails in *Morocco*, from the shabby black dress in *X.27* to the exotic bird feathers in *Shanghai Express*, from the diamonds in *Desire* to the American uniform; from port to port, from reef to reef, from wave to wave, from embankment to embankment, bears down on us, sails unfurled, a frigate, a figurehead on the prow, a flying fish, a bird of paradise, the incredible, wonderful, Marlene Dietrich!" (From his presentation of Marlene Dietrich at the "Bal de la Mer" in Monte Carlo, August 17, 1954.)

Jean Cau:

"In a world of Lolitas, small, buxom dolls in short skirts with lips pouting, whose strident voices proclaim they want to 'live their life,' and who twist and turn enough to dislocate their vertebrae, I take off my plumed hat to you, Madame Dietrich, and bow deeply to the floor.

"Most beautiful of all women, who fills my dreams with your legend, we bid you welcome, Marlene. May you be welcome all over the world, and homage be paid to your glory and timelessness.

"Whence comes this smoky voice that speaks of broken hearts, this dark voice of a thousand wishes—and from what sea rises this eternal siren that binds Odysseus forever to the mast of his ship. Because of your glory and your beauty, Madame, you are, since time immemorial, our Queen, under our countless rapt gazes that spread over the glittering scales of your body. And since time immemorial, you are our elect, as your soul rises above the legend and above the night."

Christopher Fry:

"There are legends, legendary islands, legendary cities, legends of courage, righteousness, beauty. They will always be in our innermost thoughts. Not because they are legendary, but because they hold the truth, deep-rooted like all truth. The golden legend, or a nightmare; the legend of the Lorelei, of radiant Apollo, from whose hair were fashioned the strings of his lyre, or the dream of the blond women; the legends will always be an immutable part of the world; as if Eve, herself, on leaving the Garden of Eden, had created a new Paradise of her own mystery, and with this mystery a warmth, a wisdom, a humanity, a truth and a living legend."

Kenneth Tynan:

"These are aspects of the lady as they surface in my memory, colored no doubt by fifteen years of knowing her and some thirty years of quietly lustful admiration.

"First, there is my friend the nurse—the sender of appropriate pills, the source of uncanny medical tips, the magic panacea. For this Marlene, healer of the world's wounded, I have often been thankful. Her songs are healing, too. Her voice tells you that whatever hell you inhabit, she has been there before, and survived. Some trace of ancient Teutonic folk wisdom—many would call it witchcraft—still adheres to her. For example, she can predict a child's sex before its birth. This must, of course, be inspired guesswork or shrewdly applied psychology. She calls it science, as any witch would.

"Then there is the self-punishing worker, daughter of an exacting German father, brought up to take pleasure as a prize and a privilege, not as a birthright. This is the Marlene who worships excellence—a high-definition performer who daily polishes her unrusting skills. A small eater, sticking to steaks and greenery, but a great devourer of applause. For some people (said Jean Cocteau), style is a very complicated way of saying very simple things; for others, it is a very simple way of saying very complicated things. Marlene is one of the others. Her style looks absurdly simple—an effortless act of projection, a serpentine lasso whereby her voice casually winds itself around our most vulnerable fantasies. But it is not easy. It is what remains when ingratiation, sentimentality and the manifold devices of heart-warming crap have been ruthlessly pared away. Steel and silk are left, shining and durable.

"And a tireless self-chronicler. For the first half hour of every meeting with this Marlene, you will be told how she wowed them in Warsaw, mowed them down in Moscow, savaged them in Sydney, was pelted with poppies in Ispahan. It is all true and, if anything, understated. She is merely keeping you up to date. Then she moves in—critical, probing and self-abnegating—on your own life and its problems. For the time being, you transfer your burdens to the willing shoulders of this gallant Kraut.

"As I wrote before I met her, she has sex but no particular gender. They say (or, at least, *I* say) that she was the only woman who was allowed to attend the annual ball for male transvestites in pre-Hitler Berlin. She habitually turned up in top hat, white tie and tails. Seeing two exquisite creatures descending the grand staircases, clad in form-hugging sequins and cascading blond wigs, she wondered wide-eyed: 'Are you two in love?' '*Fräulein*,' said one of them frostily, 'we are not lesbians.' This Marlene lives in a sexual no man's land—and no woman's, either. She dedicates herself to looking, rather than to being, sexy. The art is in the seeming. The semblance is the image, and the image is the message. She is every man's mistress and mother, every woman's lover and aunt, and nobody's husband except Rudi's—and he *is* her husband, far off on his ranch in California.

"She believes in the stars but makes her own luck. Impresarios unnerve her. She has no agent or business manager except herself. Where once, in the high noon of the thirties, she depended on Josef von Sternberg, she now looks to Burt Bacharach, her youthful arranger and conductor. In his absence, she frets; at his excuses, she expressively shrugs. Burt is her generalissimo, the musical overlord on whom, quite asexually, she dotes.

"She laughs a lot, making a honking sound that is not without melancholy. A special note of mournful bitchery invades her voice when the conversation turns to jumped-up starlets who need to be put down. ('What *about* that picture? She has to be out of her mind. Honey, it's to *die!*') This professional Marlene is not what anyone would call a woman's woman. I was not surprised to learn that she had never met Greta Garbo, her major rival in the World Eroticism Stakes of the prewar era. She venerates many kinds of men— great strenuous helpers of our species like Sir Alexander Fleming, who discovered penicillin; great life-enhancing performers like

Jean Gabin and Orson Welles; great self-revealing writers like
Ernest Hemingway and Konstantin Paustovsky; great masters of
timing and nuance like Noel Coward; and men of great power like
General Patton, John Fitzgerald Kennedy and—the latest recruit
to the clan—Moshe Dayan. Marlene relishes the breath of power.
She is rabidly antiwar, but just as rabidly pro-Israeli. This paradox
in her nature sometimes worries me.

"Aloof, imperious, unfeeling, icy and calculating: These are
some of the things she is not. Proud, involved, challenging, ironic
and outgoing: These are apter epithets. On stage, in the solo act
to which she has devoted the last decade or so, she stands as if
astonished to be there, like a statue unveiled every night to its own
inexhaustible amazement. She shows herself to the audience like
the Host to the congregation. And delivers the sacred goods. She
knows where all the flowers went—buried in the mud of Passchen-
daele, blasted to ash at Hiroshima, napalmed to a crisp in Viet-
nam—and she carries the knowledge in her voice. She once
assured me that she could play Bertolt Brecht's *Mother Courage,* and I
expect she was right. I can picture her pulling a wagon across the
battlefields, chanting those dark and stoical Brechtian songs, and
setting up shop wherever the action erupts, as she did in France
during the Ardennes offensive—this queen of camp followers, the
Empress Lili Marlene.

"What we have here, by way of summary, is a defiant and
regal lady with no hobbies except perfectionism, no vices except
self-exploitation, and no dangerous habits except an infallible gift
for eliciting prose as monumentally lush as this from otherwise
rational men. Marlene makes blurb writers of us all. She is advice
to the lovelorn, influence in high places, a word to the wise, and
the territorial imperative. She is also Whispering Jack Schmidt,
Wilhelmina the Moocher, the deep purple falling, the smoke in
your eyes, how to live alone and like it, the survival of the fittest,
the age of anxiety, the liberal imagination, nobody's fool and every
dead soldier's widow. On top of which, she has limitations and
knows them." (From "One or two things I know of her . . .".)

* * *

I agree with Tynan—not completely, but with his last sentence, at any rate. I do, in fact, know my limits, and never overstep them, or almost never.

I'm easily discouraged. A shrug of the shoulders is enough to send me back into my shell. On the other hand, I defend my principles like a lioness, and I defend a friend, whether or not he's in need. I've fought for my friends whenever I've felt they were being attacked, even when they themselves were utterly indifferent, even risking danger to myself, which didn't matter at all to me, either then or now. I don't think I'll ever change.

I've never been very self-confident, either in films or on the stage. On the stage, Burt Bacharach's praise gave me a much-needed feeling of security. It's already known who gave me this feeling in films. But outside of these two areas, I'm as helpless as a newborn. I'm not really strong; I have firm convictions. But, as regards a crisis, I feel unsure. I'm speaking here of my own crises; I courageously confront a misfortune that strikes my family or friends, since I feel it's my duty to help—a feeling that gives me a certain strength.

I've been unable to apply this "philosophy" to myself. When a misfortune strikes me, I sink into deep despair. Even my closest friends are not aware of this weakness, which I cannot overcome. And since I learned long ago that self-pity is strictly forbidden, I had to get used to this disaster and could not bother others with my troubles.

Death has wrested many friends from me, my best friends. I've lost my husband, my most painful loss of all. Every friend who departs from us deepens our loneliness. It hurts me to no longer be able to pick up a phone and hear a beloved voice, and I confess I'm tired of suffering.

I miss Hemingway and the jokes he would shout to me from the other end of the world; his humorous advice, which he concluded with a "Sleep well." These words haunt me, and my early rage flares up again. But that doesn't help me through the night. But is there a remedy against sleepless nights? Nobody knows any. And, although the "professors," as Hemingway called them, still write thick, learned books on this subject, no remedy exists against this nightly angst. That's the way it is.

I've spent almost all of my life with highly intelligent men. They're not like other men. Their spirit is great and stimulating. They hate strife; indeed they reject it. Their imaginations are aware of those around them. Their inventive gifts are boundless. They demand devotion and obedience. And a sense of humor. I happily gave all this. I was lucky to be chosen and clever enough to understand them.

Women who have problems (men have fewer) run to their psychiatrists and pay them to listen to them. (I know an analyst who has an earphone that he can turn on or off as he pleases, but always gives the impression that he is listening attentively to his patient's problems.) Naturally, as a realist, I've never understood how one could pay a stranger cold cash to listen to him or her.

When people of my generation look back on their lives, many of them feel they have wasted their youth. I think that, at that time, we didn't know that we were squandering our time. We lived from one day to the next; only the moment counted, as it does for all young people, then as now. "After me, the deluge . . ." That's a wonderful expression and perhaps not the worst attitude. It would have been a good title for this book, but it doesn't really communicate the feelings we experienced in our youth. We never thought of the "deluge." On the other hand, the youth of today know that such a deluge is possible.

At that time, or so we thought, everything was simpler. I'm sure that today's young people, who don't interest themselves in politics—who pursue their daily jobs, as we did then—would say the same. This wonderful attitude of youth triumphs over all. I hope it doesn't decline and that it will be able to confront the terrifying events threatening the world; that it will survive and preserve its peace of mind.

I detest modern-day "self-exiles." I've read all the books on them. Also those of Elia Kazan. Such people should find a place where there are no laws, where no restrictions disturb their aimless lives, where they can beg for their food, go utterly to the dogs. First sell their possessions and then their own bodies, and finally have themselves killed and carried off in anonymous coffins, bearing the inscription, "Family Unknown."

Since so many people ask how I spend my time, I'll be frank: I read incessantly. I receive almost all the new books published in America—good as well as bad. I've read the new god of modern literature, Peter Handke, in German. But he remains a riddle to me. He has declared that he cannot live in Germany and prefers to live in Paris. He seems to have had enough of Germany, and of life in general. Moreover, I consider him to be deeply masochistic— one of the chief reasons why I can't identify with the characters of his books. But I'm not a critic, just an ordinary reader. After his third book I felt bored, nauseated, and finally gave up. Probably my fault! Perhaps his books are better in the English translation. But I don't like to be disappointed. As for German writers, I'll have to stick with Heinrich Böll and Günter Grass. But I find it easier to read French authors. Of course, I like English and American writers most of all and spend whole nights with their books.

Time doesn't heal all wounds. Now as before, I'm astonished at the permanence of sadness and its power over humans. Perhaps time does heal superficial wounds, but it has no power over deep wounds. Over the years, the scars hurt as much as the wounds. "Keep your head high," "Chin up," "This, too, will pass," etc.— none of this advice is very useful. What is important is to spin a cocoon around your heart, to suppress the pull of the past. Don't count on the sympathy of others. You can manage very well without them. I know that.

What remains is solitude.

SELECTED CHRONOLOGY

Note

In the 1920s Marlene Dietrich performed in plays and films not mentioned in this book or listed in this chronology. Her Berlin stage credits for this period include *The Circle, A Midsummer Night's Dream, When the New Vine Blossoms, The Imaginary Invalid, Spring's Awakening, From Mouth to Mouth, Broadway, Duel on the Lido, Die Schule von Uznach,* and *Back to Methuselah.* Her film credits include *The Little Napoleon, Man by the Roadside, The Leap into Life, The Joyless Street, A Modern DuBarry, Madame Doesn't Want Children, Heads Up, Charly!, The Imaginary Baron, His Greatest Bluff, Café Electric, Princess Olala, The Woman One Longs For, The Ship of Lost Men,* and *Dangers of the Engagement Period.*

1901   born in Berlin on December 27

1906   entered Auguste Victoria School for Girls, Berlin

1918   death of father

       graduated from Auguste Victoria School for Girls, Berlin

1919   entered Weimar Konservatorium to study violin

1920   returned to Berlin and began career as actress

1921   auditioned for Max Reinhardt Drama School

1922 Widow in *The Taming of the Shrew* by William Shakespeare (Schumann Theater, Berlin)

1923 Lucie in *The Tragedy of Love* (Joe May–Film production directed by Joe May)

1924 married Rudolf Sieber on May 17

1925 gave birth to daughter Maria

1926 Micheline in *Manon Lescaut* (UFA production directed by Arthur Robison)

1928 multiple roles in *It's in the Air,* a revue by Marcellus Schiffer and Mischa Spoliansky (Komödie Theater, Berlin)

Hypatia in *Misalliance* by George Bernard Shaw (Komödie Theater, Berlin)

1929 Laurence Gerard in *I Kiss Your Hand Madame* (Super-Film production directed by Robert Land)

Mabel in *Two Bow Ties* by Georg Kaiser and Mischa Spoliansky (Berliner Theater, Berlin)

auditioned by UFA

1930 Lola-Lola in *The Blue Angel* (Erich Pommer/UFA production directed by Josef von Sternberg)

UFA refused to exercise option on contract with Dietrich

Paramount signed contract with Dietrich

emigrated to United States, settling in Hollywood

Amy Jolly in *Morocco* (Paramount production directed by Josef von Sternberg)

1931 X.27 in *Dishonoured* (Paramount production directed by Josef von Sternberg)

1932 Shanghai Lily in *Shanghai Express* (Paramount production directed by Josef von Sternberg)

brought daughter, Maria, to live with her in Hollywood

kidnap threats against Maria

Helen Faraday in *Blonde Venus* (Paramount production directed by Josef von Sternberg)

1933 Lily Czepanek in *Song of Songs* (Paramount production directed by Rouben Mamoulian)

1934 Catherine the Great in *The Scarlet Empress* (Paramount production directed by Josef von Sternberg)

1935 Concha Perez in *The Devil Is a Woman* (Paramount production directed by Josef von Sternberg)

Josef von Sternberg ended his professional association with Dietrich

1936 Madeleine de Beaupré in *Desire* (Paramount production directed by Frank Borzage)

Domini Enfilden in *The Garden of Allah* (Selznick-International production, released through United Artists, directed by Richard Boleslawski)

1937 Alexandra in *Knight Without Armour* (Alexander Korda–London Films production, released through United Artists, directed by Jacques Feyder)

Maria Barker in *Angel* (Paramount production directed by Ernst Lubitsch)

Paramount canceled contract with Dietrich

1939 Frenchy in *Destry Rides Again* (Universal Pictures production directed by George Marshall)

became United States citizen

1940 Bijou in *Seven Sinners* (Universal Pictures production directed by Tay Garnett)

1941 Clair Ledoux in *The Flame of New Orleans* (Universal Pictures production directed by René Clair)

Fay Duval in *Manpower* (Warner Bros.–First National production, directed by Raoul Walsh)

1942 Elizabeth Madden in *The Lady Is Willing* (Columbia Pictures production directed by Mitchell Leisen)

Cherry Mallotte in *The Spoilers* (Universal Pictures production directed by Ray Enright)

Josie Winters in *Pittsburgh* (Universal Pictures production directed by Lewis Seiler)

1943 performed in bond tours and radio broadcasts and made personal appearances as part of domestic war effort until departure for Europe in 1944

1944　guest appearance in *Follow the Boys* (Universal Pictures production directed by Eddie Sutherland)

　　　Jamilla in *Kismet* (MGM production directed by William Dieterle)

　　　performed in USO tour at European front until end of war in 1945

1945　death of mother

　　　repatriated to United States at close of war

1946　Blanche Ferrand in *Martin Roumagnac* (Alcina production directed by Georges Lacombe)

1947　Lydia in *Golden Earrings* (Paramount production directed by Mitchell Leisen)

　　　awarded Légion d'Honneur

1948　Erika von Schluetow in *A Foreign Affair* (Paramount production directed by Billy Wilder)

1949　guest appearance as nightclub entertainer in *Jigsaw* (Tower Pictures production, released through United Artists, directed by Fletcher Markle)

1950　Charlotte Inwood in *Stage Fright* (Warner Bros.–First National production directed by Alfred Hitchcock)

1951　Monica Teasdale in *No Highway in the Sky* (20th Century-Fox production directed by Henry Koster)

1952　Altar Keane in *Rancho Notorious* (Fidelity Pictures production, distributed by RKO-Radio Pictures, directed by Fritz Lang)

1953　mistress of ceremonies in gala charity event at Madison Square Garden

　　　debut as *diseuse* at Sahara, Las Vegas, followed by domestic and international tours until the mid 1970s

1954　appeared at Café de Paris, London

1956　guest appearance in *Around the World in Eighty Days* (Michael Todd Company, Inc., production, released through United Artists, directed by Michael Anderson)

1957　Marquise Maria de Crevecoeur in *The Monte Carlo Story* (Titanus production, released through United Artists, directed by Samuel A. Taylor)

Christine Vole in *Witness for the Prosecution* (Edward Small–Arthur Hornblow Production, released through United Artists, directed by Billy Wilder)

1958   fortune teller in *Touch of Evil* (Universal-International production directed by Orson Welles)

1960   first German tour

Israeli tour

1961   Mme. Bertholt in *Judgment at Nuremberg* (Roxlom production, released through United Artists, directed by Stanley Kramer)

1962   narrator of *The Black Fox*, a documentary on Hitler (Arthur Steloff–Image production, released by Heritage Films, Inc., directed by Louis Clyde Stoumen)

1964   guest appearance in *Paris When It Sizzles* (Paramount production directed by Richard Quine)

Russian tour

1967   Broadway debut in one-woman show at Lunt-Fontanne Theatre, New York City

1972   first television special, *I Wish You Love* (directed by Alexander Cohen at New London Theater, London)

1976   broke thigh while performing in Sydney, Australia

1978   Baroness von Semering in *Just a Gigolo* (Leguan production directed by David Hemmings)

INDEX

INDEX